OHIO HISTO — SO-AIK-884

CONTENTS FOR VOLUME 114

SUBSCRIPTIONS AND MANUSCRIPTS

OHIO HISTORY is published annually by The Kent State University Press, Kent, Ohio 44242-0001. EDITOR: R. Douglas Hurt. Copyright © 2007 by The Kent State University Press.

SUBSCRIPTIONS: Subscription orders are accepted on a three-year basis only. Prices for a three-year subscription: $59.00 individual, $83.00 institution; Canada/international: $83.00 individual, $117.00 institution. Single copies may be purchased for $21.00 ($29.50 Canada/international). Student note: 25% off the individual subscription price when the order is accompanied by a history faculty member's name, affiliation, and signature. Prepayment required. No refunds will be made except in the case of duplicate payments made in error. It will be necessary to add a service charge when necessary refunds are made. No cancellation requests will be accepted for the current year once a subscription has been entered.

NOTICE OF NONRECEIPT of an issue must be sent to The Kent State University Press, Kent, Ohio 44242-0001, within three months of the date of publication of the issue. Changes of address should be sent to this office by two months preceding publication. The Kent State University Press is not responsible for copies lost because of failure to report a change of address in time for mailing. A charge of $5.25 will be assessed for forwarding copies returned because of incorrect address.

MANUSCRIPTS and all correspondence concerning editorial matters should be submitted electronically to doughurt@purdue.edu. Books for review should be submitted to R. Douglas Hurt, Department of History, University Hall, 672 Oval Drive, Purdue University, West Lafayette, Indiana 47907-2807.

EDITOR R. DOUGLAS HURT invites articles, edited documents, and other annotated, unpublished primary materials related to all aspects of Ohio's history as well as manuscripts on the Midwest that focus on Ohio or its region. Manuscripts, including notes, must be double spaced. The documentation should be set as endnotes and prepared according to the *Chicago Manual of Style,* 15th edition. Originality of subject, general interest of the article, sources used, interpretation, and style are criteria for acceptance and publication. Manuscripts generally should not exceed 7,500 words of text, including notes. Articles accepted for publication become the property of *Ohio History* and The Kent State University Press and may not be published elsewhere without written permission.

THE EDITOR and Kent State University do not accept responsibility for statements of fact or opinion made by the contributors.

Ohio History, Vol. 114 Copyright © 2007
by The Kent State University Press
ISBN 978-0-87338-930-3   ISSN 0030-0934
0030-0934 / 114 / $01.00 / 00

It is with pride and optimism that we present this inaugural issue of *Ohio History* under the Kent State University Press imprint. The journal will be an annual, published each spring and available by subscription. In bringing this venerable journal back into print, we wish to thank the Ohio Historical Society for its many years of stewardship, Dr. Shirley Wajda for keeping *Ohio History*'s heart beating between editors, and the journal's new editor R. Douglas Hurt, head of the Department of History, Purdue University.

A specialist in American agricultural, rural, western, and midwestern history, Dr. Hurt received his Ph.D. from Kansas State University. Before coming to Purdue he was director of the graduate program in Agricultural History and Rural Studies at Iowa State University and associate director for the State Historical Society of Missouri. He served as editor for *Agricultural History* and has written, edited, or contributed to more than thirty books. We are delighted to welcome Dr. Hurt as the latest in a distinguished line of *Ohio History* editors.

WILL UNDERWOOD
Director
Kent State University Press

In June 1887 the Ohio Archaeological and Historical Society published the first issue of the *Ohio Archaeological and Historical Quarterly,* with the hardback volume entitled *Publications.* I. W. Andrews provided the lead article, "The Beginnings of the Colonial System of the United States," and B. A. Hinsdale closed with "Western Land Policy of the British Government from 1763–1785." The *Quarterly* included the Society's annual Proceedings from 1885 to 1887 and the Report of the Executive Committee for 1887–88. A publication gap occurred after volume 3 appeared in 1891 due to reasons that are not entirely clear, but it resumed with volume 4 in 1896. In these early issues the authors provided solid, descriptive narratives of their chosen subjects and thereby helped launch an authoritative source for anyone interested in the history of Ohio.

The title of the journal remained the *Ohio Archaeological and Historical Quarterly* for the next fifty-nine years, until January 1955, when it became the *Ohio Historical Quarterly.* By the mid–twentieth century it had earned a national reputation as the journal of record for Ohio's history and as a publication that journal editors at other state historical societies considered a model. The *Ohio Historical Quarterly* had evolved from a publication under the direction of an editorial board to a professional publication with a skilled editor, James H. Rodabaugh. In 1962 the title changed again to *Ohio History.* Carl M. Becker provided the lead article, entitled "Picture of a Young Copperhead." (You have perhaps noticed that the lead article in this issue comes from Carl Becker.)

In 1982 *Ohio History* became an annual publication, and in 1986 it became a bi-annual journal. In 2002, after 106 years of continuous of publication and 116 years of print since 1887, financial difficulties mandated that the Ohio Historical Society end publication of the journal in print form. Volume 111, the Winter/Spring issue, brought an end to a distinguished journal, at least in paper format. The Summer/Autumn issue appeared as an online publication that continued for the entire issue of volume 112 in 2003. Then, for the next three years *Ohio History* ceased to exist.

But there were still many who treasured the journal for its incisive articles that had made an immeasurable contribution to the history of the territory and State of Ohio for more then a century. As a result, in 2006 the Kent State University Press made a commitment to revive *Ohio History,* and Will Underwood, director of the Press, asked me to serve as editor. This offer proved daunting, and I refused several times before he and Jo-anna Hildebrand Craig, assistant director and editor-in-chief, convinced me to assume this responsibility. I was reluctant not only because I understood the amount of work involved with an editorship but also because few scholarly journals have been revived once publication ceased. In addition, the previous editors were skilled, knowledgeable professionals who knew Ohio's history and deftly wielded their editorial pens. For more than a century their cumulative work firmly established *Ohio History* as an authoritative journal on which all students of the state's history, scholars, and the reading public alike could rely with confidence for historical accuracy. If I accepted, I would follow in the wake of their considerable achievements in an attempt to reestablish *Ohio History* as the journal of record for the history of Ohio.

With this issue, I hope that you will agree that the journal has returned to its rightful place among the leading state historical journals. *Ohio History* is back, and it has a bright future.

R. Douglas Hurt

GINETTE ALEY is assistant professor of history at the University of Southern Indiana. Her publications on the early Midwest have appeared in the journal *Ohio Valley History* and in *The Boundaries between Us: Natives and Newcomers along the Frontiers of the Old Northwest Territory, 1750–1850,* edited by Daniel P. Barr (Kent State University Press, 2006). She is currently revising her dissertation for publication, "A Republic in the Making: Power, People, and Policies in the Early-Nineteenth-Century West."

CARL BECKER is professor emeritus at Wright State University, where he offered courses in the American Civil War and the United States in WWII. He has published numerous journal and reference articles and biographical essays on the Civil War and sports history and is the author of *Home and Away: The Rise and Fall of Professional Football on the Banks of the Ohio, 1919–1934* (Ohio State University Press, 1998).

RON CARDEN is professor of history and chair of the social science department at South Plains College in Levelland, Texas. A graduate of the University of New Mexico, he has written a biography of Bishop William Montgomery Brown and an article for the *Journal of Anglican and Episcopal History* on Bishop Brown's path to heresy.

MARC EGNAL is professor of history at York University, Toronto. He is completing a book on the causes of the Civil War.

KEVIN GANNON is assistant professor of history at Grand View College in Des Moines, Iowa. His current research centers on state formation and the construction of nationalism in the early republic, particularly the actions and ideas of groups critical in these processes. His essay is part of a larger project entitled "Nationalism's Opposites: States' Rights, Nullification, and the Secession in the Antebellum North."

DEBORAH MARINSKI earned her Ph.D. in history from the University of Toledo and is currently a visiting assistant professor at the University of Toledo. Her areas of interest are late-nineteenth- and early-twentieth-century U.S. history.

SARAH E. MILLER earned her Ph.D. from the University of Toledo and is assistant professor of history at the University of South Carolina Salkehatchie.

ROBERT A. WHEELER, associate professor of history at Cleveland State University, received his Ph.D. from Brown University. He is co-author of *Cleveland: A Concise History* and co-editor of *The Social Fabric,* a two-volume reader. He is also the editor of *Visions of the Western Reserve, 1750–1860* (Ohio State University Press, 2000).

The Cincinnati Football Reds

A Franchise in Failure

CARL BECKER

At their annual meeting in July 1933, the owners of the teams in the National Football League (NFL) granted franchises to the Cincinnati Reds, the Philadelphia Eagles, and the Pittsburgh Pirates. Entrepreneurship in professional football had long been risky, but as the season of 1933 approached, the NFL was moving into a new era, one that might give greater security to a fledgling franchise—in this instance the Cincinnati Reds. Professional football, once a pariah in American football, was winning respectability among sports fans; membership in the league would stabilize, offensive play would become more exciting, and attendance at NFL games would steadily rise.[1]

Organizing the American Professional Football Association in 1920 (renamed the National Football League in 1922), the owners of the charter teams sought to solve problems plaguing professional football: the rapid movement of franchises in and out of the league; players jumping from team to team for higher salaries; the use of ringers (often collegians playing under assumed names to protect their eligibility for collegiate play) to accommodate local pride and the gambling fraternity; inchoate scheduling; and the disrepute of professional football. Becoming president of the league in 1921, Joe Carr, founder of the Columbus Panhandles, one of the charter clubs, soon dealt with issues involving movement of players from team to team, the use of ringers, and, at least to some extent, scheduling. But he had to wrestle for many years with questions of membership and the reputation of professional football.[2]

1. Minutes, Annual Meeting, National Football League (hereafter NFL), July 8–9, 1933, Archives, Professional Football Hall of Fame, Canton, Ohio. All NFL meeting minutes cited are located here.

2. For the early years of the NFL, see Robert W. Peterson, *Pigskin: The Early Years of Pro Football* (New York: Oxford Univ. Press, 1997), 67ff. See also Bob Carroll et al., *Total Football: The Official Encyclopedia of the National Football League* (New York: HarperCollins, 1997); "Joe Carr," typescript, Joe Carr File, Archives, Professional Football Hall of Fame.

Ohio History, Vol. 114 © 2007 by The Kent State University Press

At the outset, the charter clubs numbered fourteen and primarily represented midsize midwestern cities—Columbus and Canton in Ohio and Hammond in Indiana, for example—and a few larger cities, notably Chicago and Cleveland. By their policy governing membership, Carr and the charter owners permitted a clutter of membership to develop down to 1926. They awarded franchises to nearly any petitioner knocking on the door, often waiving the entrance fee of $100. Nor did they raise serious questions about whether owners of a prospective franchise could weather losses at the gate for a season or so. As a result, membership in the league fluctuated substantially from 1920 through 1926. During the period, including the charter members, transactions involving franchises numbered at least fifty-six, thirteen of them by cancellation or suspension of franchises. In 1926, the peak year for membership, the number reached twenty-five. Now franchises represented small, medium, and large cities throughout the Midwest and East.[3]

In a roundabout way, Carr and the owners ultimately fashioned a restrictive policy on membership because of another problem. Through the 1920s, the league had to face the hostility of the collegiate establishment—of university administrators, coaches, and fans who asserted that the cash nexus contaminated amateurism. Amateur football, they insisted, built strength of character and manhood that served the individual, the family, and the nation. They had an eloquent spokesman in Amos Alonzo Stagg, the renowned collegiate coach. In 1923, addressing an open letter to "all friends of college football," he declared that "Sunday professional football" threatened the welfare of the intercollegiate game, corrupting as it did the amateur spirit. Perceiving professional football as a territory taken by ethnic and working-class Americans, the collegians, often middle- and upper-class old-line Americans, created another reason for disdaining the Sunday game.[4]

The amateurs attempted to call the professionals to account after Harold "Red" Grange, the sensational running back at the University of Illinois, signed a contract with the Chicago Bears only hours after playing his last collegiate game in 1925 and embarked with the team on three barnstorming tours through the East, South, and West. In response, the National Collegiate Athletic Association and the American Football Coaches Association urged administrators not to employ any coach, trainer, or official who gave his services to professional football. The NFL softened the anger by adopting a rule in 1926 prohibiting franchises from signing any collegian until his class had graduated.[5]

The barnstorming tours drew modest crowds in some cities, but attendance at games in New York City and Los Angeles numbered 60,000 and 70,000. Such numbers, though, did not signify that Americans were becoming more interested in professional football. Rather, they were curious about Grange. He was one of several mythic men—among

3. One may follow the course of membership in Joe Horrigan, "National Football League Franchise Transactions," *The Coffin Corner* 18 (Summer 1996): 3–13.

4. "Pro Elevens Hurt Sport, Says Stagg," *New York Times*, Nov. 2, 1923.

5. For an account of Grange's tour and the role that Grange played in professional football, see John M. Carroll, *Red Grange and the Rise of Modern Football* (Urbana: Univ. of Illinois Press, 1999), 117ff. "N.C.C.A. to War on Pro Football," *New York Times*, Dec. 16, 1925.

them Babe Ruth in baseball, Bill Tilden in tennis, and Jack Dempsey in boxing—who burnished the "Golden Age of Sports" in the nation. Even after a knee injury left Grange an ordinary running back, thousands of fans viewed him as the "biggest name in football." Probably his appearance on the professional stage dispelled some of the bias against the paid game. Collegiate stars, heretofore passing it by for careers in business, were now willing to wear the togs of the trade—Benny Friedman of Michigan and Ernie Nevers of Stanford, for instance.[6]

Indirectly, nonetheless, Grange endangered the very existence of the NFL. When the league denied a franchise in New York City to Grange's agent C. C. ("Cash and Carry") Pyle (the Giants of the NFL were already there), Pyle organized a competing league in 1926, the American Professional Football League. Many of its nine teams, notably the New York Yankees with Grange in their lineup, challenged the NFL in its larger markets. Though only the Yankees survived the season, NFL teams posted "anemic balance sheets," the Giants losing $40,000.[7]

Chastened by the competition, Carr and the owners decided to transform their league into a "big-city" league. By raising fees of various sorts and offering shares of the league treasury, they forced and persuaded small-town clubs to surrender their franchises. When the smoke cleared, the membership fell from twenty-five in 1926 to twelve in 1927. In the wake of the Great Depression, additional franchises folded until only eight were in the league in 1932. Despite the purge, the owners as late as 1930 were making vague overtures to three independent teams in small towns in the Ohio Valley—Portsmouth and Ironton in Ohio and Ashland in Kentucky—to join the NFL, and indeed the Spartans of Portsmouth entered the league that year. Evidently Carr and the owners saw Portsmouth as a way station where eastern and western teams could play midweek games as they traveled east and west. Thereafter, the league never again admitted a small-town franchise, and membership remained at nine and ten until 1950.[8]

Ironically, a big-city team, the Bears, and a small-town team, the Spartans, tied in the final standings. These teams met in a playoff game in 1932 for the championship of the league, one that led directly to important changes in the rules of play and structure of the league. Owing to a siege of snowstorms, the teams played indoors in the constricted confines of the Chicago Stadium, where the field was only eighty yards long, forty-five yards wide. The Bears won 9–0 on a pass thrown (alleged the Spartans) from a point near the line of scrimmage in violation of the rule requiring passes to come from at least five yards behind the line. Early in 1933 at a special meeting, the owners adopted a rule

6. Michael Oriard, "Home Teams," *South Atlantic Quarterly* 95 (Spring 1996): 449–500. One may read a discussion of sports heroes in the 1920s in Benjamin G. Rader, "Compensatory Sports Heroes: Ruth, Grange, Dempsey," *Journal of Popular Culture* 16 (Spring 1983): 11–22.

7. On losses in 1926, see Peterson, *Pigskin,* 99–101; and James Quirk and Rodney D. Fort, *Pay Dirt: The Business of Professional Team Sports* (Princeton: Princeton Univ. Press, 1992), 337.

8. For details of the "campaign" against the small-town clubs, see several sources: Quick and Fort, *Pay Dirt,* 42, 337; Peterson, *Pigskin,* 102; and Horrigan, "National Football League Franchise Transactions"; Minutes, Executive Committee, NFL, Jan. 25, 1930.

permitting passes from any point behind the line of scrimmage. They also approved another rule stemming from the game, the placing of the ball ten yards from the sidelines after an out-of-bounds play. Heretofore, a play began where the last one ended, or one yard from the sideline if the ball went out of bounds; as a result, the team on offense often had to use a play to move the ball into operating territory. Because of the narrow field at the stadium, the officials brought the ball in-bounds to an imaginary hash-mark. The owners also decided to move the goal posts from the end lines to the goal lines; now field goals, often breaking ties, could become a staple of the game. Believing that playoff games could engender more interest in the National Football League, the owners at their annual meeting in 1933 created Eastern and Western Divisions of the league, the winners of each division to meet for the league championship.[9]

Carr and the owners expected their handiwork to enliven offensive play, which, tied to power running, had long been stodgy, with the result that scoring was low and ties commonplace. In 1932 yards gained a game by passing averaged ninety; a season later, it jumped to 155 yards. Though falling to 118 in 1934 as defenses adjusted, yardage reached 159 in 1935. Field goals increased substantially in 1933, and tie games were half as many in 1932. Scoring rose from sixteen points a game in 1932 to twenty in 1933 and twenty-one in 1934. Probably the opening of the offense accounted, in part, for a steadily rising attendance at NFL games despite the depression: from about 11,000 in 1932 to 14,000 in 1934. The playoff games between the titlists of the Eastern and Western Divisions drew crowds of 26,000 in 1933, 35,000 in 1934.[10]

At once the increasing attendance reflected and contributed to the enhanced stature of professional football. Collegians were readily signing with NFL clubs, and collegiate people were far less shrill in reproving the Sunday game. A cachet of its standing came in 1934 when the Bears, the league champions in 1934, met a team of leading collegiate players in an all-star game (a scoreless tie). Obviously elated over what he viewed as a prestigious advance for the NFL, Carr declared that professional football was destined to surpass all other sports in popularity. It was, he asserted, the people's game: "The pro team provides mechanics, grocery boys, shop girls and workers of all sorts with a home aggregation over which they can yell their heads off." He was certain that the "vast number" of Americans with little schooling would support professional football.[11]

Against the rising landscape of the NFL, the Cincinnati Professional Football Club appeared, receiving a franchise in the league a few days after its incorporation in June 1933. Organizing the club were Dr. M. Scott Kearns, the coroner of Hamilton County, and Wil-

---

9. For details on the game, see Carl Becker, "The 'Tom Thumb' Game: Bears vs. Spartans, 1932," *Journal of Sport History* 22 (Fall 1995): 216–27; Minutes, Special Meeting, NFL, Feb. 25–26, 1933; Minutes, Annual Meeting, NFL, July 8–9, 1933.

10. These figures derive from Carroll et al., *Total Football*, 1649–953.

11. Thomas B. Littlewood, *Arch: A Promoter, Not a Poet* (Ames: Iowa State Univ. Press, 1990), 90ff; "Pro Football to Exceed All Sports," *Cincinnati Enquirer* (hereafter *CE*), Aug. 10, 1934.

liam McCoy, secretary of Nelson, Browning and Company, a firm specializing in investment securities. Supposedly they represented a group of "prominent" but unidentified Cincinnatians. Possibly among them was Sid Weil, owner of the baseball Reds. Weil was interested in professional football and reportedly had joined Carr as a spectator at one of the Spartans games in 1932. He had to be weary of his Reds, now on their way to a third consecutive last-place finish in the National League as they lost games and money (he sold the Reds late in the year). He rented Redland Field to the football Reds and consented to their use of the Reds name. With the franchise in Cincinnati, Carr was closer to his goal of a big-city league. He knew, too, that at Portsmouth the Spartans, sinking in a financial quagmire, might dispose of their franchise, which they did early in 1934, selling it to a Detroit magnate. Kearns became president, McCoy secretary-treasurer. Along with an unnamed stockholder, they constituted a committee directing the club; later they became the board of directors. Under its charter, the company was authorized to issue 1,600 shares of various kinds of common stock. Including Kearns's and McCoy's subscriptions to its stock, the company raised about $20,000. The public did not learn who bought shares.[12]

Kearns was effusive about prospects for professional football and the Reds. "Professional football," he asserted, "has been growing by leaps and bounds all over the country and we want Cincinnati to be on the football map." He believed that the city would "support a professional team" if it played well, and he intended to spare no expense "to field the best team possible." He had already interviewed a number of prospective coaches, among them George Trafton, a stalwart lineman of the Bears; and the committee expected to "start looking around the country for star players." Though Kearns had his "eyes on two local men" from the University of Cincinnati and Xavier University "who might make" the team, he noted that their success was "problematical, as professional football, as played in the National League, demands considerable more than the average collegiate player has to offer." He was working on a schedule calling for home games against the Bears, Spartans, Green Bay Packers, and an "outstanding" Eastern eleven.[13]

The Reds existed on paper and as promises, but whether Cincinnati was able and willing to support them was another matter. On a few counts, the city seemed to be a satisfactory host for football. Through the 1920s, fans followed the semiprofessional teams in the Greater Cincinnati Football League. The Potters and then the Home Guards were fairly strong; they had spirited rivalries with the Ironton Tanks, the Portsmouth Shoe-Steels, the Spartans, and the Ashland Armcos, all good teams playing in the Ohio Valley. From 1925 through 1930 the Cincinnati clubs met these teams eleven times at Redland

12. "Is Treasurer of Grid Team," *Cincinnati Times-Star* (hereafter *CTS*), July 11, 1933; "Giants and Spartans Will Tangle in Loop Opener" and "Huddle Whispers," *Portsmouth Times,* Sept. 25, 1932. I have been unable to locate any official records of the Cincinnati club and thus have had to make "educated" guesses on financial data derived from the charter of the Reds, 155758, Ohio Secretary of State, and a stock certificate, Sept. 4, 1934, Archives, Cincinnati Historical Society.

13. "Cincinnati to Have Team in National Pro Grid League," *CTS*, June 21, 1933; "Cincinnati to Have Team in National Pro Grid League," *Cincinnati Post* (hereafter *CP*), June 21, 1933.

Field, drawing crowds running from 2,000 to 8,000. The community had given good support to the local collegiate teams, the Bearcats of the University of Cincinnati and the Musketeers of Xavier University, and attendance at their games exceeding 10,000 on occasion. Especially, too, the Catholic high school teams drew good crowds.

On other counts, historical and demographic, the community was hardly a certain source of support for the Reds. Kearns and McCoy might have taken instruction from the experience of the Cincinnati Celts. A semiprofessional team organized in 1910, the Celts flourished for a decade and then entered the NFL in 1921. They played only four games, and all on the road. Attendance at their games never more than 2,500, they were unable to pay even the nominal league fees and lost their franchise in 1922. Few people in Cincinnati lamented the Celts' passing, and no body of citizens animated by civic pride appeared to offer balm, as was the case in Green Bay a year later when residents bought stock in the Packers to save the team. The owners could not expect the size of the Reds market to become a surety for financial success. Except for Green Bay and Portsmouth (which saw the Spartans collapse in 1933), the Queen City, with a population of about 500,000, was the smallest city in the league.[14]

Moreover, the Reds faced a market constricted in its outlook on professional football. The citizens of Cincinnati still took great pride in the claim that their city was the birthplace of professional baseball. Theirs was a "baseball town," and the football Reds, from the outset, were a cockboat sailing in the wake of a man-of-war in the baseball Reds. Even as the baseball Reds were ending another disastrous season, the feature sportswriters of the city—Nixon Denton of the *Times-Star* in his daily column "Second Thoughts," Lou Smith of the *Enquirer* in "Sports Sparks," and Naylor Stone of the *Post* through an intermittent and untitled column—were giving the lion's share of their print to the Reds and major league baseball.

The sportswriters were a piece of a pattern complementary to the primacy of baseball. Before radio and television brought professional football to a national audience, residents of a large city without an NFL franchise paid little attention to the game. It had no "local rootedness," no "local presence" in communities like Cincinnati. In Cincinnati readers of the sports pages learned little about the NFL teams and players in the 1920s; about all they knew derived from the wire service reports on the Sunday games appearing in the daily newspapers. What "local rootedness" football had in the city came from the two collegiate teams and the high school elevens. Beat reporters and stringers could file stories about the Red's recruiting, practices, and games, but the feature writers had to institutionalize the team in the community in speculative and reflective prose on the team and its players.[15]

To challenge the dominion of baseball, to surmount the limits of the market, to establish a local presence for the NFL and the Reds, and to muster support from the fea-

14. For an account of the Celts, see Keith McClellan, *The Sunday Game: At the Dawn of Professional Football* (Akron: Univ. of Akron Press, 1998), 161ff.

15. On the concept of local rootedness, see Oriard, "Home Teams."

ture writers—all interrelated elements—Kearns and McCoy needed a sovereign remedy: the Reds had to post victories, not in the long run but at the advent of their play. That would be difficult. The owners apparently had limited funds for signing collegiate stars or purchasing outstanding players from other league teams. They were not wealthy men who could bankroll their team, as could several other owners in the league, among them George Preston Marshall of the Boston Redskins and Tim Mara of the Giants. Nor did they have the experience in semiprofessional or professional football, as did the owners of the clubs entering the league with the Reds. Art Rooney of the Pirates was a madcap gambler who simply converted his semiprofessional team, the Rooneys, into the Pirates. The co-owners of the Eagles, Bert Bell, scion of a wealthy family, and Lud Wray, both experienced men in football, had bought the franchise of the Frankford Yellow Jackets, which had a body of fans around Philadelphia. Neither Kearns nor McCoy was a dynamic leader. Kearns, the spokesman for the Reds, was a rather colorless and bland man who could not present an appealing face to the community. They had wonders to perform to make the Reds viable.

Early in July, Kearns and McCoy began to prepare the Reds for play. They appointed as head coach William "Al" Jolley. Jolley had played tackle for Marietta College and for five NFL clubs from early in the 1920s into the 1930s. Though not given the title, he functioned as a general manager, negotiating contracts with players, hiring game officials, arranging travel for the team, and more. He had as an assistant coach Myron "Mike" Palm, who was expected to play as a quarterback. Palm had played that position for Penn State in 1925 and 1926 and for the Giants and Brooklyn Dodgers for a few years. A reporter for the *Times-Star* believed that he could make the Reds a contender for the NFL championship.[16]

Only days after his appointment, Jolley began "scouring" the "original thirteen states" for players. He left Cincinnati with a "nice new checkbook" handed to him by McCoy, who said, "Go as far as you can" but then added, "I mean in your car." Jolley anticipated signing several "famous players" and had "designs" on John "Shipwreck" Kelly of the Giants, a colorful halfback who had played for the University of Kentucky. He would not divulge the names of the other men whom he wished to sign.[17]

No more reports on Jolley's progress appeared in Cincinnati newspapers until early in September, when candidates for the team gathered at Friarhurst Field for tryouts. Of the forty-four identified in a reporter's story, all but one had played collegiate football—at Ohio State, the University of Kentucky, Centre College, and so on (Kelly was not among them). At least fourteen had played for other NFL teams; significantly, perhaps, none had been with a league team for more than a year or two, an implication that they were hardly outstanding players, that they were hand-me-downs. But noting that he had strong tackles, Jolley predicted that fans would have much to cheer.[18]

16. "Appointed Head Coach of Pro Football Team," *CTS*, July 13, 1933; "Former All-American Star to Be Jolley's Assistant," ibid., July 14, 1933; "Mike Palm Signs to Help Coach Cincy's Pro Eleven," *CP*, July 14, 1933.

17. "Appointed Head Coach of Pro Football Team," *CTS*, July 13, 1933.

18. "'Pro' Footballers Strive for Berths on Cincinnati Reds," ibid., Sept. 5, 1933.

Jolley sent the candidates through two strenuous workouts a day and soon had pared the squad down to forty-two and had two "picked" elevens scrimmaging. Less than a week after the opening practice, the picked teams met in a game at Avoca Park. Before a crowd that a *Times-Star* reporter estimated at 6,000, the teams played forty minutes under a blistering sun. Each team ran from the Notre Dame box; neither could score. The crowd, even if not as large as reported, suggested considerable interest in the Reds, at least for the moment. Following the game, Jolley cut players without "fear or favor," reducing the roster to the league limit of thirty. Altogether, he had seen as many as seventy-nine men.[19]

The Reds were preparing to play through a strange, jumbled schedule. Kearns, working with other owners, seemingly picked up leftover scraps for his team. Owners of teams drawing good crowds ordinarily attempted to schedule primarily teams also drawing well, with the inevitable result that poor-drawing teams had to play many games against teams of their own kind. Veteran owners also drove hard bargains against new owners in determination of guarantees for visiting elevens. In any case, though, in the Western Division of the league, the Reds had on their schedule home and away games with only two teams in the division, the Spartans and the Chicago Cardinals. They had no games with two teams in the Western Division, the Bears and the Packers, which might draw large crowds. In the Eastern Division, the Reds would meet three teams in home and away games: the Pirates, the Eagles, and the Dodgers, all then weak at the gate. Of course, the Reds might post a winning record against such teams. They would meet three nonleague elevens.

In mid-September the Reds opened their season, traveling to Portsmouth to meet the Spartans. The Spartans were a strong team coming off a good showing in 1932 when they lost to the Bears in the playoff game for the championship. They had the nucleus of that eleven returning, including Glenn Presnell and Earl "Dutch" Clark, both triple-threat halfbacks. The Reds roster now numbered twenty-nine; nineteen had played for NFL clubs, and ten were with their first NFL team. Of the starting lineup for the game and a few games thereafter, seven men had been with NFL elevens, and four were rookies. Among the NFL men, the outstanding players were Les Caywood, a lineman who had played for five different NFL teams in the past seven years, and George Munday, a lineman coming to his own after playing but eight games for the Giants and Cleveland Indians in 1931 and 1932. As it turned out, Les Corzine, a halfback from Davis-Elkins College, proved to be the leading rookie. By bulk, the Reds had little to fear from the Spartans. The Reds line averaged 219 pounds, the Spartans 214; the Reds backfield averaged 210, the Spartans 208. Throughout the season, the Reds were never at a pronounced disadvantage in weight against their opponents. By age, the Reds averaged twenty-six, the Spartans twenty-five.[20]

Attired in bright-red helmets, jerseys, pants, and stockings, all trimmed in white, and

19. "Coach Reduces 'Pro' Grid Squad," ibid., Sept. 8, 1933; "6,000 Grid Fans Watch Pro Team," ibid., Sept. 11, 1933; "Lightner Survives Pruning Session," ibid., Sept. 13, 1933.

20. See lineups in "Cincinnati Red Gridders Drop Opener to Champion Spartans at Portsmouth," *CTS*, Sept. 18, 1933; "Red Gridders Easily Defeat Troy Eleven," ibid., Sept. 25, 1933. I arrived at these figures from an entry-by-entry reading of the "Players Register" in Carroll et al., *Total Football*, 547–1442.

their numbers ten inches high, enabling "near-sighted men" in the stands to identify them, the Reds took the field at Portsmouth before a crowd of 5,000 sweltering under a burning sun. Their slight advantage in weight did little for the Reds as the Spartans methodically ground out a 21–0 victory. The Reds, said a Cincinnati reporter, revealed a "distinct lack of organization," a failing he attributed to their few days of practice. They were often fatigued because of the heat.[21]

Their loss to the Spartans, then a premier eleven in the league, did not necessarily spell a dismal season for the Reds, and their next two games must have heartened them and prospective fans. First they went to Troy, Ohio, to face the Flyers, a semiprofessional team of former collegians from Ohio State, the University of Illinois, the University of Dayton, and Ohio Wesleyan. The collegians notwithstanding, the Reds easily won 54–0, with Gil "Pretzel" Lefebvre, the smallest man in the NFL at 156 pounds, running for four touchdowns. A good crowd of 5,000 marveled at his running. The Reds did incur a loss of sorts at Troy. After the game, Jolley chastised halfback Vernon "Chief" Elkins, a Native American, for throwing a "spot" pass to an "undesignated" receiver. Elkins left the Reds in high dudgeon, but Jolley gave him a release to play for the Memphis Tigers, coincidentally the next opponent of the Reds. At Memphis, the Tigers, perennially one of the better independent teams in the South (in recent years they had defeated the Packers and the Bears), gave the Reds a "tussle" at first; but then, exhibiting a "versatile" and "savage" attack, the Reds scored two touchdowns and a field goal for the win, 17–0. They impressed the crowd of 1,500 with their "form as a unit," and a reporter for the *Memphis Press-Scimitar* praised them for their "smooth efficiency." Now they had to return to Cincinnati to showcase their efficiency in their first home game, their foe the Chicago Cardinals.[22]

From their opening days of practices to the eve of that game, though, the Reds scarcely left a mark on the feature sportswriters. Through that period, Smith of the *Enquirer* wrote not one word on their progress. He described in detail play in the National Amateur golf tournament taking place at a course in Cincinnati. He discussed the prospects for the football teams at Notre Dame, Ohio State, the University of Cincinnati, and Xavier University. He commented on the coming season for the baseball Reds—but nothing on the football Reds. At the *Times-Star,* Denton followed a similar tack. Stone at the *Post* did offer a few casual remarks about the Reds, and his newspaper ran a few pictures of Reds players in one issue. Otherwise, the football Reds were a cipher among the three writers.

The Reds were optimistic as they prepared to meet the Cardinals. They had won two games in a row; a big tackle, Lloyd Burdick, injured earlier, was on the mend; and reports had Jolley about to sign Jim Bausch, a line-smashing back with the Bears who had won

21. "Cincinnati Red Gridders Drop Opener to Champion Spartans at Portsmouth," "Spartans Win 21–0," and "Reds Fall in First Start," *CE,* Sept.18, 1933.

22. "Red Gridders Drill at Redland Field," *CTS,* Sept. 22, 1933; "Troy Trojans Next for Reds," *CP,* Sept. 22, 1933; "Red Gridders Easily Defeat Troy Eleven," *CTS,* Sept. 25, 1933; "Elkins Quits Cincinnati, to Play with Local Pros," *Memphis Commercial Appeal,* Sept. 30, 1933; "Reds Win, 17–0, in Dixie Game; Victors Impress," *CE,* Oct. 2, 1933; "Grid Reds Show Real Power," *CP,* Oct. 2, 1933; "Reds Defeat Tigers In Season's Opener," *Memphis Press-Scimitar,* Oct. 2, 1933.

the decathlon in the Olympic games of 1932. Even the gridiron, though improvised at Redland Field, seemed to be inviting them to play, its lines distinctly and carefully limed. It was laid out east and west immediately adjacent to the first base grandstand, with the right field bleachers and third base grandstand at the rear of the end zones.

The game could have been a festive civic event but for the weather. Several high school football teams were on hand as guests of the Reds, and the Shillito Reds Club, all wearing white shirts, were ready to cheer for touchdowns. The mayor of Cincinnati was also a guest. Unfortunately, the Reds and Cardinals had to play in an icy rain on a soggy field before only 1,500 fans. The Reds could not score, and the Cardinals won on a field goal, 3–0, their only league victory of the season. The game resulted in a "heavy loss" at the gate. As Carr once noted, professional football, dependent as it was on ticket sales on the day of a game, was hostage to weather conditions.[23]

Marring or enlivening the game was a fight between Joe Lillard, a black Cardinals halfback who kicked the winning field goal, and the seasoned Reds linebacker Caywood. Evidently after Caywood hit Lillard with his fist after a play, Lillard struck him in the jaw. Both men were ejected from the game. The crowd, coming from a community with ethnic and old commercial ties with the Upper South, offered Lillard no empathy. Wherever he played, Lillard, one of two blacks then playing in the NFL, endured racial slurs or worse. According to his coach, Paul Schissler, he was the victim of racism, a "marked" man, southern and northern players throughout the league giving him the "works." Because the "rest of the league took it out on us [the Cardinals]," Schissler let Lillard go after the season ended. No blacks would play for an NFL team until 1946.[24]

Two days after the game with the Cardinals, the Reds entrained early in the morning for Pittsburgh on their first extended road trip. That night they met the Pirates at Forbes Field with a crowd of 5,000 on hand. The Pirates dominated play, chalking up twenty-one first downs to the Reds' four, and won 17–3. The following Sunday, playing before 12,000 spectators, the Reds met the Brooklyn Dodgers at Ebbets Field. With Benny Friedman passing for three touchdowns, the Dodgers won 27–0. The Reds could record but five first downs.

The Reds returned to Cincinnati a "sadder but wiser" team, said a *Times-Star* reporter. They had lost four league games scoring only one field goal. Coach Jolley, believing that the backfield lacked power, released two backs, shoring it up with the acquisition of "Jarring Jim" Bausch, the Olympic champion. Also joining the team were Jim Mooney, a tackle who had played for the Dodgers and had worked out with the Reds at Ebbets

23. "Professional Team to Use Modified Notre Dame System in Opener Sunday," *CTS,* Oct. 4, 1933; "Field Goal Defeats Reds in 'Pro' Football Debut," *CE,* Oct. 9, 1933; "Sparkling Machine Like Football Features Opening of Professional Football in Queen City," *CTS,* Oct. 9, 1933.

24. When the *Spartans* and Cardinals met at Portsmouth in 1932, police had to come on to the field twice to quell fighting with Lillard, the subject and often the victim of the conflict. Local newspaper reporters employed racial allusions throughout their reports on the game. Lillard was "Massa Lillard," the "ace of spades," a "dark black cloud" hanging over the Spartans, an "Ethiopian in the woodpile." "Cardinals handcuff Spartans to 7–7 Tie Score," *Portsmouth Times,* Oct. 3, 1932; *Morning Sun* (Portsmouth), Oct. 3, 1932. Quoted in Peterson, *Pigskin,* 179.

Field, and Cookie Tackwell, a lineman who had been with the Frankford Yellow Jackets and Bears since 1930.[25]

Thus "reconstituted," the Reds practiced for a game against the Pirates at Redland Field. Saying that expenses for the game would be about $8,000, Kearns looked for a crowd of 7,000 to 8,000. But neither on the field nor at the gate did the Reds succeed. Again, inclement weather—and probably the Reds' record—held down the crowd, and only about 900 fans braved a constant drizzle. The Pirates, though outgaining the Reds in yardage, 211 to 131, could not cross the goal line. Bausch carried the ball eighteen times for forty-one yards, but none for a touchdown. Together the teams missed five attempts at field goals. The result was a scoreless tie.[26]

Concerned about the Reds' failure to score, Jolley then shifted players from one position to another and installed new plays into the offensive repertoire. Then the Reds traveled to St. Louis to play the St. Louis Gunners, a good independent team then contemplating entrance into the NFL. The Reds, noting that six or seven men released by Jolley were on the Gunners roster because they had showed "little ability," expected to capture an easy victory. They did win, but only 7–0 after a fiercely fought game. Evidently the pay-off was good: a crowd of over 6,000 populated the stands.[27]

Their offense sputtering, Jolley declared that the Reds would mount a passing attack against another fledgling team, the Philadelphia Eagles, at Redland Field the next Sunday. He expected Bausch to pace the aerial offensive. Kearns again hoped for a good crowd—if the weather was favorable. It was not. The rains came, soddening the field, especially the baseball infield. Only 300 to 500 spectators were in the stands. Line-battering marked play. Bausch attempted few passes. Ironically, the Eagles scored on a touchdown set up by a pass and won 6–0.[28]

In the wake of another scoreless game, Jolly announced his resignation, explaining that it was in the best interest of the team. One report, though, had Kearns forcing his resignation. Nonetheless, "good feelings" existed on "both sides." But a story surfaced alleging that dissension was rife among the Reds, many players feeling humiliated by their weak offensive showing against the Gunners. Taking over as coach was Mike Palm. Palm immediately

25. "Reds' Gridiron Team Being Reconstituted," *CTS*, Oct. 18, 1933; "Jim Bausch, World's Greatest Athlete Signs with Cincinnati Pro Grid Team," ibid., Oct. 19, 1933; "Cincinnati Reds All Ready for Pittsburgh Tilt Sunday," *CE*, Oct. 21, 1933.

26. "Cincinnati Professional Team Ready for Pittsburgh Fray," *CTS*, Oct. 21, 1933. "Cincinnati Reds Battle Easterners to Scoreless Tie," ibid., Oct. 23, 1933; "'Jarring Jim' Bausch Impresses Fans in Debut," *CP*, Oct. 23, 1933.

27. "Red Gridders Show Pep at Workout Camp," *CTS*, Oct. 25, 1933; "New Players Appear," *CE*, Oct. 25, 1933; "Redlegs Leave for Mound City," *CTS*, Oct. 28, 1933; "Reds Play Gunners at St. Louis Sunday," *CE*, Oct. 28, 1933; "Cincinnati Reds Defeat St. Louis," *CTS*, Oct. 30, 1933; "Hard Fought Win by Red Eleven," *CE*, Oct. 30, 1933; "Redlegs Win from Gunners by Touchdown," *CP*, Oct. 30, 1933; "Cincinnati Reds Take Measure of Gunners, 7–0," *St. Louis Globe-Democrat*, Oct. 30, 1933.

28. "Coach Jolley of Reds Living Up to Name," *CTS*, Nov. 2, 1933; "Phil. Eagles Will Flash Sandlotters on Way to Stardom," ibid., Nov. 3, 1933; "Red Football Team to Battle Today; Hopes to Down Philadelphia Eagles," *CE*, Nov. 5, 1933; "Reb Russell Lived Up to Reputation as Star," *CTS*, Nov. 6, 1933; "Touchdown Put Over by Eagles," *CE*, Nov. 6, 1933; "Reds Again Are Victims of Rain and Opposition," *CP*, Nov. 6, 1933.

initiated changes. He abandoned the Notre Dame box in favor of the more popular single-wing, asserting that with its unbalanced line it afforded more power, especially as a team moved closer to the goal line. He released two players and acquired John "Tex" Burleson, a burly lineman who had played for the Pirates. He also moved players to different positions. For some reason, he moved practices from the afternoon to the morning.[29]

What Palm had wrought was tested on short notice. Entraining for Chicago on a Saturday morning to meet the Cardinals at Wrigley Field, the Reds were "full of Pep" and had a "new lease on life." And seemingly they did. Surprising a crowd of 7,000, they defeated the Cardinals 12–9. Lew Pope ran forty-eight yards for a touchdown, and Myers Clark drop-kicked two field goals. Lillard led the Cardinals to their only touchdown. The Reds' attack, despite the victory, was hardly powerful, yielding only ninety-four yards rushing, none passing. Certainly it was not the "savage attack" portrayed by the reporter for the *Time-Star*.[30]

The Reds came home exuding confidence as they made ready for the "cocky" Spartans again, this time at Redland Field. Palm ran his men through scrimmages incorporating new "line formations," "drilling them in the overhead game," and running receivers "hop-legged" snaring passes. Probably spurring on and agitating the Reds was a report that the Spartans had called them a "collection of pot-bellied and washed-up old men." Undoubtedly, the game marked the high point of the season for the Reds. The largest home crowd of the season, 4,500 or 7,000, depending on what newspaper one read, came to Redland Field. Among them was a trainload of fans from Portsmouth. They saw the game as a lark and seemed more interested in taking lunch at the new Union Station. Recalling the game years later, Presnell said that his team, like the fans, was overconfident. The Spartans fumbled twice in the second quarter, and the Reds converted the miscues into a touchdown and a field goal and then turned back numerous Spartan drives to win 10–7. For once the Reds heard their fans cheer them on; the Spartans heard their fans denounce them for "apathetic" play. At the invitation of Kearns, Stone sat on the Reds bench. He was astonished at the Reds' spirit: the players engaged in "backslapping" and manifested the "old college try" throughout the game.[31]

The victory, though heady wine, did not lead to a third consecutive win. Going to Philadelphia, the Reds reverted to their old form. Momentarily, they took the lead 3–0. Then the Eagles, stirred on by a crowd of 10,000, gathered momentum and won 20–3. Now the

29. "Jolley Resigns as Reds' Coach," *CTS*, Nov. 7, 1933; "Mike Palm Named," *CE*, Nov. 8, 1933; "Jolley Released as Coach of Cincinnati Grid Reds," *CP*, Nov. 7, 1933; "Reds to Change System, New Coach Declares," *CTS*, Nov. 8, 1933; Charles O'Conner, "Time Out," *CTS*, Nov. 9, 1933.

30. "Red Gridders Leave for Windy City Trip," *CTS*, Nov. 11, 1933; "Reds Break Into Win Column in Hard Game," ibid., Nov. 13, 1933; "Reds Defeat Chicago Cards," *CE*, Nov. 13, 1933; "Redlegs Land First League Victory," *CP*, Nov. 13, 1933.

31. "Reds to Take to Air," *CE*, Nov. 17, 1933; "Cincinnati Reds Are Confident of Holding Spartans in Professional Grid Struggle at Redland Field Today," ibid., Nov., 19, 1933; "Redlegs Jolt Portsmouth 10 to 7 as 7,500 Fans Look On," ibid., Nov. 20, 1933;. C. Robert Barnett, *The Spartans and the Tanks* (North Huntingdon, Pa.: Professional Football Researchers Association, 1983), 28; "Reds Beat Spartans as Week-End Winds Up 'Swell' for Local Fans," *CTS*, Nov. 20, 1933; Naylor Stone, *CP*, Nov. 29, 1933.

Dodgers came to town for the last game of the season. The outlook was not good for the Reds. They had already lost decisively to the Dodgers and had three men unlikely to play because of injuries, while the Dodgers were at full strength. A fairly good crowd (3,500) saw the Reds turn the tables on the Dodgers, lifted by one of the great runs of the season. In the fourth quarter, with the Reds leading 3–0, Lefebvre fielded a punt on his own two-yard line and in a spectacular broken-field run raced into the end zone for a touchdown. For many years the run stood as the longest punt return in NFL history. The Reds held on and won 10–0.[32]

Thus the Reds completed the season with a league record of three wins, six losses, and a tie; their nonleague victories evened out their wins and losses. They finished in fourth place in the Western Division, ahead of the last-place Cardinals. With three or four good men, they might reasonably expect to improve their record in 1934. Their talent already thin, they could not, however, hope to trade for outstanding players. They would have to purchase capable players already in the league or sign on good men coming out of the collegiate ranks.

Their ability to add such players depended, at least in part, on their financial status. If the record for 1933 was any sign, that would not be easy. No reporter ever provided any specific details on their ledger, either as the season progressed or at its conclusion. Perhaps the Reds nearly broke even or realized a small profit on road trips, a loss on home games. On road trips they received guarantees of $3,000 to $3,500 a game from the home teams. That sum would cover players' salaries—in the neighborhood of $2,750 at $125 a player a game—and expenses for travel and lodging. But home games had to wreck the Reds budget. For their five home games, the Reds had to expend around $15,000 to $17,000 in guarantees while meeting their own payroll of $12,000 to $14,000. They also had to pay fees to game officials and rent for fields of play and practice. Revenue from home games, drawing about 14,000 fans each paying $1.50 a ticket, was about $21,000. Thus their loss at home could have been as high as $10,000. Months after the season ended, a Reds officer acknowledged that it had been "big." A reporter for the *Times-Star*, noting the attendance at Redland for the Dodgers' games, asserted that "evidently" Cincinnati "did not care for professional football."[33]

If Cincinnatians did not "care" for professional football, Kearns and McCoy did little to move them to another view. Not once did they place a display advertisement in local newspapers informing readers of the upcoming Reds games. They did not publicize

---

32. "Reds Lose Star End as Result of Injury," *CTS*, Nov. 28, 1933; "Coach Palm Is Hard Put for Subs for Squad," *CE*, Nov. 29, 1933; "Reds Wind Up Pro Grid Season Against Dodgers," *CTS*, Dec. 2, 1933; "Fast Little Red Stirs Fans with Run of 98 Yards," *CTS*, Dec. 4, 1933; "Lefebvre in 98 Yard Touchdown as Redlegs Beat Dodgers 10–0," *CE*, Dec. 4, 1933.

33. I built these figures, which are quite approximate, from consultations with Bob Carroll, director of the Professional Football Researchers Association, Dec. 14, 2000, and Glenn Presnell, Dec. 15, 2000. "Chili Walsh Here to Bid High for Reds' Franchise," *CP*, Aug. 14, 1934; "Fast Little Red Stirs Fans with Run of 98 Yards," *CTS*, Dec. 4, 1933.

their teams outside of Cincinnati, in the many small communities in southwestern Ohio and northern Kentucky. Aside from inviting Stone to sit on the Reds bench at one game, evidently they did not attempt to elicit support from the principal sportswriters in the city. In their columns on sports, which commanded large readerships, the feature writers gave the Reds short shrift. Through the season, Denton referred to the Reds in "Second Thoughts" but twice, complaining in one column that he was unable to buy a chocolate bar in the reserved seat section. As he had just before the opening of their season, Smith did not spend one word on the Reds in "Sports Sparks." Even though the baseball Reds were completing a dismal season as the football Reds played their first four games, Denton and Smith were writing about baseball. Only the *Post* gave print to the NFL, summarizing the principal games that the league teams played and publishing standings. The residue of local rootedness was at work. Reading the *Times-Star* and *Enquirer,* one would hardly have known that the NFL existed.[34]

If the Cincinnati Professional Football Club faced straitened circumstances in the months following the season's play in 1933, no one noted the problem in public print. No one—no civic leader, no club official—proposed a public campaign to sell season tickets to games or stock in the club, as typically was the case in Portsmouth or Ironton when the Spartans or Tanks were in financial trouble. As though he fully intended to see his team play out the season of 1934, Kearns attended the NFL owners' meeting early in July, negotiating trades for and purchases of seven players, none of whom played even one quarter for the Reds in 1934.[35]

Nevertheless, the Reds were looking for some sort of support from the community. Late in July Kearns announced that the George W. Budde Post, No. 507, of the American Legion had assumed sponsorship of the Reds. The commander of the post, John Duffy, explained the decision as one tying the future of professional football in the city to civic virtue: "Our great belief in the future of professional football is the big reason why myself [*sic*] . . . and other members of the Price Hill Budde Post have undertaken the sponsoring of the Reds this years. We are entering the field because we are at all times anxious to put our names behind a great civic enterprise, and we feel that our names backing the Reds will be a forward step." He was certain that the Reds would "advertise" Cincinnati. To hasten the good work, Edward Boyle, a past commander of the post, said that he intended to direct ticket sales from Reds headquarters in the Metropole Hotel. He expected to make a "thorough canvass" of the "city's business spots to help foster the idea." No one indicated that the post would provide direct subventions to the franchise.[36]

As the legion assumed sponsorship of the Reds, whatever it was, Myron Greentree, a former business associate of McCoy and now general manager of the team, announced

34. Nixon Denton, "Second Thoughts," *CTS,* Oct. 9, 1933.

35. Minutes, Annual Meeting, NFL, June 30–July 1, 1934; "Reds Land Seven Gridders," *CE,* July 2, 1934.

36. "Budde Post to Sponsor Reds' Pro Football Team," *CE,* July 22, 1934; "Legion Post to Back Grid Team," *CTS,* July 23, 1934; "Legion Backs Grid Reds," *CP,* July 23, 1934.

that he had signed nineteen players to contracts. At least seven had been with the Reds in 1931: Corzine, Lefebvre, Tackwell, Pope, Mooney, John Rogers, and Hillary Lee. He had also received letters from Clark, Munday, and Les Mulleneaux saying that they expected to sign contracts soon. Of the nineteen, five did not make the team, and four or five played in only one or two games.

Despite Duffy's rhetoric and the post's sponsorship, the Reds' place in Cincinnati was not secure. Two weeks after the announcement of the post's decision, Charles "Chili" Walsh, coach of the St. Louis Gunners and one of the club's owners, was in town attempting to purchase the Reds franchise for the Gunners. Dressed in a white linen suit and "scorching red tie," he was prepared, said the *Post*, to make a "big" offer to the Reds. But Kearns declared that only a huge offer, one wiping out the Red's debt, would result in a sale and that otherwise the club would continue to play in Cincinnati, perhaps as a member of the newly organized American Football League. Initially Walsh did not meet Kearns's figure, whatever it was; but then he raised his offer, and Kearns agreed to sell the franchise to the St. Louis club. Kearns did not disclose the terms, but reports had the Gunners paying $20,000. All nine other NFL clubs had to ratify the sale. But their approval was not forthcoming. They took no vote appearing on any official record. Reportedly, though, they believed that travel expenses for Eastern and Western Division teams ruled out play in St. Louis. Greentree had another explanation: the Reds' stockholders voted unanimously to abandon the sale because the "wail of fans began to echo north from the Kentucky hills and south from Hamilton." They would have as soon sold the Tyler Davidson Fountain in downtown Cincinnati, said Greentree. Conferring with Greentree in Cincinnati, Carr applauded the decision. Stone rejoiced in the vote, saying that fans of football in Cincinnati would be happy.[37]

"Wails" alone did not halt the sale. Rumors had it that several prominent businessmen had purchased enough stock to forestall a sale. More than a month after the sale fell through, Greentree revealed the names of the men—the "mysterious forces"—who had "saved" professional football for the city. The men—Charles Kroger, Charles Hinsch, Polk Lafoon, Thomas Wood, and Charles Wilson—were all reputable businessmen affiliated mostly with insurance and investment companies. What number of shares they bought no one revealed. Evidently they purchased enough to give the Reds an infusion of about $7,500. In any case, Greentree believed that the Reds' "financial worries" were at an end and that they could compete for players.[38]

37. Lou Smith, "Sports Sparks," *CE*, Aug. 6, 1934; "Chili Walsh Here to Bid High for Reds' Franchise," *CP*, Aug. 14, 1934; "Deal for Sale of Football Reds Held Up," ibid., Aug. 4, 1934; "Franchise Sold to Gunners, Official Says," *St. Louis Post-Dispatch*, Aug. 7, 1934; "Cincinnati Agrees to Transfer National League Franchise to Gunner," *St. Louis Globe-Democrat*, Aug. 8, 1934; "Professional Football Team Franchise to Remain Here," *CTS*, Aug. 17, 1934; "Directors Decide to Keep Grid Reds in Cincinnati," *CP*, Aug. 17, 1934; "Gunners Not to Get Cincinnati Grid Franchise; Fans Object," *St. Louis Post-Dispatch*, Aug. 1, 1934; "Red Eleven Again in Field; Pro Franchise Remains Here," *CE*, Aug. 1, 1934; "Joe Carr is Visitor," ibid., Aug. 22, 1934.

38. "Here Are Cincinnatians Who Saved Pro Football," *CE*, Sept. 9, 1934. Kroger was a "Special Agent" for the Atlantic Life Insurance Company, Hinsch a bond salesman for the Fifth-Third Securities Company, Polk a vice

Soon Greentree did indeed sign some new players to contracts. From Green Bay he acquired Norman "Buster" Mott, a quarterback, and expected him to become the "foundation" of the Reds' passing attack. Frank Thomas, Mott's backfield coach at the University of Alabama, once called him the best passer he had seen in ten years. The manager purchased Earl Elser, a tackle, from the Spartans. He also signed four men just coming out of universities: Talmadge "Sheriff" Maples, Jim Dildie, Bo Kirkland, and Jim Bushby. Of Maples, a lineman at the University of Tennessee, his coach, Bob Neyland, supposedly had said "honestly, it sometimes hurts me to see the sheriff drive on and meet the runner head on." Dildie and Kirkland, also linemen, had been on an eleven at the University of Alabama that played in the Rose Bowl. Bushby had a reputation as a good running back at Kansas State. Altogether, though, they were a disappointing lot. Their coaches' praise notwithstanding, Mott and Maples played just a few games for the Reds. Neither Dildie nor Kirkland suited up for even one game. Bushby and Elser did not play out the season with the Reds and were only journeymen at best.[39]

Not until late in August, only a few days before practices began, did the Reds name a coach. Palm having taken a coaching position at West Virginia University, Greentree turned to Myers "Algy" Clark, a quarterback for the Reds in 1933. The manager called him an "inspired" leader, his ability "outstanding." Clark did not promise victories but was certain that he would direct the "hardest fighting club in the league. . . . I guarantee my eleven will be there fighting every minute of the game and will play heads-up football all the time." He had as his assistant coach Caywood, the "Dean" of the Reds.[40]

The Reds opened practices at the end of August with about forty men trying out for berths. Coaches and reporters all were roseate at what they saw: the line was stronger than in 1933; the backfield was faster; the Reds were improved at all positions; Bushby and Mott would cure the weakness of passing in 1933 when the passers handled the ball as though it were a hot iron; the Reds would "go places"; they were 50 percent better than they were in 1933; they would be strong contenders for the league championship. So went the litany of acclaim. Perhaps coaches, sportswriters, and fans all could feel even more optimism at learning that the Reds had made some kind of arrangement with the Louisville Bourbons of the American circuit calling for them to serve as a "farm" club. The Reds had already sent a tackle, Vernon Bryant, to the Bourbons for "seasoning" and reportedly

---

president for the Union Gas and Electric Company, Wood president of Safeway Insurance Underwriters, and Williams president of the Western and Southern Life Insurance Company. See *William's Cincinnati Directory 1933–1934* (Cincinnati: Williams Directory Company, 1934), 774, 946, 960, 1744, 1774. This figure comes from a certificate of stock, Sept. 4, 1934, in Archives, Cincinnati Historical Society, suggesting that Charles Williams paid $1,500 for fifteen shares of stock. If the four other men who "saved" the Reds purchased the same number of shares, as they probably did, altogether the five men turned over $7,500 to the club.

39. "Mott, Former Georgia University Star, to Be Foundation of Reds Passing Attack," *CTS,* Aug. 23, 1934; "Reds Well Supplied with Husky Tackles," ibid., Aug. 30934.

40. "'Algy' Clark Is New Coach of Cincinnati Redleg Eleven," *CE,* Aug. 20, 1934; "Redleg Pro Gridders Begin Training Grind," *CTS,* Aug. 28, 1934.

were looking over the Kentuckians' roster for players. The arrangement, though, proved to be meaningless, no movement of men between the clubs taking place thereafter.

Contemplating their schedule, the Reds had another reason for optimism. For years past, as in 1933, the owners had had considerable leeway in constructing schedules. Now, though, Carr called on owners in each division to arrange a "balanced schedule," to play home and away games with every other team in their division. They had the option of playing two or three games against teams in the other division as well as nonleague games. As a result, the Reds expected to play eight games in the Western Division and two in the Eastern Division. They had two nonleague opponents. Though they might face stronger teams in the Western Division, the Packers and the Bears, than they had in 1933, the Reds had the prospect of realizing greater revenue.[41]

Soon enough optimism gave way to reality. Going to Pittsburgh to play the Pirates for their first game, the Reds used nearly the same starters as they had in 1933, Elser and Bushby being the only newcomers. The Pirates, playing for a large crowd of 14,000, sent their fans home in a good mood, forcing the Reds to walk the plank 13–0. At best, the Reds could take consolation in their ability to move the ball on occasion; but they squandered all their scoring opportunities. Though one reporter called the Reds' line "impregnable," another asserted it was weak at one tackle. Disappointingly, Mott did not prove to be an effective passer.[42]

The "purchase and trade winds" already beginning to howl, Greentree signed three new linemen in a few days, Basil Wilkerson, Benny Sohn, and Ed Aspatore, all NFL veterans. They brought no balm to the Reds in their next game, a nonleague encounter with the Bourbons. Kicking a field goal in the last minute of play, the Bourbons won 9–7. Greentree was so distraught that he caught the first train to Cincinnati, leaving the team behind and refusing to be interviewed or to order dinner. The three linemen proving inadequate, he released them soon, none playing more than three games. He also sent Mott packing.[43]

More or less, the Reds played a home game the next Sunday. Originally their schedule called for them to go to Chicago to meet the Cardinals. But the Cardinals could not use the "larger parks" in the city. The Cubs were playing the St. Louis Cardinals at Wrigley Field, while the White Sox were meeting the Philadelphia Athletics at Comiskey Park. The Cardinals agreed to play the Reds at a "neutral" site. Greentree, taking the initiative, arranged for the game to be played in Dayton at the stadium of the University of Dayton under the auspices of the Dayton Industrial Athletic Association. Seeking to bolster the Reds' passing game, he signed Mike Sebastian, a halfback who had played at the University of Pittsburgh. Sebastian's coach there, Jock Sutherland, supposedly had declared

41. "Cincinnati Eleven to Play 11 Games in 'Pro' Circuit," *CTS*, Aug. 24, 1934.

42. "Pro Team Loses Season Opener," *CTS*, Sept. 10, 1934; "Pittsburgh Defeats Reds in Opening Game," *CE*, Sept. 10, 1934.

43. "Pro Eleven Is Seeking New Men," *CE*, Sept. 11, 1934; "Professional Football Team Management Continues Drive to Strengthen Eleven," *CTS*, Sept. 12, 1934; "Former Red Kicks Goal to Make Bourbons Victors," *CE*, Sept. 17, 1934; "Pro Footballers Lose Non-League Game to Louisville Team in Last Minute of Play," *CTS*, Sept. 17, 1934.

him the best passer whom he had seen in "many days." He also acquired Foster Howell, a tackle, at the recommendation of his former coach at Texas Christian, Francis Schmidt. The *Dayton Daily News* and the *Dayton Journal* gave considerable coverage to the coming game, and a crowd of 5,000, reading about the prowess of both teams, came to the stadium to see the "pros." The game began in a dramatic way as Reb Russell of the Cardinals ran the kickoff 102 yards for a touchdown; later the Cardinals added a field goal to win 9–0. Sebastian did little for the Reds. Aside from the touchdown, the crowd, said a *News* reporter, saw no "abundance of sensations." The Cardinals played with "finesse and precision" while the Reds were "ragged." If any profit derived from the gate, the Athletic Association took a good share of it.[44]

Then the Bears, champions in 1933, came to town for the Reds' first true home game. And for the only time during the season, reporters for the *Times-Star* and *Enquirer* gave substantial coverage to a coming game because of the stature of the visiting team. They wrote in detail of Red Grange, the "Galloping Ghost," as though he were still in his prime and of the "brilliant" array of talent on the Bears' eleven. Of the Reds they commented largely on their new uniforms—red jerseys with gold letters and red helmets—and on Cole Gilging, a recent graduate of Xavier University who was exuberant at starting as an end for the Reds: "Boy I love it. In pro ball you run up against a lot larger and tougher men." The writers may have stirred up some interest in the game, for more than 5,000 fans were at Crosley Field (Redland had been renamed for the new owner of the baseball Reds). They heard two American Legion bands and a postal employees' band play fight songs and Russell Wilson, the mayor of Cincinnati, deliver a short speech extolling the Reds. Then they saw the Bears, starting their second-stringers, handily defeat the Reds 21–3. Beattie Feathers of the Bears ran up and down the field twenty times, gaining anywhere from two to thirty-two yards. The Reds were "woefully weak" on offense but did kick a field goal, their first points in league play.[45]

Still seeking their first victory and touchdown in league play, the Reds next met the Cardinals in Cincinnati in a game marked by novelty. For the first time, a professional football team played a night game on Sunday and, to boot, at a university facility, Cochran Field at Xavier University. For some reason, apparently the Reds could not play at Crosley Field. Clark drilled the Reds in "more deception" and in their blocking and tackling in prepara-

44. "Bears, Cards, in Final Drill for Openers," *Chicago News*, Sept. 21, 1934; "Cards Off for Grid Opener Against Reds," ibid., Sept. 22, 1934. The *Chicago Herald-American* had the Cardinals playing at Crosley Field, Sept. 22, 1934; "Mike Sebastian, All American Back at Pitt, Joins Reds to Help Bolster Aerial Game," *CTS*, Sept. 18, 1924; "Chicago Cardinals Boast of Fine Array of Stars," *Dayton Journal*, Sept. 21, 1934; "Cards-Reds Roster Proves Scouts Don't Always Like All-American Footballers," *Dayton Daily News*, Sept. 22, 1934; "Cards Win Thriller at Stadium," *Dayton Journal*, Sept. 24, 1934; "102 Yard Run High Spot as Cards Win," *Dayton Daily News*, Sept. 24, 1934; "Cards Beat Red Gridders," *CE*, Sept. 24, 1934.

45. "Chicago Bears, Outstanding Pro Team to Be Reds' Next Foe in Initial Home Game," *CTS*, Sept. 25, 1934; "Grange, Galloping Ghost of Gridiron, to Play Against Cincinnati Eleven," ibid., Sept. 26, 1934; "Cincinnati to See Brilliant Array of All-American Talent," ibid., Sept. 27, 1934; "Former Xavier Ace to Play Flank Post in Redleg-Bear Tilt," ibid., Sept. 28, 1934; "Pro Football Gets into Action Today; Bears Led by Grange, Meet Red Club," *CE*, Sept. 30, 1934.

tion for the Cardinals. They resolved that Russell would not repeat a long run against them. They were apprehensive, though, about stopping Lillard, the "Ebony Flash," the "swarthy colored boy." Astonishingly, though they had played the Cardinals once, they did not seem to know that Lillard was no longer with the Cardinals. The game would be a test of another sort, too. Greentree let it be known that he was ready to "start building for [the] next season" and that "men found wanting against the Cardinals" would be released. Though the advance sale of tickets indicated that a large crowd would be at Cochran, it numbered only about 2,500. The fans had little to cheer about. Unleashing a strong running attack yielding 287 yards, the Cardinals ground down the Reds 16–0. The Reds, netting but eighty-four yards, were "absolutely hopeless" on offense and would not, predicted a reporter, rise out of the "maiden ranks" until they found reinforcements. Coach Clark never bore the blame for the Reds' performance. Greentree, the recruiter, seemingly assumed responsibility for the skein of losses. Good as his word, soon after the game Clark let four men go, including the diminutive Lefebvre, saying that he would replace them later.[46]

The Reds then journeyed to Green Bay to play the Packers with only eighteen men on the roster, two of them injured and hardly able to play. The Packers, smarting over recent losses, gave the eighteen a 41–0 shellacking. From Green Bay the Reds went to Chicago to meet the Bears. Greentree had signed a new back, Pete Saumer, reputedly a strong runner, but he could not stay the avalanche. The Bears buried his new teammates 41–7, with Feathers scoring two touchdowns. Finally, though, the Reds did score a touchdown on Corzine's short run. Returning home, the Reds had the Detroit Lions on their schedule. But Greentree, pessimistic about the gate, arranged for the game to be played at Portsmouth, where the former stars with the Spartans might show their wares. Undefeated, the Lions, wrote a reporter for the *Detroit Free Press,* regarded the trip to Portsmouth as a "triumphant" homecoming. Before a crowd of 4,800, the Lions, their erstwhile Spartans no doubt remembering the embarrassing loss to the Reds in 1933 and playing in front of many old friends, overwhelmed the Reds 38–0. Dutch Clark sparkled as he passed, punted, and ran the ball. The only redemptive aspect of the game for the Reds was Mooney's excellent punting. Recalling the game years later, Presnell of the Lions called the Reds "rejects."[47]

As the Reds absorbed their beating, Greentree again explored the prospect of selling the franchise to the Gunners. He and Walsh met with Carr in Columbus to discuss the subject, and Carr, who had earlier opposed the proposed sale to the Gunners, now gave his assent. But Greentree denied that the club would be sold immediately, explaining

46. "Redlegs Tuning Up for Game with Cards," *CTS,* Oct. 2, 1934; "Former Hughes Backfield Flash May Carry Pigskin for Reds on Professional Field," ibid., Oct. 4, 1934; "Russell Feared by Reds, Working to Stop Cardinals," *CE,* Oct. 5, 1934; "Reds Meet Cards at Cochran Field Tonight," ibid., Oct. 17, 1934. "Members of Reds on Toes for Scrap with Chicago Team," *CTS,* Oct. 6, 1934; "Grid Reds Play for Jobs," *CP,* Oct. 6, 1934. "Chicago Cards Defeat Redlegs Under Lights," *CTS,* Oct. 8, 1934; "Red Eleven Is Defeated by Chicago Cardinals, 16–0," *CE,* Oct. 8, 1934; "Red Grid Team Drops Four Men," *CTS,* Oct. 10, 1934; "Redleg Gridders Off for Wisconsin," ibid., Oct. 11, 1934.

47. "Green Bay Packers Massacre Redlegs," *CTS,* Oct. 15, 1934; "Bruders, Packers' Star in Reds' Defeat, 41–0," *CE,* Oct. 15, 1934; "Bears Once Again Win Over Redlegs," *CTS,* Oct. 22, 1934; "Reds Downed at Chicago, 41–7," *CE,* Oct. 22, 1934; "Lions Keep Record Unmarred by Trouncing Cincinnati, 38–0," *Detroit Free Press,* Oct. 29, 1934; "Detroit Gridders Overwhelm Reds," *CTS,* Oct. 29, 1934; interview with Glenn Presnell, Nov. 9, 2000.

that "we have just cleared the way for possible sale of the Reds later." The Reds owners would not sell the franchise, he asserted, unless attendance was poor at home games during the remainder of the season. His words were a sham. As he purportedly opened a door to keeping the Reds in Cincinnati, Greentree was in fact closing it. Continuing to negotiate terms with the Gunners, he agreed to give the Gunners the Reds' two remaining home games against the Pirates and Packers.[48]

Now the Cincinnati newspapers hardly gave the Reds any coverage. The *Times-Star* and *Post* barely noted their next loss, 35–7, at St. Louis to the Blues, a member of the American League, and the *Enquirer* did not even mention the game. Greentree, who had suddenly arranged the game and was in St. Louis, told a reporter for the *St. Louis Post-Dispatch* that he could not understand what was wrong with the Reds: "It's a strange thing. We have a great collection of individual stars. As a unit we don't seem to score." His lamentation was nonsense. Not one Red had recognition among fans, coaches, and players as a "star." Of the thirty-six men who were on the Reds roster at one time or another in 1934, only seven played any games in the NFL in the following years, four for no more than four games. Apparently the players had no illusions about their failure to score. Decades later Corzine recalled that the offense had "no deception whatever"; another player asserted that the "ends and backs didn't run good patterns, I guess they didn't know a helluva lot of them."[49]

Through his seeming puzzlement over the Reds' play, Greentree may have been attempting to raise the ante for the Reds. At St. Louis he met with Walsh and Edward Butler, a co-owner of the Gunners, and agreed to sell the franchise to the Gunners for $20,000, a sum probably close to the Reds' indebtedness. The *Post-Dispatch* reported the purchase in a front-page story, saying that another planet had made its appearance in the sports firmament. Setting aside their concern about travel expenses, the NFL owners gave their unanimous consent to the sale, probably hoping that the Gunners would prove a stronger franchise than the Reds. The Gunners picked a few Reds—Corzine, Munday, Mooney, Rogers, and Elser—for their roster.[50]

Even as the ink dried on the contract for the sale, the Reds completed their play in an appropriate way. At Philadelphia the Eagles gave them a terrible whipping, 64–0, then the worst loss any team suffered in the NFL since its organization. The Reds thus ended their play with a league record of no wins and eight losses, scoring but ten points. The Gunners went on to complete the Reds' schedule, winning one game and losing two; for the first time in the history of the NFL, one team played out a defunct team's schedule. Financially, the Gunners did no better than the Reds. At the end of the season, they could not meet a debt of $9,000. The NFL then revoked their franchise in 1935.

48. "Way is Clear for Red Sale," *CP,* Oct. 20, 1934.

49. "Blues Gain 35 to 7 Victory Over Cincinnati Eleven," *St. Louis Post-Dispatch,* Nov. 1, 1934. I derived these figures from a reading of the players' entries in the "Players Register" in Carroll et al., *Total Football,* 547–1442. Quoted in Paul Stillwell, "The Team Nobody Wanted," *Pro!* Nov. 10, 1974, 3D–6D.

50. "St. Louis Sportsmen Purchase Cincinnati Football Franchise," *St. Louis Post-Dispatch,* Nov. 6, 1934; "Gunners Buy National Football League Franchise," ibid., Nov. 6, 1934; "$20,000 Reported Paid for Transfer of Reds' Franchise to St. Louis," *St. Louis Globe-Democrat,* Nov. 6.

. . .

At the news of the sale, Reds fans did not protest in "wails," as supposedly they did a few months earlier at the reports of a similar sale. No one whimpered about the decision. No one raised questions about the Reds' financial condition, which obviously led to the sale. Surely it was not good, akin to what the club had experienced in 1933. On the road, with guarantees awaiting them, probably they covered expenses. But at home, again the figures appeared in red ink. The Reds played but two games in Cincinnati, a telling sign that they did not see much support coming from fans there. They drew about 8,000 fans in the two games and derived about $12,000 in revenue. Taking into account the guarantee that they had to post, the payroll that they had to meet, and the expenditures for staging a game, the Reds probably lost $3,000 to $5,000. Coupled with the dismal record in play, it was too much for the owners to bear.

The Reds needed a fistful of dollars to bid for good players who could have touched the heart of fans and scored victories. Never did they recruit a player who became a "star"— an Ernie Nevers, an Arnie Herber. Never did they announce that they had acquired an established player in the league or a promising rookie—a "name"—coming out of college. Meanwhile, in 1933 and 1934, the Bears brought to their roster outstanding young players Jack Manders, Bill Karr, and Beattie Feathers; the Giants could boast of Harry Newman and Ken Strong and the Redskins of Glen "Turk" Edwards. The Reds were in the business of entertainment but did not entertain as did movies and radio of the day.

Unable or unwilling to keep the Reds afloat by their own resources, Kearns, McCoy, and other stockholders, whoever they were, did not urge the leading sportswriters in the city—Denton, Smith, and Stone—to sound an alarm to the community on the imminent loss of their franchise. (In any case, as in 1933, the scribes had hardly given the Reds the time of day in 1934.) They did not reach out to the citizenry, arguing that civic pride called for the rescue of the Reds. Vigorous owners and journalists might have acted otherwise, as they did in Green Bay in 1923 and 1933 and in Portsmouth in 1931.

As it was, the Reds were an anachronism in the new era of the NFL—indeed, a drag on the league. Almost a fly-by-night team, they were an island of instability in the mainstream of stability. Besides the Reds and Gunners, only one franchise, the Spartans, shut down from 1933 through 1939. Considering the Reds' financial base and the economic conditions of the time, probably the NFL should not have granted the Kearns and McCoy a franchise. On the field, they could not exploit the new rules rewarding diversity in offensive play. On average over two years, the Reds scored just three and one-half points a game; excluding the Reds, all other teams averaged nearly eleven points a game. They could not share in or contribute to the rising popularity of professional football. Their home attendance averaged just 2,800 a game through two years, even as average attendance for all the other teams in the league was nearly 14,000. The Reds never had kinship with the ledger, the goal line, or the community.[51]

51. These figures come from a summary of scores in Carroll et al., *Total Football,* 1750–51.

A Republic of Farm People

Women, Families, and Market-Minded Agrarianism in Ohio, 1820s–1830s

GINETTE ALEY

On April 31, 1832, forty-eight-year-old Aaron Miller departed his native Louden County, Virginia, home on horseback, accompanied by his brother Daniel, to travel westward to Ohio. Their expressed purpose was to seek out and purchase farms capable of profitable wheat production for several of the Miller brothers and their families. Over the next month and a half, Miller recorded his detailed observations about Ohio and its agriculture, farm people, and overall state of economic and material development. Certainly, whatever Thomas Jefferson had envisioned within his agrarian ideology regarding the future growth and prosperity for the young United States and its "republic of farmers" was alive, well, and commercially succeeding in Ohio by the 1830s, major elements of which were documented by Miller.[1]

Even before crossing into the state, on a route that would traverse central Ohio counties primarily along the National Road and briefly into Indiana, Miller met almost daily with two, three, or five droves of Ohio cattle bound for the Baltimore and Philadelphia

---

1. Aaron Miller's diary is held by the Ohio State Historical Society, Columbus, and cataloged as "Aaron Miller Diary, VOL 549." I quote it here as he wrote it; it was also published verbatim as "Diary of Aaron Miller," *Ohio Archaeological and Historical Quarterly* 33 (Jan. 1924): 67–79 (hereafter Miller Diary). Apr. 31, 1832, Miller Diary, 69; see brief biographical sketch in Miller Diary, 67–68. On the history of Ohio, see Andrew R. L. Cayton, *Ohio: The History of a People* (Columbus: Ohio State Univ. Press, 2002), R. Douglas Hurt, *The Ohio Frontier: Crucible of the Old Northwest, 1720–1830* (Bloomington: Indiana Univ. Press, 1996), Robert Leslie Jones, *History of Agriculture in Ohio to 1880* (Kent: Kent State Univ. Press, 1983), and Andrew R. L. Cayton and Stuart D. Hobbs, eds., *The Center of a Great Empire: The Ohio Country in the Early Republic* (Athens: Ohio Univ. Press, 2005). Especially useful was Francis P. Weisenburger, *The Passing of the Frontier: 1825–1850* (Columbus: Ohio State Archaeological and Historical Society, 1941). A general history of American agriculture is Paul W. Gates, *The Farmer's Age: Agriculture 1815–1860* (Armonk, N.Y.: M. E. Sharpe, 1960). On the strength of agrarianism in the new republic, see Drew R. McCoy, *The Elusive Republic: Political Economy in Jeffersonian America* (New York: Norton, 1982).

Ohio History, Vol. 114 © 2007 by The Kent State University Press

markets. At every turn he sought the "knolage and good sense" of the local farm people on matters including what kinds of agriculture were practiced and had flourished,
land value per acre, market access, and the general health of the country. The negative
condition of the latter in particular, though infrequent, was enough to dissuade Miller
from even looking at farms in an area of that character. Upon coming into Champaign
County, for example, Miller learned that the land there was "filled with a certain something" that the locals could not identify and only knew that if the cattle ate "it" in the
woods, what was termed "milk sickness" would prevail upon them. This sickness often
brought on an agonizing death to both cattle and unsuspecting humans who drank the
sick cattle's milk. That being the case, he and his brother rode on.[2]

. Miller was primarily guided in the search for his and his relatives' new Ohio farms by a
calculus, or rationalization, of "advantage." After all, these were going to be cash purchases
that would form the basis of family farming enterprises whose owners had aspirations of
profitability. Miller also knew that his determination of selecting the site with the best advantages for wheat growing would set into motion the relocation of numerous family members and several neighbors from Virginia, a move that in all likelihood would be permanent.
Among the advantages he noted about the places he passed were their fine grass, soil quality,
good spring water (as opposed to well water), the overall state of cultivation, the level of
activity in the county seat, and even the abundance of "nice farmers," such as those he found
in Germantown (in Montgomery County). Of particular interest to Miller was the advantage of water navigation, and in his diary he offers important insight on the influence of
Ohio's canal-building era on the development of the state's agriculture as well as on the lives
and livelihood of its farm people. Newark, situated on the canal, appealed to him because
flour was regularly shipped out from there for the New York market. Also, there seemed to
be no limit to the growth potential of Chillicothe, which was "improveing verry fast" as a
result of the canal being constructed twenty miles south of the town, with the contractors
having committed to extending it northward by the fall. This convinced Miller that the farm
people there "will have the advantage of the new york market *and* the new Orleans market."
He added, "Certainly verry great are the advantages of this canal of the state of Ohio."[3]

2. May 3–6 and 20, 1832, Miller Diary, 69–70, 74. A discussion of milk sickness is found in the entry for May
13, 1832, and includes the following: "the cattle will be turned out in the morning well and healthey[,] and in
the evening will be found verry sick[;] they take with a trembeling . . . and continue so a few [h]ours and die . .
. and any person using the milk[,] freaquently done before it is discovered in the cow, takes with a sickness on
the stomach and commence with a pukeing and die without remedy, in a verry short time."

3. Miller's remarks about "advantages" are made throughout his entries, but see, for example, May 15 and
18, 1832, Miller Diary, 73; May 10 and June 1, 1832, Miller Diary, 71, 77 (emphasis added). On Ohio's canal period see Harry N. Scheiber, *Ohio Canal Era: A Case Study of Government and the Economy, 1820–1861* (Athens:
Ohio Univ. Press, 1987). On the transformative effect of the canal-building era on neighboring Indiana farm
people and the complex politics behind it, see Ginette Aley, "'Bringing About the Dawn': Agriculture, Internal
Improvement, Indian Policy, and Euro-American Hegemony in the Old Northwest, 1800–1846," in Daniel P.
Barr, ed., *The Boundaries between Us: Natives and Newcomers along the Frontiers of the Old Northwest Territory,
1750–1850* (Kent: Kent State Univ. Press, 2006): 196–218; and Ginette Aley, "Westward Expansion, John Tipton,
and the Emergence of the American Midwest, 1800–1839" (Ph.D. diss., Iowa State University, 2005).

Market-minded agrarianism pervaded Miller's diary in his search for the most economically advantageous situation for his family and clearly served as the major ideological and economic context for his perception of Ohio and the emerging Midwest. It apparently resonated as well with the numerous farm people from whom Miller gathered
information and with those whom he merely observed in their agricultural activities.
This state of affairs in Ohio and the West during the 1820s and 1830s is in sharp contrast
to the scholarly argument that the market of the expanding republic was something
"feared" or avoided by agriculturists. Rather, as Miller's diary and the following accounts
make plain, it was recognized as a force to engage in with "knolage and good sense" and
one that could *improve* the family's situation, not just meet the demands of it. Indeed,
market-minded agrarianism, when coupled with transportation innovations like canal-
building, offered exciting new possibilities for commercially successful farming. This
idea supports the conclusions of historians such as Daniel Vickers who assert that the
market transactions of early Americans "bespoke a clear commercial sensibility" and a
"mode of production geared to considerations of use *and* sale."[4]

One can see this commercial sensibility, for instance, in Miller's observations about his
ride through Madison County, "a low barron country." It had the appearance of being "a
great place for graizing cattle," and the "people here make it a beusiness." They would buy
their cattle low elsewhere, bring them back, and then every fall drive a large portion of
them east to sell as stock cattle. Their efforts garnered the farmers a considerable quick
profit. "From what I can learn," Miller wrote, "they make about fifty percent clear on their
money annually." Not surprisingly, given the family orientation of American agriculture,
the labor of young boys was essential to the success of the cattle enterprise. The boys tended
the cattle while on horseback, he related, "with their basket of provisions on their arms[,
riding] after them all day to keep them together and at knight pen them up."[5]

It is also within the context of the market that Miller's interactions with two farm

4. Daniel Vickers, "Competency and Competition: Economic Culture in Early America," *William and Mary
Quarterly* 3d ed., 47 (Jan. 1990): 3–29 (quoted at 6; emphasis added). My characterization of "market-minded
agrarianism" parallels R. Douglas Hurt's conclusion that early Ohio settlers were "a profit-minded people"
(*Ohio Frontier*, 210). A major influence of the fearing-the-market argument is Christopher Clark, *The Roots of
Rural Capitalism: Western Massachusetts, 1780–1860* (Ithaca: Cornell Univ. Press, 1990), and, recently, in a Mid-
west context, Richard F. Nation, *At Home in the Hoosier Hills: Agriculture, Politics, and Religion in Southern Indiana* (Bloomington: Indiana Univ. Press, 2005). It is difficult to reconcile, for example, Miller's shrewdness with
Clark's assertion that "when farmers traded more of their produce outside the region, their chief purpose was
not to engage in the market economy but to satisfy the demands placed on them by the household economy"
(*Roots of Rural Capitalism*, 84). In a similar vein is the portrayal of the market as something of a negative, mag-
netic force that "drew farmers" in, instead of casting farm people as positive, even ambitious, decision makers
with regards to profitable transactions. See Christopher Clark, "The Ohio Country in the Political Economy of
Nation Building," in Cayton and Hobbs, eds., *Center of a Great Empire*, 146–65.

5. May 12, 1832, Miller Diary, 71–72. On the rise of Ohio's beef-cattle industry, see Jones, *Agriculture in Ohio*,
chap. 5, and R. Douglas Hurt, "Bettering the Beef: Felix Renick and the Ohio Company for Importing English
Cattle," *Timeline* 10 (Mar./Apr. 1993): 24–29. Another example of the importance of boys' labors in both the
domestic and farm economies is found in Ginette Aley, "Grist, Grit, and Rural Society in the Early Midwest:
Insight Gleaned from Grain," *Ohio Valley History* 5 (Summer 2005): 3–20.

women reveal the nature of their role in the family farming enterprise as well as their participation in market transactions. In the first encounter, Miller inquired of a Butler County farmer named Morres if it was true that he desired to sell the family's 180-acre farm. Morres answered in the affirmative, explaining that all but one of his children had married and left "and that he was giting to old to manage the farm." He drove a hard bargain, but Miller thought it a highly desirable farm with seventy acres of it being cleared, a "verry fine stone house," and the land well watered by springs. So Miller agreed to meet his price of $2,000 cash. Obviously nervous, Morres went down to the dairy "where his wife was putting away her milk" to discuss the matter with her. Miller had to wait until the next morning to learn that in fact the sale would not go through because Morres said that his wife "was not willing." While Miller believed that it was Morres himself who had developed cold feet concerning the sale, Morres's wife was clearly an integral part of the decision-making process when it came to the market status of the family farm. His second notable encounter with a farm wife occurred during Miller's investigation of land closer to Cincinnati where he came upon a substantially improved farm owned by "Jersey people." The farm wife was preoccupied with "packing up marketing to load a wagon which was agoing to start the next morning to cincinnati." The couple told Miller that their farming generated about $300 a year in this way, despite being forty-five miles from the market. This statement impressed Miller. It affirmed to him "that none are so far from market as those who have nothing to sell."[6]

Miller eventually bought a 252-acre farm from a dissatisfied Dunker south of Hillsborough in Highland County. The clincher for him was its distinct market advantage: "I am told that on the Ohio river they will give from five to ten cents a bushel more for the wheat raised in Hiland county than for aney other." Subsequently, Miller, four of his brothers and their families, a neighbor and his four sons and their families migrated from Loudon County, Virginia, to Highland County, Ohio, via a caravan of wagons. They resettled and essentially lived out their lives on farms in close proximity to each other, none further than fifteen miles apart.[7]

Aaron Miller's farm-buying journey and subsequent family-based migration illustrate a number of the major themes and experiences in the emerging agrarian Midwest. Given the estimation that by 1840 as many Americans lived west of the Appalachian Mountains as lived east of them, the process of migration was a widely shared experience. In Miller's diary we also observe the extent to which Ohio agriculturists were becoming attuned to and willingly, if not eagerly, integrated into the expanding transportation and market structures in the 1820s and 1830s. Ohio historian Andrew Cayton characterizes this period as one of "Improving Ohio," that Ohioans viewed their interests as being "intertwined" with that of the development of the state. Certainly, accounts like that of Miller bespeak a widespread and somewhat enthusiastic participation in the expanding market. Market-minded

6. May 20 and 21, 1832, Miller Diary, 74–75.
7. May 27, 1832, Miller Diary, 76–77; see also 67–68 for brief comments about the Millers' migration to Ohio.

agrarianism was the springboard for many to join the stream of westward migration and the peopling of Ohio and the Midwest, just as it was for the extended Miller family.[8]

Central to a nexus linking farming, migration, and the market was the family, the entity by which migration and settlement were managed, the mechanism by which farms were developed and marketed, and the medium through which social and community interactions (including religious affiliations) were carried out. The family was a person's first and primary identity. For women, it often signified their entire identity and the stage upon which their lives played out. However, historically, and historiographically, the roles of agrarian women and children have been overshadowed by the more readily available male-authored manuscript materials, such that historians continue to point to the relative dearth of studies focusing on women during this period, specifically regarding Ohio.[9]

Part of the problem may also be in our conceptualizations as well as lack of perspectives. In a provocative 2000 article, historian Patricia Cline Cohen notes that the era of the early republic, especially between 1790 and 1830, is still relatively quiet when it comes to U.S. women's history, which frequently manifests itself as silence in college textbooks. Cohen attributes this to the common traditional rendering of the period's history as one driven by "an unrelenting masculine narrative" of political and economic events; these events, she points out, "of so masculine a cast, appeared to leave little room for attention to women." Yet, economic events of the early nineteenth century *do*, or at least *should*, invite discussions about the labors of rural agrarian women. Equally important is the need to incorporate these women's views of the market. It seems that with regards to economics, we are not yet acknowledging women (and children) loudly enough where they most certainly were present.[10]

Most Americans of the young republic were farm people, and, perhaps inadvertently, scholars seem to minimize the importance of agriculture to the lives, activities, and perspectives of women and their families. Given the prevalence of farming, and that farming was a family enterprise typically aimed toward the market, how can we justify the continued downplaying of rural women and their children as major contributors to the

---

8. In his demographic study of the early American frontiers, James Davis found that "the settlement process prior to 1840 was almost wholly a family activity, the family sometimes being altered a bit by the process." James E. Davis, *Frontier America 1800–1840: A Comparative Demographic Analysis of the Frontier Process* (Glendale: Arthur H. Clark, 1977), 24. "Introduction," Edward Watts and David Rachels, eds., *The First West: Writing from the American Frontier, 1776–1860* (New York: Oxford Univ. Press, 2002), xiii; Cayton, *Ohio*, 49.

9. Hurt, *Ohio Frontier*, 407. An important (non-Ohio) model for studies on rural farm women during this period is Joan M. Jensen, *Loosening the Bonds: Mid-Atlantic Farm Women, 1750–1850* (New Haven: Yale Univ. Press, 1986). On interpreting the roles of women and children in the context of changing family relations in the decades after the Revolution, see Anya Jabour, *Marriage in the Early Republic: Elizabeth and William Wirt and the Companionate Ideal* (Baltimore: Johns Hopkins Univ. Press, 1998); Steven Mintz and Susan Kellogg, *Domestic Revolutions: A Social History of American Family Life* (New York: Free Press, 1988); Carl N. Degler, *At Odds: Women and the Family in America from the Revolution to the Present* (New York: Oxford Univ. Press, 1980); and Mary P. Ryan, *Cradle of the Middle Class: The Family in Oneida County, New York, 1790–1865* (New York: Cambridge Univ. Press, 1981).

10. Patricia Cline Cohen, "Women in the Early Republic," (Organization of American Historians) *Magazine of History* 14 (Winter 2000): 7–11 (quoted at 7).

expanding market economy prior to 1850? For that matter, why do we continue to employ a phraseology that separates women from their agricultural responsibilities, expertise, and accomplishments, such as "the farmer and his wife"? They were both farmers. Agrarianism, even more than migration, was a broadly shared experience among women, men, and families until well into the nineteenth century. It offers an inherently relevant, ongoing context for studying changing socioeconomic patterns (in this case, the developing market structure) as they relate to gender and deserves closer investigation. Miller's diary is only one example that demonstrates how the farming-migration-market nexus can offer unique opportunities to document and assess the involvement and perspectives of early-nineteenth-century farm women, and their children, engaged in the agricultural development of their state and region. As is evident throughout Miller's writings, women were remarkably market minded and exhibited a variety of responses to market interactions.[11]

To some degree men and women faced migration differently, largely as a consequence of the different roles they played within the family unit. Yet at the same time, both remained committed to their vision of improved circumstances for the family. As two of the male family members capable of securing the cash purchase of farms, Aaron and Daniel Miller embarked on the lengthy, farm-buying journey on behalf of their kin in Virginia. Beyond keeping the family close by, of primary interest to the brothers in relocating were the prospective market advantages they would gain. Sustaining familial ties and networks was clearly important to the Miller brothers, and this would be true of women as well. Yet women's writings reflect the excruciating pain of severing kinship ties, since usually not all family members migrated, as seen in the Millers' case.

It was also generally believed that migration and the separation were permanent. Minerva Tupper Nye expressed this sentiment when she wrote to a friend in 1788 soon after migrating from Massachusetts to the Ohio Country: "We now live in the city of Marietta where we expect to end our days." For some women the separation from family and friends was like an open wound, the constant ache of a heavy heart. From her extensive research in nineteenth-century women's personal writings, historian Lillian Schlissel found this pain and separation to be a common feature of nineteenth-century life, surmising that "a family on an American frontier—wherever that frontier might be—was a family separated from some part of itself." Expanded more broadly, migration had the effect of breaking off and transplanting portions of regions, sub-regions, and affiliated groups of

11. See Ginette Aley, "Review of Richard F. Nation, *At Home in the Hoosier Hills: Agriculture, Politics, and Religion in Southern Indiana, 1810–1870*," H-Indiana, H-Net Reviews, May 2006, URL: http://www.h-net.org/reviews/showrev.cgi?path=232491153163558. On farm women in a later period, see Deborah Fink, *Agrarian Women: Wives and Mothers in Rural Nebraska, 1880–1940* (Chapel Hill: Univ. of North Carolina Press, 1992); see also Elizabeth Fox-Genovese, "Women in Agriculture during the Nineteenth Century," in Lou Ferleger, ed., *Agriculture and National Development: Views on the Nineteenth Century* (Ames: Iowa State Univ. Press, 1990), 267–301; and Nancy Grey Osterud, "Gender and the Transition to Capitalism in Rural America," *Agricultural History* 67 (Spring 1993): 14–29. On childhood in the agrarian Midwest, see Pamela Riney-Kehrberg, *Childhood on the Farm: Work, Play, and Coming of Age in the Midwest* (Lawrence: Univ. Press of Kansas, 2005).

people in the creation of reconstituted societies in newly claimed places, like in Ohio and the emerging Midwest.[12]

The effects of migration were also felt by Anna Briggs Bentley. In May 1826, six years before the Millers departed Virginia for new Ohio farms, thirty-year-old Bentley, her husband, their six children (born at two-year intervals), and a black servant named Henry made the long, difficult, and emotionally wrenching journey from Sandy Spring, Maryland, to Columbiana County, Ohio, in desperate hopes of developing a prosperous farm. They left behind her mother and sister as well as one buried child. But as Quakers they were able to join an established, though still developing, Quaker community in eastern Ohio. In that year, approximately eight thousand others of their faith were already engaged in building up that region of Ohio. Bentley's anguish over the separation from her mother, sister, and former home led to a profusion of incredibly detailed and insightful letters that reveal the arduous life of an agrarian wife and mother and that of her family.[13]

One series of responses attests to the disruption of kinship ties. When her husband, Joseph, first considered moving the family away from Sandy Spring, Bentley implored her father not to encourage the move because "it would be a trial too great for me to bear a separation so distant from my dear parents." After migrating, her written remarks ranged from "Oh, can it be that I am so far from you? I think of it sometimes and fall to wondering how I ever could have consented to it" to "There are several waggons going from here to Alexandria and Baltimore in 2 or 3 weeks. Oh, how I wish I could go in one of them." Children were equally traumatized by migration. As the Bentleys were leaving Maryland, an acquaintance came to say good-bye to five-year-old Thomas Bentley but became overwhelmed with emotion. The family "left him leaning against a tree." Anna Bentley later wrote her mother that "Thomas has cried about it this evening and asked, 'Mother, did [Kirk] cry because he would never see me again?'"[14]

12. The Minerva Tupper Nye correspondence is held at the Ohio Historical Society as MSS 210 and is quoted in part in Mildred Covey Fry, "Women on the Ohio Frontier: The Marietta Area," *Ohio History* 90 (Winter 1981): 55–73 (quoted at 58). Less useful but interesting is Hermina Sugar, "The Role of Women in the Settlement of the Western Reserve, 1796–1815," *Ohio State Archaeological and Historical Quarterly* 46 (Jan. 1937): 51–67; Lillian Schlissel, "Introduction," in Lillian Schlissel, Byrd Gibbens, and Elizabeth Hampsten, eds., *Far from Home: Families of the Westward Journey* (New York: Schocken Books, 1989), xv. An alternative view of midwestern family and farming life that emphasizes a rigid hierarchical and patriarchal set of relationships, see John Mack Faragher, *Women and Men on the Overland Trail,* 2d ed. (New Haven: Yale Univ. Press, 2001).

13. Anna Briggs Bentley's many letters are cataloged as the Briggs-Stabler Collection, MS 147, Maryland Historical Society, Baltimore, and many are also published as Emily Foster, ed., *American Grit: A Woman's Letters from the Ohio Frontier* (Lexington: Univ. Press of Kentucky, 2002). I have chosen to quote the letters verbatim, including her tendency to use emphases, but have translated the dates from the Quaker format (i.e., "1st month 16th day 1830") to the more conventional month/day/year style. Bentley's biographical information is in the "Introduction." Foster's interpretations as editor must be used with care. One particularly obvious error is in her statement that Bentley gave birth to daughter Caroline in 1834 "only ten months after her son, Edmunds" (156). As Foster herself noted earlier, and the letters confirm, Edmunds was born in 1831, a fact that is also noted in Appendix Three. She makes another error relative to Edmunds' age upon his death in 1842, inaccurately saying that he was twelve years old (202), although he could not have been. See Dec. 12, 1830, and July 18, 1831, Foster, ed., *American Grit,* 118, 131, 132n1. Cayton, *Ohio,* 43.

14. Bentley's letter to her father is quoted though not cited in Foster, ed., *American Grit,* 14. On the way to Ohio and May 22, 1826, Jan. 16, 1830, ibid., 22, 26, 107. One of Bentley's letters is also published in Marks,

Migrating away from family members was just as wrenching as the experience of one's own grown children and grandchildren moving west to pursue better economic opportunities. In this way migration cut like a double-edged sword across generations. Bentley used her correspondence to bridge the distance between separated family members, so that "as I am journeying on through time in my distant habitation I may keep up a kind of acquaintance and not feel like a stranger in my own dear native land." Others, such as farm woman Sarah Adamson of Fayette County, Ohio, felt compelled to ease the pain through creative literary expressions, including poetry. In 1838 fifty-one-year-old Adamson was forced to say good-bye to several of her children who were emigrating to Lee County, in what is known today as the State of Iowa. She remained inconsolable to the point of distraction. To many women, migration had deeply personal consequences:

> Who can describe the painfull parting scene
> Which passed between us at the gateway green
> The heartaching sorrow still retains its place
> Nor months, nor days, nor friends can it erase.
> My Sidney, Mary Jane and William, Oh adieu
> I[t] grieves me to the heart to part with you.

After a daughter and several grandchildren succumbed to death there, Adamson and her husband joined their remaining offspring in Iowa in 1850. Bentley herself enclosed in an 1829 letter a poem entitled "Broken Ties" that expressed her regret about how the "dissevered chain" that bound a family "in sparkling ruin lies."[15]

Despite the depth of anguish that migration and separation from kin, friends, and home provoked, Bentley's letters evince that remarkable ability, that "pioneering spirit," to shake off personal disappointments and face the new world into which the family had just imposed themselves. No doubt some women held tightly to their bitterness. Bentley's letters, however, reveal not only her resignation to this new life ("I do strive after resignation") but also her awe and optimism at participating in the transforming of a new place into an agriculturally productive region, which she believed would in turn improve their economic situations as well. The migration journey in May of 1826 was threatening in and of itself. "Oh, that wearisome, trying journey," she lamented, "it would be *no* hardship without little children, but we were so crowded and overloaded . . . I little knew how harassed the mind would feel and wearied the body when each day's travel was ended and after much bustle the supper was over and the poor children put to bed." Yet within the same letter, which in practice would often span several days, Bentley

---

Bayly Ellen, ed., "Correspondence of Anna Briggs Bentley from Columbia County, 1826," *Ohio History* 78 (Winter 1969): 38–34.

15. July 14, 1827, Foster, ed., *American Grit*, 61. A reference to Bentley's poem is found in a letter dated Feb. [?], 1829, ibid., 83. A portion of Adamson's untitled poem is reprinted in Glenda Riley and Carol Benning, eds., "The 1836–1845 Diary of Sarah Browne Armstrong Adamson of Fayette County, Ohio," *The Old Northwest* 10 (Fall 1984): 302–4; see also 286–89 and 302 for Adamson's biographical information.

assured her loved ones of her hope: "I know if we can only get through *this* summer the worst will be over." Characteristic of rural people balancing a hard reality with optimism, she conceded that "I do find it hard to do for all with so few conveniences and *no help,* but I have all reason to expect better times soon." Her resourcefulness included churning pounds of butter without a churn and using a sugar trough as the baby's cradle.[16]

Improving one's circumstances in a republic of farmers required a cooperation-based labor regimen that came at a premium in terms of physical health, and it still did not guarantee that all would go well for the family. Women's health was already strained by the frequently recurring pregnancies and childbirths that constituted their reproductive labors. As noted, Bentley had already borne seven children and buried one by the time she migrated to Ohio at the age of thirty. She then gave birth to six more children at roughly three-year intervals, the last one arriving in 1842 when she was forty-six. Child care was an ongoing element of women's lives, and, as Bentley's literary conversations make plain, it gave many women the most joy and sense of identity and purpose. She believed that a "mother's heart" connected women in a unique and meaningful way. Nevertheless she became understandably weary and depressed after bearing so many children. At the prospect of having her tenth child, she admitted to her sister that she had held out hope after the ninth child that she "never should have that trial to undergo again"; coming to grips with this pregnancy "has been a trial almost too hard for me to bear with any degree of resignation." Her gloom would eventually lift, though it did not completely dissipate. Bentley's letters show that while she took pleasure and pride in her children, she also took an immense personal satisfaction and sense of achievement in her agricultural abilities and activities.[17]

But Bentley regularly bore a great deal of pain. She often complained, for example, of being plagued by a debilitating back pain made worse when she continued with her work. Working despite the pain resulted in a subsequent curtailing of her labor that affected the entire household, given that a woman's role was to meet the immediate daily needs of her family. Bentley's husband, Joseph, would sometimes come home and find her unwell. "He threw down his load of wood," she wrote on one such occasion, "and when he looked at my full [wash] tubs and pale face covered with a cold sweat he began to *scold* me for undertaking all at once. 'It is just like thee overdoing the matter and then [be] good for nothing.'" He proceeded to step in and help the children set the table, make supper, feed the baby, clean up, and "spread the beds." Agrarianism demanded that everyone work, and the laborer was valued to the point that those who could not do so were labeled "good for nothing": "I am very 'crippling,' as Mother used to say, with my hip and back, some-times [I] can scarcely walk at all and am getting to be almost good for nothing." Ironically,

16. May 22 and July 30, 1826, Foster, ed., *American Grit*, 24, 25, 39.
17. Appendix Three, ibid., 317–20; Aug. 14, 1836, ibid., 173. Examples of health issues that Bentley seems to associate with reproduction are Feb. 24 and June 15, 1834, and Dec. 31 [1836], ibid., 156–57, 159–60, 178. Her understanding of how a "mother's heart" connects women is expressed in Oct. 21, 1832, ibid., 146.

even Bentley seemed unaware of the value of women's reproductive labor, as she made the preceding self-deprecating comment while pregnant with her ninth child.[18]

The same standards and expectations of farm men and women applied to children. At an early age, the children assisted their mother with domestic and farm chores regardless of gender, just as they had witnessed their father doing. Nine-year-old Maria was adjudged "very useful" for her ironing ability, care of younger siblings, bringing in of nearly all of the household's water, and dish washing. Thirteen-year-old Granville at times took over his mother's washing, baked the corn pones his sister mixed up, made the coffee, and brought over milk given by neighbors. Fourteen-year-old Franklin assisted with the household's sewing when a wounded foot kept him confined indoors. A decade earlier, William Cooper Howells was also an agrarian boy in eastern Ohio. His responsibilities included sorting wool, obtaining flour at the local mill, minding the cow and pig, keeping up the family's supply of firewood, and helping his mother with the baking, all the while envying the other "big boys" who got to tend the fires for boiling the sugar water at the sugar camps. Howells's account confirms that the sexual division of labor beyond the basic household and field dichotomy is more aptly characterized as flexible and ad hoc; intense labor needs encouraged an outlook toward labor that was often age and gender blind. "The rule was," he insisted, "that whoever had the strength to work, took hold and helped." His account is also replete with examples of farm people, young and old, seeking and devising ways to make a profit however they could.[19]

Yet the larger, more laborious tasks associated with actually establishing the new farming enterprise were typically divided along gender lines. "The men and boys leave at daybreak and return at sundown," Bentley related. "They are engaged in felling, grubbing, mauling, and burning and expect *very* shortly to have 3 or 4 acres fenced in and planted in potatoes, turnips, &c." She added that their work turned their clothes "literally black" thus adding substantially to her laundry labors. Childhood was short, from Bentley's daughter Maria's perspective. When she was fifteen she wrote to her cousin about a typical day: "Father is now out in the clearing at work & Thomas too. Franklin is hauling wood, and I just done [shooing] the children out to play." She added that she felt tired and stiff, "as I suppose an old plough horse must feel after a hard day's work." The common use of children, especially boys, to assist with strenuous labor and dangerous chores was the cause of many serious accidents and injuries. Within a short period of time, three of Bentley's sons were suffering with serious injuries ranging from an ax to the foot, a pitchfork prong to the neck, and a gunpowder explosion to the face. Bentley

18. June 14, 1826, and Mar. 13, 1831, ibid., 27, 124. Clearly at wit's end after trying to nurse sick children and believing her labors in general to be of little use, Bentley signed one of her letters "I am your own stupid, weary, good-for-little, A[nna]" (Apr. 8 [1832], ibid., 140). A useful study that details the roles and responsibilities of frontier women is Glenda Riley, *The Female Frontier: A Comparative View of Women on the Prairie and the Plains* (Lawrence: Univ. Press of Kansas, 1988).

19. May 22; June 14, 20, 1826; and July 26, 1829, Foster, ed., *American Grit*, 26, 27, 30, 97; William Cooper Howells, *Recollections of Life in Ohio From 1813 to 1840* (Cincinnati: Robert Clark Comp., 1895; reprint, Delmar, N.Y.: Scholars' Facsimiles & Reprints, 1977), 44, 45, 50, 55, 58–59, 80 (quoted at 157).

expressed her distress about the potential dangers to children who labored with their family in building a farm.[20]

Agrarian women labored in and out of their households. In these developing farm communities they often came together to coordinate the massive food preparation required to feed the rounds of harvesters, "raisers," logrollers, etc. This was a daunting responsibility that originated from a "custom of the country," meaning that the scarcity of laborers and the cash to pay them was overcome by the widely accepted social obligation of reciprocity. Coming from the upper south, a region accustomed to servants and slaves, this situation was new for the Bentleys, as it also would have been for the Millers of Virginia. "They have a custom here in harvest or other busy times," she explained, "to collect as many neighbors as they can, and they will pay back in work . . . they prefer that to paying money."[21]

When it was Bentley's turn to feed the almost forty hands gathered to raise their house, she was assisted in numerous ways by neighbor women, including one who came the day before to do her regular domestic chores and care for the baby so that she could concentrate on food preparation. Other women came and one by one took on a portion of the huge task—that is, taking the fruit and flour home to make the pies, roasting her meat, baking her bread, making the applesauce. Another arrived at daybreak on the day of the raising to help feed the early workers. The final dinner spread included a ham, the mutton from half of a sheep, two large pieces of beef, a half-bushel each of potatoes and beets, seven loaves of bread, thirty pies, and two gallons of applesauce. The reciprocal labors of women and men were intertwined, and were both fundamental and essential to the early farm-building years in Ohio and the emerging Midwest. Bentley's repeated references to these labor-sharing events as "the custom here" qualifies them as being an important element in defining the roots of midwestern identity.[22]

Bentley found much to admire in her new world and in these "pie-eating people." Their neighbors were kind and sociable, extending all kinds of assistance to ease the privations faced by "New begginers." Bentley described the situation in one of her letters: "Our garden affords us as yet no vegetables, but then our neighbours send us cucumbers, beans, potatoes, in *abundance,* and I make an *abundance* of nice puddings and pies." As William Cooper Howells and many others had done, Bentley marveled at "how luxuriantly things grow" there. Typical of her and other agrarians' descriptions was her account of feasting on plums "so large and delicious they grow in the greatest abundance from about 50 yds from the house—large trees almost breaking down with them." Of all the hardships they faced, starvation would not be one of them. By July Bentley was already envisioning how the family's labor coupled with the land's obvious fecundity

20. June 14, 1826; June 29, Aug. 1, 1829; and Apr. 15, 1832, Foster, ed., *American Grit,* 27, 95, 99–101, 141, 142. Maria is an expressive teen who offers an interesting perspective of a daughter who often labored as a mother in letters that she starts and her mother finishes. See for example, Jan. 5, 1834, ibid., 154–55.

21. July 20, 30, 1826, ibid., 35–36, 38–39.

22. Sept. 18, 1826, ibid., 47–48.

would bring about an improvement in their circumstances: "I sat on a log and cast my eyes around on the beautiful hills, the majestic Oaks, and the traces of labour around me . . . here *is* an inheritance for my children where they *may* earn their bread if it *is* by the sweat of their brow." The farm was the family's future. Once the initial farm-building years were over and the farming could begin producing surpluses, they could seek out profitable market connections.[23]

Just as Aaron Miller based his decision to migrate and purchase a farm on a calculus of advantages, Bentley employed a rationale of improving one's circumstances in how she offered encouragement to family and friends who considered joining them. She firmly believed the Marylanders could do better for their families in eastern Ohio, but she and her neighbors cautioned others to seek the inner light (a common admonishment among Quakers) and guard themselves against rash decision making because inevitably some did fail in their efforts. And it was no easy life. When Bentley offered advice it was with an eye toward profitability, such as when she relayed the opinion "about what would be the most profitable commodity for Bro Isaac to bring out" to Ohio (leather) and the most remunerative trade he could engage in (tanning). Notably, after the family's first year of difficulties was over and Bentley gained the live-in help of a neighbor's teenage daughter and an elderly seamstress, her letters from 1827 on contain an increasing number of references to market-minded agrarianism, one of the first of these being about the area's thriving grapevines and the promise of viticulture. They were, she observed, "becoming a matter of speculation and is thought will be more profitable than farming. We have an ex[c]ellent spot for a vineyard and intend planting one sometime."[24]

Like their neighbors, the Bentleys were adept at identifying various commodities that held the potential to provide much-desired items to trade, barter, or sell for cash. A coal bank on the Bentley's land, for example, quickly yielded a fortunate opportunity to help expand their farming enterprise. For collecting seventy bushels of coal valued at a total of $11, they were able to procure a three-year-old bull, a young steer, and a ton of clover hay. "The coal bank," Bentley reported to her family, "seems to be opening a source of great proffit to us, as it is in great demand as being the best in the country and appears to be inexhaustible." Bartering was an important practice to rural people, especially to those who had only recently established new farms and were in need of many things. Even so, their newness was often a hindrance even to bartering because, as Bentley pointed out in early 1828, "we have not been here long enough to raise anything" with which to trade. What she had to work with at that particular moment was "*6 dozen eggs* for 2 lb of rice, which I have not seen in this country, or 3 fat hens for a lb of coffee or 3 bushels of turnips for an *old* check apron." The next year, the more marketable commodities were flax,

23. May 22, July 30, and Aug. 17, 1826, ibid., 37, 39, 41, 43.

24. July 20, 30, 1826; Feb. [?] and May 30, 1827, ibid., 34–35, 37, 38, 56, 60. Bentley's perception about the cultivation of wine grapes being of keen interest to Ohio growers by the mid-1820s is an accurate reflection and is the topic of R. Douglas Hurt, "The Vineyards of Ohio, 1823–1900," *Northwest Ohio Quarterly* 55 (Winter 1982–83): 3–16.

butter, and linen, all of which the Bentleys were struggling to cultivate and process. But they continued to be handicapped by the early stage of their farm building. In the spring of 1829 Bentley's husband, Joseph, could not afford the $35 to buy a yoke of oxen to plow his fields; ironically, he was only a yoke of oxen away from being able to haul away the hundreds of bushels of coal at his disposal for immediate sale.[25]

Implicit in Bentley's letters is the idea that bartering beyond the occasional neighborly trading was only temporary—until the passage of time and focus of labor enabled the enterprising agrarians to achieve significant commodities to market. As a side commodity, Bentley believed that the prospects for sugar making were quite good, although rather laborious, and she pursued it with an overtly competitive spirit. During the "good sugar days," she and several children would trudge through the early spring mud with a bucket on each arm for water, along with her "spiles," augur, and brush to clear the troughs and tap the widely scattered trees for sap. Bentley had only one ten-gallon kettle and one four-gallon pot with which to boil and stir off the sugar, yet her first day of sugaring netted thirteen pounds of "good sweet sugar." She added with pride that "many with 3 times as many trees and 6 kettles did not make more than 6 lb." The four days of sugaring totaled sixty pounds of sugar and inaugurated the Bentley family's sugar production; however, additional pregnancies caused Bentley to cut back. Bentley had every intention of marketing her surplus and did not hesitate to do so. "If we can make more than with great [frugality] is enough for our own use," she reasoned, "why, it will help to extricate us from debt." Her desire to use the surplus to improve their financial circumstances distinguishes this activity from one done to simply meet the demands of the household to one for profit. This entrepreneurialism also involved her butter making. In the same letter she noted that she had sent two and a half pounds of "nice butter" to the store the previous week. She was paid only eight cents per pound but took satisfaction in believing "every little [bit] helps."[26]

An ambitious, market-minded agrarianism is evident throughout Bentley's letters, appearing to grow stronger as their farm, now called Green Hill, became more productive. She seemed particularly eager for the farm to produce enough surplus to repay what the family owed on bartering terms and subsequently sell the remainder for cash. In a letter written three years after starting the farm, Bentley and the children were pulling flax in the field. Her husband oversaw the "excellent" wheat harvest, much of which was already committed toward paying back a debt. However, the larger story in the letter seemed to be how well a particular neighbor was doing. "He will have a *great deal* of wheat, rye, oats, and corn *to sell*," she wrote enthusiastically to her family. To her and their community this prosperity was an admirable testament to "the united labour of his wife and self. . . . They

25. Bentley's reference to the steer is unclear, whether she means one or two that were obtained along with the bull and hay (Dec. 20, 1827, Foster, ed., *American Grit,* 68; Mar. 2, 1828; Mar. 1 Apr. 5, 1829, ibid., 73, 85, 89).

26. Mar. 15 and Apr. 5, 1829, ibid., 87–88, 89, 90, 91. Interestingly, Bentley wrote that she would be "thrown out of making sugar" in the spring of 1831, "as I shall have other fish to fry about the middle of the 4th month," meaning the birth of her ninth child (Dec. 12, 1830, ibid., 118).

are gaining esteem everywhere." Clearly, early Ohioans were a market-minded people and labored ambitiously toward this end. Especially important was the degree to which farm women not only considered the market structure (and that it was a positive force capable of improving the family's circumstances) but were also agriculturally skilled and knowledgeable decision makers in deciding to interact with it—a consideration that too often escapes the notice of scholars of both the period and the region.[27]

Nineteenth-century farm women were actuated first by family responsibilities and considerations. It is therefore not surprising that this worldview, far from precluding market interactions, would actually shape, guide, and even *encourage* these women. Bentley reasoned that if they can produce more than "with great economy is enough for our own use," then why not seek to market the rest to improve their situation? The bottom line, and often the deciding factor, was ensuring that the family's immediate needs were met first. This inclination toward family-first marketing would be in sync with the broader interpretation of safety-first agriculture that scholars associate with the pioneering phase of farm building; however, the problem has been a failure to recognize farm women as being market minded or to seek out their perceptions of market interactions. Acknowledging the prevalence of market-minded agrarianism among women and men in the development of the early Midwest is evident in Bentley's letters and other accounts and draws both farm women and their children into discussions about the nation's integrating market economy.

Little research has yet been done on the conversations and opinions farm women had concerning their market involvement during this period. Yet they appear to have been constructing a market culture that would be governed by the standard of meeting family needs first before selling surplus commodities. However, women who shunted this aside in order to obtain cash at the expense of their family's well-being would be upbraided by other women for violating this standard. A contemporary of Bentley named Sara Ames Stebbins illustrates this point. Compared to Bentley, Stebbins's migration and settlement experiences were miserable yet in some ways hopeful to a woman determined to establish a farm.

In January 1839 Stebbins wrote to her mother-in-law back home in Massachusetts about her family's struggling new life in Richfield, Illinois, in the west-central part of the state. "We have laboured under every disadvantage sence we have been here," she complained, including having to go two miles for cooking water. More offensive to her was that some of her fellow agrarians seemed to have forsaken their family obligations, observing how "people are not obliged to live as they do here on hog and hominy. They can have all the luxuries if they ha[ve] a mind to. Evry kind of sauce or grain will grow [in abundance]." According to Stebbins, these rural women cared little about feeding their families well, yet they were quite willing to market their produce: "Women [here] know nothing a bout cooking and [are] lasy. If they have poltry[,] eggs or butter it is for

27. July 26, 1829, ibid., 97–98. See earlier reference to Aley, "Review," in note 11.

sale.... You cannot call this living." She felt that given these women's apparent neglect of their families and kitchen tables, their market transactions were condemnable.[28]

Stebbins objected to what she believed was an unbalanced, if not irresponsible, approach to the market taken by her Illinois neighbors. Other agrarian women such as Sarah Adamson of Fayette County, Ohio, however, displayed a far more sophisticated outlook than the previous assessment at handling varied and complex market transactions. Her actions and notations indicated, among other things, that she maintained an active partnership with her husband in managing the household and farm. She was also the mother of seven biological children and five stepchildren. For a decade beginning in 1836, Adamson kept a diary detailing her and her family's extensive economic activities, ranging from the bartering of livestock for farm equipment to the purchasing of items she needed for domestic food production with the cash she made from selling her butter, eggs, or goose feathers. These entries were often side by side with others noting the community and personal events that framed her world, such as church meetings, the children's schooling, marriages, illnesses, deaths, and the like. But the business of the family's farm and side economic activities were transacted nearly every day.[29]

Simple transactions during 1836 are exemplified by entries on August 11 ("Sold to Wm Hawk 9 1/2 lb. of bacon at 8 cents") and August 26 ("Pd. Matilda Pinkerton for weaving blankets 1.50 [and] Henry hauled [for] Mr. Ott to the amoun[t] $6.00"). A degree of complexity and independence in financial matters is discernible in three entries she made between September 1836 and January 1837. In these accounts, Adamson recorded paying for a pair of shoes for her daughter with the feathers she plucked from twenty geese, along with a small amount of cash; purchasing seven dollars' worth of materials to make a cloak for someone who would pay her with seventy pounds of lard; and receiving cash for the sale of stock hogs, "the balance 40$ to be credited on my Note given for colts bought at the sale." Bentley, too, referred to purchasing livestock, such as when she bought two pigs for twenty-five cents each in 1832. Adamson also noted in her diary when her sons plowed and engaged in other farm chores. As stated by historian Glenda Riley, one of the diary's editors, Adamson was not "a person to miss an economic opportunity."[30]

In fact it could easily be argued that early Ohioans embraced and sought out economic opportunities on a number of levels, and, in this pursuit, agrarian women were often as savvy and as attuned to the market as their husbands were. State and regional market horizons changed during the 1820s and 1830s on account of growing enthusiasm for canal building, which in reality tended to promise more prosperity than it actually

28. Sara Ames Stebbins to Mother, Jan. 6 [1839], reprinted in Donald F. Carmony, ed., "Frontier Life: Loneliness and Hope," *Indiana Magazine of History* 61 (Mar. 1965): 53–57 (quoted at 54, 55, 56); Carmony explains that Stebbins's reference to "sauce" was an expression meaning those garden vegetables eaten with meat and thus was used as an adornment for the meat.

29. Adamson's biographical information is found in "Sarah Adamson Diary," 285–89.

30. Aug. 11, 26 and Sept. 6, 1836; Jan. 11, 13, 1837, ibid., 291, 293 (Riley's quote at 292); Jan. 22, 1832, Foster, ed., *American Grit*, 137.

delivered. Nevertheless, the significance of canal building may lie in that it greatly encouraged productivity at a time when many farm people were finally able to participate. Canal building had the simultaneous effect of inciting boosterism and jump-starting the development of adjacent towns in anticipation of profits, although some of these would go bust after the Panic of 1837.

In March 1831, the year before the Miller brothers' farm-buying journey, Anna Bentley remarked to her family about the "rapidly improving times in prospect for the farmer now for this particular section of the country" as a result of the "locating" of a portion of the canal system in their area. By the end of 1834 canal talk had become canal building, and with it "[a] great change is taking place in our neighbourhood." Buildings were going up in nearby Hanover, and lots that had sold for $80 the previous summer were then being sold for $280. Many canal-building related jobs opened up as well, offering additional employment opportunities. Bentley's oldest son, for example, contracted to supply thirty wheelbarrows for canal workers. Of course, canal building was not without its environmental consequences, causing some citizens like the Bentleys to view "the rushing on with this canal[,] tearing up the trees by the roots, &c" with mixed feelings.[31]

By the mid-1830s signs of prosperity in Ohio were becoming conspicuous in a number of ways. In Columbiana County one aspect of this success that struck Bentley was the way that women in particular were dressed, as opposed to the earlier farm-building days: "Then 1 decent calico and plenty of homemade was sufficient; now there is scarcely an old woman of my acquaintance that could not count 3 nice dresses to my 1." These women had their fine array of silks and more, "while poor me is as contented as any of them when I can put on a clean, whole (ragged and dirty I will not go) calico dress with cape of the same." Despite her insistence on being content, Bentley was acutely aware that others had surpassed their family in terms of success in their farming enterprises and were clearly enjoying the fruits of their labors. While her letters do not reveal the extent to which access to the canal system directly improved their circumstances, they do point toward an explanation as to why the family seemed to struggle at least as often as they prospered throughout the 1830s.[32]

When the Bentleys migrated to Ohio in 1826, their oldest boys, Granville, Franklin, and Thomas, were thirteen, eleven, and five, respectively. In the early 1830s, as the farm was beginning to produce comfortably, the family's labor dynamics changed significantly when Granville and Franklin left to learn trades (wagon making and carpentry). Although daughter Maria was often "called out" to assist her father, she was more badly needed to help her mother with the younger children. Not only was there a deficit in male laborers, but the once-energetic and ambitious Anna Bentley had become worn down by her other labors—reproductive, domestic, and, increasingly, neighborhood (i.e., births, deaths, illnesses). In an 1833 letter she complained that because of overwhelming child care demands

---

31. Mar. 13, 1831, and Dec. 14, 1834, Foster, ed., *American Grit*, 125, 160–61.
32. Aug. 14, 1836, ibid., 173.

she was "often bowed down with cares and sorrows, so many to clothe, to *make, mind, knit, patch, and darn for.*" Her buoyancy is clearly missing from her writing at this point. Elsewhere, after describing a host of recent disappointments, Bentley added that she "could fill another whole sheet with little grievances and discouragements but will not now."[33]

Compounding the labor problem was a series of setbacks and occurrences, the kind that seem to be rather endemic to agrarianism. In the early 1830s the Bentley farm comprised roughly six acres of corn, eight of oats, three of barley, five of clover, and about fifteen of wheat. Their livestock consisted of ten head of cattle, three calves, fifteen sheep, eight hogs, and, at one point, 200 chickens. Anna Bentley also maintained an extensive kitchen garden, in which the major crop was potatoes, and an array of fruit trees (primarily apple and peach), from which she derived some earnings through sales. Throughout the 1830s, however, the Bentleys' productive efforts were hampered by major and minor events: lawsuits for debt, rounds of illnesses and injuries (some devastating), rattlesnakes in the cornfield, smut on the wheat, a serious threat from a neighbor's spectacular fire that was fed by the practice of building thatch cowsheds, the plow breaking "all to pieces" during one season's plowing, and the death of a "faithful" ox that "laid down & died just in the midst of the Fall work which was very *inconvenient* indeed." The hard times seemed to outweigh the easy; an obviously weary Bentley wrote in 1844, "it is pinching times for us to get anything now we don't raise, and we live so far from the store."[34]

As it was true of agrarianism, life and labors were bound up together such that the vicissitudes of life had a ripple effect on a farm's ultimate agricultural production. It is hard to imagine this being any more the case than it was for the Bentleys. The farm struggled with the loss of the eldest sons' essential labor and with Bentley's diminished capacity from continued childbearing. This struggle was magnified in the 1840s when Joseph, now in his fifties and in failing health, could hardly manage the farm because he was essentially alone. The biggest blow came in 1842, when the family was deeply affected by the deaths of three of their children (ages eleven, three, and less than a year) from "the dreaded Scarlet fever." For Bentley, what was left of the pioneering spirit and market-mindedness was channeled into mothering her growing brood of grandchildren and participating as much as possible in the day-to-day running of the family farm.[35]

Market-minded agrarianism coursed through the early republic. It prompted migration, the establishment of new farms and communities in Ohio and elsewhere, the promotion of transportation innovations, and the ambitions of farm men, women, and families. As is evident from Anna Bentley's letters, success was never assured, but hope was sown each spring. Little attempt has been made to recover the perspectives of early-

---

33. Dec. 10, 1831; July 22, 1832; and Jan. 24, 1833, ibid., 132, 133, 142–43, 149.

34. July 18 and Dec. 10, 1831; Apr. 8 [1832]; July 22, 1832; Jan. 24, 1833; May [1833]; Dec. 14, 1834; Nov. 22, 1836; Oct. 23, 1844, ibid., 130–31, 132–33, 139–40, 142–43, 149–50, 150–51, 162, 176, 216.

35. [December 1842] and [Fall 1845], ibid., 202–5, 220.

nineteenth-century women about their market interactions or to try to interpret from their writings what the market held out for them and their families. Acknowledging their agricultural labors and aspirations as vital components of the expanding national economy brings them back into this important discussion. Embedded within market-minded agrarianism are such things as ambition, decision making, a desire to improve one's circumstances, and agricultural skills, knowledge, and expertise—attributes early-nineteenth-century agrarian women clearly possessed in abundance.

"Send Sisters, Send Polish Sisters"

Americanizing Catholic Immigrant Children in the Early Twentieth Century

SARAH E. MILLER

In the 1920s, Father John Hewelt of Dearborn, Michigan, complimented Mother Adelaide Sandusky and the Sisters of St. Francis, Sylvania, Ohio, in their efforts to teach the students of their parish schools the English language. He wrote, "I am deeply impressed with the American spirit of your reverend sisters. All spoke the English Language perfectly. Of course we love our Polish, but we are educating American children to make their bread in America."[1]

The sisters, like many other contemporary orders, understood the importance of preparing immigrant children for a successful future in the United States. The Polish background of many of the Sisters of St. Francis, Sylvania, initially drew them to their mission of education in the Polish parish of St. Hedwig in Toledo, Ohio, and also allowed them to empathize with students as they eased them into American society through their teaching.

A growth in immigration during the late nineteenth and early twentieth centuries developed two opposing views pertaining to immigrant Catholic parishes. The immigrant communities strove to retain their old-world customs, language, and religion while the established society hoped to "Americanize" these immigrants into mainstream culture. Catholic immigrants throughout the United States formed parish schools to retain their native culture and to buffer the Americanization process. However, public pressure caused even the hierarchy of the Catholic Church to call for a reduction of nationalism

---

1. Mary Dunstan Klewicki, *Ventures for the Lord: A History of the Sylvania Franciscans* (Sylvania, Ohio: Sisters of St. Francis, 1990), 38, 40. Requests for teachers coming to the Sisters of St. Francis of Sylvania would often specify the desire to have Polish sisters fulfill the requirement. This letter is not dated but was probably written in the 1920s. The Sylvania Franciscans closed this mission in 1931.

Ohio History, Vol. 114 © 2007 by The Kent State University Press

in the parish and for English to be the language of these schools during the first quarter of the twentieth century.

Many religious orders had learned that survival in America meant speaking English and conforming to American norms in public situations. Although immigrant parish neighborhoods preferred to retain old-world culture, the immigrant teaching-sister facilitated the transition of children into American culture through the parish school without uprooting them from their national culture. The sisters taught English, civics, and customs but did not take away or ignore the ethnic customs important to the community. Parish schools throughout the United States sought out first- and second-generation immigrants to be teachers because of their old-world connections. At St. Hedwig of Toledo, the sisters increased the children's probability of success in American society while maintaining many of the old-world traditions of the Polish neighborhood.

The teaching-sisters of the early twentieth century had developed from a long tradition of Catholic service dating from the Middle Ages. Catholic nuns pledged vows of chastity, poverty, and obedience and lived among their sisters and essentially governed themselves. The ability of these women to operate in society in this way was unique. They were not confined to traditional roles given to females; the church allowed women-religious to work outside the home and to have administrative responsibilities, which created a level of respect from others despite their sex. The Nineteenth Ecumenical Council at Trent, which met between 1545 and 1563, mandated that women-religious be confined to "strict enclosure," meaning they must stay cloistered. In defiance of this Council, new communities of noncloistered nuns emerged throughout Europe and became involved in teaching, nursing, and charitable work. These new communities called many women into the Catholic sisterhood and allowed them to escape the restrictive roles within the family and to work actively outside the home in service to others. Within the convent, women could develop and employ all of their talents and abilities. In the nineteenth and early twentieth centuries, many immigrant women joined religious orders based in America to serve in the United States.[2]

The increase in the number of European immigrants amplified the need for Catholic services for a population that did not speak English. The Catholic Dioceses in America requested different religious orders to come to the United States and minister to the growing immigrant population. Soon these religious colonies of orders based in Europe actually outnumbered the orders already in existence. These immigrant orders realized the need to Americanize to accomplish their mission goals, especially teaching and social services.[3]

Various immigrant women-religious across the United States saw the need to communicate in English to fit into American society. The Sisters of St. Joseph of Carondelet,

---

2. Carol K. Coburn and Martha Smith, *Spirited Lives: How Nuns Shaped Catholic Culture and American Life, 1836–1920* (Chapel Hill: Univ. of North Carolina Press, 1999), 13, 68–70; Karen Kennelly, ed., *American Catholic Woman: A Historical Exploration* (New York: Macmillan, 1989), 27.

3. James A. Burns, *Growth and Development of the Catholic School System in the United States* (New York: Arno, 1969), 20.

who arrived in St. Louis from France in 1836, translated their constitution into English in the 1850s. This made the order more attractive to potential candidates and provided a common language that would be used within the congregation and in mission work. The Sisters of Notre Dame of Namur arrived in Cincinnati, Ohio, on October 30, 1840, and opened a school in January of the following year. At that time, only one of the eight sisters spoke English fluently. She traveled from classroom to classroom to help out until the other teachers had learned enough English to communicate adequately with their students. The Adorers of the Most Precious Blood arrived in the Midwest from Germany in the 1870s. The sisters requested permission from the bishop to do something that was not permitted in Germany: to teach boys in addition to teaching girls. They reasoned that "America was different." Granting permission, the bishop urged the sisters to learn English so they could teach in parishes other than those of German immigrants. Learning English to function professionally in America was often hard on immigrant nuns. Mother Anselma Felber of the Adorers of the Most Precious Blood wrote letters home to Germany asking, "please pray that God may loose my tongue and let me hear right," to pray "that the Holy Ghost may come and teach us the English language," and professing, "without a miracle I shall never know English." These immigrant orders, and others like them, quickly perceived the importance of conducting their mission in English in the United States.[4]

When the Sisters of St. Francis from Rochester, Minnesota, started their province in Sylvania (near Toledo) in 1916, ten of the forty-eight sisters were immigrants from Poland or Prussia, and at least another nineteen were daughters of Polish immigrants. Many of the sisters came from the Minnesota farm country and had a strong sense of their Polish heritage, and they were eager to join the province for its original mission: serving the Polish population. Early retreats were delivered in both English and Polish; however, by August 1918, the retreats were conducted only in English. All official functions were conducted in English, and a class in "Spoken English" was taught on Friday nights from four until six o'clock. This class was mandatory for all teaching-sisters, thus showing they understood the importance of communicating in English with others. These sisters bridged the divide between Polish nationalism in Toledo and conformity to American society.[5]

The immigrant teaching-sister became an essential link between the old-world traditions and new-world society across the United States. Between 1865 and 1915, as many as 25 million immigrants came to America. They were from a variety of backgrounds, many of which were Catholic, and formed national enclaves in cities. Each nationality created ethnic parishes to preserve the thoughts and culture from the Old World.[6]

4. Colburn and Smith, *Spirited Lives*, 53; Burns, *Growth and Development*, 130; Linda Schelbitzki Pickle, *Contented Among Strangers: Rural German-Speaking Women and Their Families in the Nineteenth-Century Midwest* (Urbana: Univ. of Illinois Press, 1996), 169; 176–77.

5. Registry of Sisters, Archives of the Sisters of St. Francis, Sylvania, Ohio; Klewicki *Ventures for the Lord,* 8, 11, 32–33.

6. Jay P. Dolan, *In Search of an American Catholicism: A History of Religion and Culture in Tension* (New York: Oxford Univ. Press, 2002), 90–91.

Religion and its continuity gave Catholic immigrants "the strength to live in a new world of strangers. The key element in this religion was language, the language of home." Dr. Ernst Lieber, a politician from Germany, spoke to a group of German immigrants about retaining their native language. He told them, "Make your dollars in English but converse with our Lord God in our good old German language!" Lieber, like Father John Hewelt, understood that in the United States business transactions required knowledge of the English language. It is important to note, however, that neither man advocated the eradication of native language or culture. This same attitude was demonstrated by teaching-sisters as they strove to facilitate immigrant children's acceptance into American society without quashing their national identity.[7]

The parish schools formed by immigrant enclaves eliminated the need for the children to attend public schools. Many immigrant and first-generation parents feared the anti-Catholic attitudes of some Americans and sought to shield their children from such negativity. One way these parish schools preserved the old-world way of living was by orienting them around the community. Bishop Bernard McQuaid viewed the parish school as a fortress to guard against the "wolves of the world." Parish communities called on Catholic nuns, especially those of immigrant background, to teach in their schools. Familiarity with the cultural background of the parish neighborhoods gave teaching-sisters the legitimacy to encourage Americanization.[8]

For most immigrants, religion "was not an abstract entity but a localized one based on region, family, neighborhood and even social class," and teaching-sisters contributed to the retention of Catholicism for the many groups of immigrants who settled in the United States. The parish school was one important way for immigrants to retain their Catholic values, as described in a pastoral letter dated December 1884: "Therefore the school which principally gives knowledge fitting for practical life ought to be pre-eminently under the holy influence of religion. . . . No parish is complete until it has schools adequate to meet the needs of the children." In teaching and administering parochial schools, teaching-sisters created American-Catholics generation after generation. This charge was greater for sisters teaching in parishes populated by immigrants who wished to retain not only their Catholicism but also their national heritage. Acclimating immigrant children to life in America improved their probability of success in the United States, which meant teaching-sisters needed to find a balance between adjusting the students to their new society and maintaining their connection to their heritage.[9]

The first wave of Polish immigrants came to Toledo in 1871, along with immigrants

7. Timothy Walch, ed., "The Ethnic Dimension in American Catholic Parochial Education," *Immigrant America: European Ethnicity in the United States* (New York: Garland, 1994), 141–42; Dolan, *In Search of,* 94.

8. Walch, "Ethnic Dimension," 143; Mary Ann Donovan, *Sister as Power: The Past and Passion of Ecclesial Women* (New York: Crossroad, 1989), 48.

9. John Bodnar, *The Transplanted: A History of Immigrants in Urban America* (Bloomington: Indiana Univ. Press, 1985), 148; Klewicki, *Ventures for the Lord,* 1; Timothy Walch, *Parish School: American Catholic Parochial Education from Colonial Times to the Present* (New York: Crossroads, 1996), 151.

from Russia, Italy, the Balkans, Austria-Hungary, and the Near East. By 1900 these groups made up a cosmopolitan city. The Polish founded St. Hedwig Parish "to establish a community where they and their children would be free to practice the religion and preserve language that was oppressed in their native land." The parish school was staffed for the 1884–85 school year by the Felician Sisters of Detroit, a Polish teaching order; however, for reasons not clearly enumerated, they left the school. Father Wieczorek requested aid from the Sisters of St. Francis in Rochester, Minnesota, a predominately Polish congregation. A year later, they sent three sisters to teach the 150 students. Enrollment at St. Hedwig's School soared to 350 by 1889; by 1903 the parish school taught 1,000 students.[10]

In the fall of 1916, Bishops Joseph Schrembs and Patrick Heffron proposed that the sisters in Rochester establish a Toledo province (it was located in Sylvania). Since the sisters were already teaching in Toledo, Bishop Schrembs felt that "the establishment of a Polish province subject to the motherhouse, will be a step toward far-reaching results for [their] community and [his] diocese." The Polish background of so many of the Franciscan sisters contributed to the bishop's desire to retain these sisters and to further their province's growth in the Toledo area. Mother Leo of the Rochester motherhouse wrote in a letter to the province that "the principal purpose of this foundation is to conduct efficiently our Polish schools."[11]

Many of the sisters who taught at St. Hedwig were immigrants themselves; others were children of immigrants. Sister M. Salome was born in Poland and was the music teacher at the school from 1904 to 1918. Sister Henrica, who was born in Gross Suchorcz, Poland, translated several Polish books into English and taught at St. Hedwig from 1907 to 1915. Sister Isidore of Strasburg, Prussia, taught the 1917–18 school year. Sister Ethelreda taught grades one through four from 1911 to 1916 and again in 1917–18. Sister Clarita, born in Poland, started her teaching career at St. Hedwig in 1917 and taught for three years. A Chabowski, Poland, native, Sister Alveria was at St. Hedwig during the 1917–18 and 1926–29 school years. Sister Eugenia entered the order with "no English education" in 1916, began teaching at St. Hedwig the next year, and remained at the school until 1925. Mother M. Stanislas came to the United States when she was only two months old and taught grades three, six, eight, and nine at St. Hedwig from 1913 to 1917. In addition to these sisters who had personally immigrated to the United States, many of the other teaching-sisters grew up in Polish households. The understanding of Polish society allowed these sisters to shape the futures of the children at St. Hedwig while still respecting their culture.[12]

10. Morgan Barclay and Charles N. Glaab, *Toledo: Gateway to the Great Lakes* (Tulsa, Okla.: Continental Heritage Press, 1982), 64; St. Hedwig Parish Centennial Anniversary Committee, *The First Hundred Years, 1875–1975: A History of St. Hedwig Parish* (Toledo: St. Hedwig Parish, 1975), 39, 191.

11. Klewicki, *Ventures for the Lord*, 3; Mother Leo, Rochester, Minn., to the Province in Sylvania, Ohio, "Concerning the Province," Feb. 26, 1919, Archives of the Sisters of St. Francis.

12. Sister M. Salome, "Personal File"; Sister Henrica, "Personal File"; Sister Isidore, "Personal File"; Sister Ethelreda, "Personal File"; Sister Clarita, "Personal File"; Sister Alveria, "Personal File"; Sister Eugenia, "Personal File"; and Mother M. Stanislas, "Personal File," all in Archives of the Sisters of St. Francis.

Movements within the U.S. government and the Catholic Church strove to reduce the immigrants' desire to maintain their native way of life. In the late 1880s, as part of the Americanization movement, states began increasing the compulsory school laws in an attempt to curb the number of students in parish schools, particularly ones in ethnic communities. Many states required parents to receive permission from public boards of education before enrolling their children in private schools. The Compulsory Education Law of Ohio required that each student enrolled at a Catholic school report to the public board of education. This law was challenged but upheld by the Ohio Supreme Court in 1892 in *The State of Ohio vs. The Reverend Patrick Francis Quigley.* By 1909 most states had child labor or compulsory school laws. Nineteen of these states, including Ohio, required that a child be able to read and write English before being legally employed. In 1910 the Ohio state legislature additionally required a child to pass a fifth-grade-level test in reading, writing, spelling, English, grammar, geography, and arithmetic before obtaining employment. States were increasingly taking more interest in students' school attendance. These laws not only decreased the number of children in the labor force but tried to guarantee a degree of literacy and Americanization. Even poor immigrant families could not legally send their children to work without knowledge of the English language.[13]

In the 1880s and 1890s, public debate over the Americanization of the Catholic Church ensued within its hierarchy and was debated in newspapers and journals. Archbishop John Ireland fully believed that the Catholic Church must "become American without ceasing for an instant to be Catholic." In 1916 foreign languages were used exclusively in more than 12,000 parishes across the United States; another 3,000 offered mass in a foreign language as well as in English. The papacy initiated a revision of the Code of Canon Law in 1918 that prohibited the future development of a national parish without special permission. Tension between the goals of the diocese and the goals of the immigrant parish escalated. The Church advocated an American Catholicism, but many immigrants felt their language and culture was just as important as their religion.[14]

George Mundelein, a strong advocate of Americanization, became archbishop of Chicago in 1915. A local Chicago newspaper announced his appointment by stating, "He is fitted for the Archbishop of Chicago where the Gospel is preached in twenty-five languages, but where Catholics are all Americans in the making." In a step away from his predecessors and against the desire of many immigrant communities, Mundelein took a new approach toward parish organization and established parishes according to geography and not by nationality. He also mandated English as the language of instruction in all parochial schools. The Polish population across the United States stood firm against these instructions. A common thought among the Polish was "a Pole who says he is a Catholic but who is ashamed or neglects the Polish language is not a true Catholic." The priests of the Polish communities of Chicago petitioned the pope against this policy. In

---

13. Burns, *Growth and Development,* 219, 297
14. Dolan, *In Search of,* 74; Walch, "Ethnic Dimension," 142.

Mundelein's rebuttal, he said: "It is of the utmost importance to our American nation that the nationalities gathered in the United States should gradually amalgamate to fuse into one homogeneous people and without losing the best traits of their race, become imbued with the one harmonious national thought, sentiment and spirit." The pope sided with Mundelein, but the archbishop was unable to control the Polish parish schools that continued to be the main institution sustaining the Polish language among second- and third-generation immigrants. However, this retention did not nullify the Americanizing advantages of a bilingual school that also offered instruction in English. In the mid-1910s, more than 2,200 Polish teaching-sisters upheld the Polish cultures in parish schools in more than twenty-four states, including St. Hedwig's School in Toledo.[15]

World War I contributed to the fear of all things foreign, and the public became less tolerant of "different" during the 1910s. The U.S. government issued laws that attempted to eradicate national identities, hoping to complete the notion of the melting pot. The Catholic Church, and even the pope, believed that a unified Church emphasizing the English language would be beneficial in the United States. Bishop John Ireland, a leader in this campaign explained, "ours is the American Church, and not Irish, German, Italian, or Polish—and we will keep it American." Father Joseph M'Clancy also articulated this view: "Americanization is the endeavor to make America a united people; to eliminate alienism and radicalism, to turn out of our lower school boys and girls the men and women of tomorrow, who will shed all foreign tastes and admiration, and action. It is a noble project, into which our Catholic schools are quick to enter." Thus the hierarchy of the Catholic Church clashed with the ethnic parishes, including the Polish parishes, that wished to retain their national identity.[16]

In the 1918 First General Report of the Provincial Community, Mother Adelaide Sandusky included a section entitled "Problem of Languages," in which she wrote:

> We are meeting with much difficulty in the way of giving the proportionate value and relative importance to the study of the two languages in our schools. It is impossible to give the proper training in the English language to the children in the school. We are trying to meet the difficulties as well as we can. The policy is to limit the study of the foreign language to reading and writing, taught in the 3, 4, 5 and 6th grades. In time most of the Sisters will get around to that point of view; but just at present it would be disastrous for us to attempt anything so radical, both with the Sisters and with the people; and especially with the clergy.[17]

While trying to comply with the wishes of the Catholic hierarchy, Mother Adelaide pointed out that at that time it would have been "disastrous" to implement the policy.

15. Dolan, *In Search of,* 140, 222; Walch, "Ethnic Dimensions," 147, 150.

16. Walch, "Ethnic Dimensions," 152, 155.

17. Mother Adelaide Sandusky, "First General Report of the Provincial Community, Sylvania, Ohio, October 1, 1918, " p. 11 (photocopy), Archives of the Sisters of St. Francis.

Like the Polish parishes in Chicago that petitioned the pope, the sisters at St. Hedwig's School knew that the Polish community in Toledo would not easily give up their language; they considered it an essential part of their identity. Although limiting Polish study was policy, Mother Adelaide realistically understood that an abrupt change to using English only would disrupt the community. The respect given by the teaching-sisters to the Polish culture lessened many of the complaints against the use of the English language.

The immigrant teaching-sister stood as a bridge between the Americanizing forces of both the government and Catholic Church and the immigrant populations' desire to retain their national cultures. As early as 1840, Governor William H. Seward of New York declared that it would be advantageous for children of immigrants to be taught by teachers of the same language and religious backgrounds. The State of New York rejected his advice for public schools; however, the immigrant Catholic parishes agreed with Seward and looked to teaching-sisters of similar ethnicities to teach in their schools. Even seventy years later these parishes believed that by requesting teaching-sisters with foreign backgrounds, parish schools could smoothly make the transition from a foreign-language school to a school with classes taught primarily in English. This Americanization of young students did not necessarily negate respect for native language and customs but, rather, prepared students for life in the United States after they left school. Because of this respect, the sisters were able to teach immigrant children the required American civics lessons without too much of a culture shock.[18] In 1907, Cardinal James Gibbons of Baltimore said:

> Our Catholic schools afford a much easier pathway for the foreigner to enter the American life than is the case in the public school. There a child must enter at once upon the use of the English language—perhaps under the guidance of one who does not know the habits and customs of the immigrant child, and hence cannot enter into complete sympathy with his work. . . . In Catholic school they come under the instruction of those who know the respective language and can understand their peculiar idioms of thought and speech. With English language as a constantly enlarging part of their course, they are gradually, almost unconsciously, brought into complete sympathy with American ideals, and readily adapt themselves to American manners and customs. This assimilation is constantly going on in our Catholic schools, and is quite an important factor in our national development.[19]

While the students at St. Hedwig's School, Toledo, were taught in both English and Polish, Mother Adelaide maintained her hope of restricting the amount of Polish used in certain grades. For example, the curriculum of the second grade at St. Hedwig for the year 1917–18 was taught in both languages. Catechism was taught in Polish and arithmetic in English, and spelling, reading, and writing were taught in Polish and English.

---

18. Burns, *Growth and Development*, 198–99, 294, 295, 296.
19. St. Hedwig Parish, *The First Hundred Years*, 193; Burns, *Growth and Development*, 317.

The goal was to move away from the teaching in Polish in the upper grades. As students became accustomed to this curriculum, they would often use English with their friends outside of school and use Polish with their families at home.[20]

During the early 1920s, the students at St. Hedwig used a book called the *Fundamentals of Citizenship* for their 100-minute civics class each day. The introduction to the book taught students that "The success of a democracy depends on knowledge and moral character. If all the people are not acquainted with their civic and social responsibilities they cannot act intelligently on the common affairs. The right of suffrage means very little if the people do not have some knowledge of the issues passed on at the polls. . . . The Catholic Church has always taught the fundamentals of citizenship. It has emphasized the social rights and responsibilities of citizens."

The accompanying workbook, *Civics Catechism on the Rights and Duties of American Citizens,* was developed for upper-elementary-school students and also for adult immigrants preparing for the naturalization examination. Teaching them the responsibilities of citizenship, *Civics Catechism* was published in several different versions for different immigrant groups. The English-Polish edition, called *Katechizm Obywatelski,* enabled "non-English speakers to obtain a knowledge of the English language at the same time they are being instructed" in the foundations of American society and institutions. An understanding of the English language was essential for carrying out civic duties, and the two-column format of the book allowed the student to develop skills in both areas simultaneously. Some of the chapter topics included American democracy, education, health, naturalization, the Declaration of Independence, and the Constitution of the United States. The sisters taught these subjects to the students of St. Hedwig to provide the students with a better understanding of American society, government, and laws—items that would prepare them for real-world experiences after they finished school.[21]

Younger children learned civics from *Lessons in Civics for the Six Elementary Grades of City School,* by Hannah Margaret Harris. This booklet presented situations that a student might encounter in his or her daily life. For example, the book for first-year students dealt with "the daily walk to and from school" and "coming into contact with certain persons who represent authority and the service of organized authority." The fourth-year situations included "receiving books and material for school work as loans from the city" and "visiting public places" Through these textbooks, teaching-sisters guided their Polish students into an understanding of expected conduct in the United States.[22]

20. Sister M. Leocadia (principal), "Statistical Report for Parochial Schools Conducted by the Sisters of St. Francis, Sylvania, Ohio" (Feb. 1, 1921), pp. 1–2, Archives of the Sisters of St. Francis; Committee on Special War Activities, *The Fundamentals of Citizenship* (Washington, D.C.: National Catholic War Council, 1919), 5–6; *Katechizm Obywatelski: Pouczajacy Prawach I Powinnosciach Amerykanskiego Obywatela / Civics Catechism on the Rights and Duties of American Citizens,* English/Polish ed. (Washington, D.C.: National Catholic Welfare Conference, n.d.), 3.

21. Leocadia, "Report for Parochial Schools, 1921," 1–2; Hannah Margaret Harris, *Lessons in Civics for the Six Elementary Grades of a City School,* Department of the Interior, Bureau of Education (Washington, D.C.: Government Printing Office, 1918), 11, 58.

22. Leocadia, "Report on Parochial Schools, 1921," 1–2; Margaret S. McNaught *Training in Courtesy: Suggestions for Teaching Good Manners in Elementary School,* Department of the Interior, Bureau of Education (Washington, D. C.: Government Printing Office, 1918), 5.

Throughout the 1920s, all grades at St. Hedwig School used *Training in Courtesy*, by Dr. Margaret Schallenberger McNaught, commissioner of elementary schools of California. This book aided in teaching students about American culture. The introduction states that "the importance of education in manners is due to the fact that a knowledge of social customs and social usages is almost as necessary to a civilized man as a knowledge of how to earn a living. If men and women did not know and observe the rule of the road "turn to the right," their movements along any street or highway would be a continuous disturbance of traffic, not only annoying, but liable to be dangerous at an unexpected moment. So it is with every social custom." The goal was teach students the importance of good conduct, cleanliness, neatness, common courtesies, and manners. The sisters believed that the students at St. Hedwig who learned and followed these suggestions would become accepted into American society, which sometimes discriminated against immigrant cultures.[23]

Another book the sisters at St. Hedwig used in the early 1920s was called *Games and Other Devices for Improving Pupils' English*, compiled by W. W. Charters and Harry G. Paul. Each chapter dealt with a grammatical problem and addressed it through stories, dramatization, games, exercises, and drills. This book and others used at St. Hedwig were also used in public schools. By utilizing similar textbooks, teaching-sisters instructed their students with much of the same material learned in public schools, hoping that by doing so they would be able to give their students the same opportunity to succeed in future ventures as the native-born student already had. Parish schools, however, objected to the popular McGuffey Readers because they taught Protestant morals. Instead, St. Hedwig's School assigned the Expressive Readers, written by James Baldwin and Ida C. Bender, and the Elson Readers, written by William H. Elson. The Elson Readers for the younger grades contained chapter topics such as patriotism, stories, and duty. The fifth reader in the Expressive Readers series contained the old fable "The Cricket and the Ant," "Pandora" by Nathaniel Hawthorne, and stories about Benjamin Franklin.[24]

Immigrant women-religious understood the practicality of being able to speak English when conducting business, teaching classes, and providing social services. Most foreign orders changed some of their customs and initiated English as their congregational language, thus allowing the immigrant sisters to converse and work with native-born Americans outside of the convent.

The immigrant parish, however, was much more rooted in the native language and culture of their followers. Immigrant sisters who spoke native languages were called to teach in parish schools. By using English with the old-world language, sisters were able to ease the children into the English-speaking process. Their educational efforts were

23. Sister M. Leocadia, "Statistical Report for the Parochial Schools Conducted by the Sisters of St. Francis, Sylvania" (Feb. 1, 1923), pp. 1–2, Archives of the Sisters of St. Francis; W. W. Charters and Harry G. Paul, *Games and Other Devices for Improving Pupils' Education,* Department of the Interior, Bureau of Education (Washington, D.C.: Government Printing Office, 1923), iv.

24. Leocadia, "Report on Parochial Schools, 1923"; William H. Elson, *The Elson Readers: Book Four,* revision of *Elson Primary School Reader, Book Four* (Chicago: Scott, Foresman, and Co., 1920) ii; James Baldwin and Ida C. Bender, *Reading with Expression: Fifth Reader* (New York: American Book Co., 1911), iv.

successful; often second- or third-generation immigrants insisted that English become the primary language in bilingual parish schools. For example, by the late 1920s, most Polish teenagers in New York spoke Polish only at home but still retained the Polish community customs. This pattern repeated itself across the United States, including in Toledo, where English was used more often in everyday life outside the home, especially at school. Immigrant teaching-sisters often used the same education materials provided by the state to instruct the children of the parish while perpetuating and respecting their native culture.[25]

Policies of the United States encouraged immigrants to become American. To compete in the American economy, politics, and society, an immigrant had to function as well as a native-born American. Though the Catholic Church also saw the importance of Americanizing Catholic immigrants, parish communities fought hard to retain their old-world customs. The teaching-sisters, particularly those with immigrant backgrounds, provided a link between the Old World and the New World. The Sisters of St. Francis, Sylvania, teaching at St. Hedwig's School in Toledo, Ohio, eased students into American society by teaching English, civics, and customs but all the while retaining a respect for the language and traditions of the immigrant community. These sisters gave students the ability to compete with native-born Americans in the United States without eradicating their ethnic identity.

25. John J. Bukowczyk, *And My Children Did Not Know Me: A History of the Polish Americans* (Bloomington: Indiana Univ. Press, 1961), 71.

The Connecticut Genesis of the Western Reserve, 1630–1796

ROBERT A. WHEELER

Connecticut's long, successful fight for land in the west was impressive. For years prospective settlers and investors, thwarted at nearly every turn, continued to fight. They survived rival claims of other colonies, particularly New York and Pennsylvania. They cleverly expanded the seemingly innocuous requests of several Connecticut townsfolk for more land into a claim for a huge tract of land in Pennsylvania supported by a large land company. Indians and Penamites threatened them constantly over a thirty-year span, but they either fought them off or retreated only to return in greater numbers. The fight that left a cadre of wounded and partially abandoned Connecticut residents in Pennsylvania continued in the Continental Congress. Here a savvy Connecticut delegation summoned all its powers to claim other land in the west in compensation. A private deal confirmed the sagacity of the policy of "firmness and prudence" that gave the state a western reserve in Ohio. Even then the fight was not over. Disagreement over who would benefit from the sale of the land raised hackles in Connecticut. Finally, in 1796, the reserve was sold and was soon ready for settlement. Its dimensions and north-south geographical position copied the size of the colony of Connecticut. So, in one sense, the struggle ended when the state acquired and then sold a virtual duplicate of itself farther west.

THE CHARTERS AND THEIR WESTERN LIMITS

The first portion of the struggle pitted rival claims of several colonies against each other. The precise bounds of the colony of Connecticut were unclear from the beginning. Its western edge was particularly vague. The initial grant of land that became Connecticut,

Ohio History, Vol. 114 © 2007 by The Kent State University Press

called the Warwick Patent, was probably made in 1631 by the Council of New England to a group of eleven proprietors. It gave "all that part of New-England, in America, which lies and extends itself from a river there called Narraganset river, the space of forty leagues upon a straight line near the sea shore towards the southwest, west and by south, or west, as the coast lieth towards Virginia, accounting three English miles to the league; . . . north and south in latitude and breadth, and in length and longitude of and within, all the breadth aforesaid, throughout the main lands there, *from the western ocean to the south sea.*" Significantly, this 120-mile (forty league) length remained constant throughout the colony's subsequent evolution and was applied to later claims for its reserve in the west.[1]

The Warwick Patent included some land occupied by Dutch inhabitants from the colony of New Amsterdam. In an attempt to affirm English control over the lands and to allay fears that the original patent was not valid, a new grant was sought. A failed attempt in 1645 was resubmitted in 1661 after the restoration of Charles II to the English throne. The new charter, issued by Charles II in 1662, described boundaries differently than had the Warwick Patent, but, like the earlier document, it mentioned the western ocean. The colony encompassed "all that parte of our Dominions in Newe England bounded on the East by Norrogancett River comonly called Norrogancett Bay where the said River falleth into the Sea, and on the North by the Lyne of the Massachusetts Plantation and on the South by the Sea, and in longitude as the Lyne of the Massachusetts Colony runinge from East to West that is to say, from the said Narrogancett Bay on the East *to the South Sea on the West parte.*"[2]

This new charter was on much firmer legal ground than the earlier patent, even though these boundaries were understandably vague. Charles II complicated matters when he continually granted lands that overlapped with the borders of Connecticut. He gave a generous charter to his brother, the Duke of York, after the English captured the colony of New Amsterdam from the Dutch in the late 1660s. The document fixed the eastern border of New York far inside Connecticut along the western bank of the Connecticut River and named the same South Sea as the western boundary of the new colony.[3]

1. While this document has long been disputed, current consensus is that it did exist and was authentic. See Mary Jeanne Anderson Jones, *Congregational Commonwealth; Connecticut, 1636–1662* (Middletown, Conn.: Wesleyan Univ. Press, 1969), 159–60, 173–75 (emphasis added). This is an appendix where the entire Warwick Patent is reproduced. Other studies, like Alfred Chandler, *Land Title Origins: A Tale of Force and Fraud* (New York: Robert Schalkenbach Foundation, 1945), 122, alter the text of the patent. For an early treatment of the charters, see Thomas D. Webb, "Connecticut Land Company: A Partial Sketch of the History of the Original Titles of the Lands in That Part of the State of Ohio Commonly Called the Connecticut Western Reserve," *Historical Collections of the Mahoning Valley* 1 (1876): 142–65.

2. Jones, *Congregational Commonwealth,* 160–61; *The Charter of Connecticut, 1662,* Tercentenary Commission of the State of Connecticut (New Haven: Yale Univ. Press, 1933), 20–21 (emphasis added). A series of meetings between Connecticut and Rhode Island fixed the eastern border with Rhode Island at the Pawcatuck River rather than the Narragansett River, but the dispute with Rhode Island continued well into the eighteenth century. See Robert J. Taylor, *Colonial Connecticut* (Millwood, New York: KTO Press, 1979), 56–59; Roland Mather Hooker, *Boundaries of Connecticut,* Tercentenary Commission of the State of Connecticut (New Haven: Yale Univ. Press, 1933), 3–15; Chandler, *Land Title Origins,* 134–35.

3. Clarence W. Bowen, *The Boundary Disputes of Connecticut* (Boston: James R. Osgood, 1882), 69–71; Hooker, *Boundaries,* 30–31; Chandler, *Land Title Origins,* 135.

Skirmishes between the two colonies came quickly. New York, which did not consider the Connecticut River a realistic eastern border, used the charter provision to obtain concessions from Connecticut. The final agreement set the eastern edge of New York twenty miles east of the Hudson River. The charter, then, either fixed Connecticut's western boundary along the Hudson or merely interrupted it on the way to the "South Sea."[4]

The attack on Connecticut continued when, in 1681, the Crown gave away more of its lands, this time to the new colony of Pennsylvania. William Penn received territory west of New York and parallel to Connecticut further compromising the western portion of Connecticut's charter boundaries. Connecticut did not object, for some unknown reason. There were no real grounds for protest, argued the English attorney general at the time, Sir William Jones. He believed provisions in the sea-to-sea clauses of the charters of Connecticut and other New England colonies were "real but impractical."[5]

Subsequent appeals by Connecticut would argue that the 1662 charter established Connecticut's western boundary prior to the creation of either New York or Pennsylvania. In any dispute, the older English colony reasoned, it would have priority. In the short term, the overlapping boundaries in the charters laid the groundwork for continuing conflict.[6]

WESTERN LAND FEVER

The conflict over land rights continued throughout much of the seventeenth century. At the same time Connecticut expanded slowly within its charter boundaries. By 1737 the last of its lands, a tract of 300,000 acres in the northwestern portion, opened for settlement. Just as in later ventures, the land was purchased by speculators who sought profit—not settlement—and sold it quickly. By midcentury virtually all land in Connecticut was owned.[7]

The short supply of land was only one element in the land speculation mania that swept Connecticut. Forces unsettling people included economic reasons, such as high taxes, lack of commerce, poor transportation facilities, rivalry between eastern and western portions of the colony, and the declining values of farm acreage. Connecticut was changing as the perceived homogeneity of its religious and political life began to crumble. The first Great Awakening split believers into "New Lights," who had been born again, and "Old Lights," who had not, and initiated an attack on the established church, further dividing the colony.[8]

4. Taylor, *Colonial Connecticut*, 55–56.

5. Charles J. Hoadley, *The Public Records of the Colony of Connecticut* (Hartford, 1876; reprinted, Johnson Reprint Corporation, New York: 1968), 9:593–96; Julian P. Boyd, "Connecticut's Experiment in Expansion: The Susquehannah Company, 1753–1803," *Journal of Economic and Business History* 4 (1931): 39.

6. Mary Lou Conlin, *Simon Perkins of the Western Reserve* (Cleveland: The Western Reserve Historical Society, 1968), 4.

7. Julian P. Boyd, ed., *The Susquehannah Company Papers* (Ithaca: Cornell Univ. Press, for the Wyoming Historical & Geological Society, reissued 1962–71), 1:xliii, 1–2. For a good discussion of the venture from a Connecticut perspective, see Richard T. Warfle, *Connecticut's Western Colony: The Susquehannah Affair*, Connecticut Bicentennial Series (Hartford: American Revolution Bicentennial Commission of Connecticut, 1979, ca. 1980).

8. Boyd, "Connecticut's Experiment," 41; Warfle, *Connecticut's Western Colony*, 9–10.

Complicating this turmoil, the impressive fertility of Connecticut residents and the declining fertility of Connecticut soil created further demands for fresh land. The choices were few. Patterns established a century before when Connecticut was founded were replicated. Some residents left, this time for western Massachusetts and Vermont. Others followed the lead of their forefathers and petitioned the Connecticut legislature in town groups, applying for new townships to settle because the town continued to be the only conduit for land grants. Some complained that their town had "Grown full of Inhabantants so that a Great many must unavoidably move to Sum other Place." Others protested that they had "Great & Expensive Family's & being Confined to very small Inheritances, are Led, by a Paternal Care for their Children, to make Enquiries How, & Where they may Find Englargement." This growing demand was different from earlier pressure for more land in one important way: Connecticut would have to seek land beyond its functional borders to satisfy these requests.[9]

In 1750 the first petition specifically requesting western lands was presented to the Connecticut General Assembly by a group of ten residents of the town of Simsbury. The petitioners requested a township grant of ten square miles "within the bounds of this Colony as described in the Royal Charter Lying west of Hudsons River which is not Included in any of the Charters to any neighbouring Governments which Lands Ly unsettled and which if they were Setled with Good Inhabitants from this Colony would be a Considerable Inlargment to the Trade and business of this Government as well as a Security of the Rights and Intrest of this Colony." The appeal to charter rights revitalized the issue of the colony's western border that had been nearly dormant since the 1680s. However, the petition was rejected probably because the legislative committee did not find the "least Probability of this Colonys ever recovering the Possession of any Lands Westward."[10]

Despite this opinion, a change was about to take place. From 1750 to 1753 requests for land were made by town groups seeking farm land for themselves. By September 1753 the potential for additional land and large profits prompted others, including many land speculators and prominent political figures from eastern Connecticut, to join groups of hopeful settlers petitioning for western lands. Slowly, as the size and importance of the membership in these groups expanded, so too did the size of the parcel requested. From several townships in the west, the focus shifted to a large tract of land in the fertile Wyoming Valley, which stretched twenty-five miles long and three miles wide along the Susquehannah River in Pennsylvania.[11]

9. Larry R. Gerlach, "Firmness and Prudence: Connecticut, the Continental Congress and the National Domain, 1776–1786," *Connecticut Historical Society Bulletin* 31 (1966): 65; Boyd, ed., *Susquehannah Company Papers,* 1:intro., esp. lxiv; Christopher Collier, *Sherman's Connecticut: Yankee Politics and the American Revolution* (Middletown, Conn.: Wesleyan Univ. Press, 1971), 38; Boyd, "Connecticut's Experiment," 41–42; Boyd, ed., *Susquehannah Company Papers,* 1:25–26.

10. Boyd, ed., *Susquehannah Company Papers,* 1:1–2. The response to the Simsbury petition is not recorded, but this rejection a year later to a similar request probably expresses the correct rationale (Boyd, "Connecticut's Experiment," 40).

11. Boyd, "Connecticut's Experiment," 42–44; Parker B. Nutting, "Charter and Crown: Relations of Connecticut with the British Government, 1662–1776" (Ph.D. diss., University of North Carolina, 1972), 79–80.

THE SUSQUEHANNAH COMPANY

The Susquehannah Company was formally organized at Windham in July 1753 to "spread Christianity as also to promote our own Temporal Interest." Its investors, among them many powerful figures, expanded several times, so that by mid-1754 the Company had absorbed many smaller groups of speculators and was the only important land company in Connecticut with an authorized size of 500 members. The Company, which unsuccessfully petitioned the legislature for approval of its project, actually expected something more significant than a small settlement. The *London Magazine* reported that the tract in Pennsylvania "will be in a short time a distinct Government," a new Connecticut.[12]

The proponents of this new colony argued that it had many advantages. It would promote English interests by extending the borders of the British colonies. Moreover, it would link the Six Nations Indian tribes to the British cause at the expense of the French, and it would enhance the Indian trade. Convinced by these arguments, the governor of Connecticut, Roger Wolcott, formally approved the projected colony in early 1754 as an important act of imperial policy.[13]

The Company, encouraged by Wolcott's support, authorized its agents to purchase land from the Indians at the Albany Congress held in June 1754. At the meetings Company agents had to compete with representatives from Pennsylvania who tried to purchase the Wyoming tract from Mohawk representatives and thus thwart the Susquehannah Company but failed. Through a series of maneuvers, the Connecticut representatives overcame the Pennsylvania challenge. First, they backed a resolution validating the South Sea portion of the royal charters of both Connecticut and Massachusetts Bay that allowed Connecticut control over the Wyoming area. In addition, they conducted a series of raucous, successful meetings with Indians. As a result, the Company purchased the Indian rights to a large tract of some five million acres extending westward along the southern border of New York and stretching sixty miles south of the line. The deed, of dubious validity, covered "a large Tract of Land on About and Adjacent to the River Susqueannah between the fourty first & fourty Third degrees of North Latitude and *being within the Limits and bounds of The Charter and Grant of His late Majesty King Charles 2nd To The Colony of Connecticut.*" The size and shape of the purchase simply extended Connecticut west after ignoring the intrusion of New York along the Hudson River. Like Connecticut, it was sixty miles wide.[14]

The Connecticut legislature began what would be a slow gradual process of recognition when it allowed the Company to ask for a royal charter covering the land but skirted

12. Boyd, "Connecticut's Experiment," 41; Warfle, *Connecticut's Western Colony*, 10. At this time speculators formed the First and Second Delaware Companies to settle land "disputes" between the Susquehannah Company lands and the Delaware River in Pennsylvania. Throughout the discussion that follows, these two companies were affected by the same events as the Susquehannah Company. Boyd, "Connecticut's Experiment," 38; Boyd, *Susquehannah Company Papers*, 1:lxiv, lxvii, n127.

13. Boyd, ed., *Susquehannah Company Papers*, 1:lxvii.

14. Nutting, "Charter and Crown," 82; Boyd, ed., *Susquehannah Company Papers*, 1:lxviii; Boyd, "Connecticut's Experiment," 44–45; Boyd, ed., *Susquehannah Company Papers*, 1:101–3.

the issue of its own recognition of the Indian deed. Governance, financing, and protection were left up to the Company.[15]

The Susquehannah Company now had land, but development began tenuously. Actual settlement, delayed because of the French and Indian War, did not begin until 1762 when the Company sent a group of 100 members to the Wyoming Valley. These first settlers arrived only to be annihilated in Indian attacks. Further colonization was blocked by a royal order of 1763 forbidding settlement in the west.[16]

These unfortunate beginnings left some undeterred, and they were soon rewarded. In 1765 and 1766 an upheaval in Connecticut politics ousted the ruling party because of its religious views, its grudging support of the Stamp Act, and its opposition to the Susquehannah Company. The new officeholders favored the Company, and one was a member of its board.

This renewed positive outlook at home was accompanied by a renewed attempt to secure a royal charter in England. After considerable energy and time, the effort by Susquehannah Company agents failed because Pennsylvania's representatives succeeded in keeping their claims before the crown.[17]

Undaunted, the Company went ahead with a series of inducements to settlers in the form of so-called gratuity townships. These tracts were offered free to shareholders in exchange for settlement, but, perhaps in order to make the settlement more compact, the size of the townships was reduced from the original ten square miles to only five square miles. This smaller size was adopted generally by the Company in the 1770s. Lots within towns were divided by lottery based on the quality and type of land.[18]

Settlement along the Susquehannah increased partially because of these inducements. The real boost to the nascent colony came in 1768 when the treaty of Fort Stanwix placed the Indian boundary west of the Susquehannah Company tract, making it much safer to settle. The *New London Gazette* of December 2, 1768, carried the Company's notice that it would attempt to gain the lands released by the treaty. The treaty also prompted Pennsylvanians to increase their own efforts to claim and settle the area. Some would-be Pennsylvania settlers were inspired to live "in the very tract of land the New Englanders threaten to take from us." In fact, a contingent of Pennsylvanians defeated and expelled the Connecticut settlers in 1769.[19]

Throughout the next several years, as the Pennsylvanians increased pressure to rid the Wyoming country of the Company's settlers, the tenacity of the Susquehannah Com-

15. Boyd, "Connecticut's Experiment," 56.

16. Boyd, ed., *Susquehannah Company Papers,* 2:130. See also ibid., 2:xxxiv–xxxv, xli; Boyd, "Connecticut's Experiment," 45–46.

17. Warfle, *Connecticut's Western Colony,* 12–16.

18. Boyd, ed., *Susquehannah Company Papers,* 3:xxi–xxii; Boyd, "Connecticut's Experiment," 51–53. This provision could be the origin of the size of townships in the Western Reserve, or it could merely be coincidental; as would be the case further west.

19. Boyd, ed., *Susquehannah Company Papers,* 3:xiv–xviii; Warfle, *Connecticut's Western Colony,* 19–21.

pany only intensified. More threats meant more settlers. In Connecticut, opposition in the General Assembly's lower house mounted because many felt that the colony should not support a private land company. Seemingly spurred on by this attack, the Company went ahead with its plans and sent a series of petitions to the legislature asking to have the area made a Connecticut county. Perhaps, more importantly, Jonathan Trumbull, a Company member, became governor of the colony.[20]

None of these developments brought success quickly. Consequently, in a seemingly desperate move, the conservative New Englanders in the Wyoming area made a curious alliance with a group of Scotch-Irish frontiersmen known as the Paxton Boys in January 1770. The frontiersmen, who had a reputation for lawlessness and had massacred peaceful Indians several years earlier, agreed to chase the Pennsylvanians from the Susquehannah Company lands in exchange for a township in the Wyoming Valley. The agreement alienated Pennsylvania authorities, who called the "Paxton Boys a band of fifty or sixty . . . lawless villains." They feared that the area would become "an Asylum to all the Villains & Robbers." The alliance also created objections to the Susquehannah Company in Connecticut and considerable unrest within the settlements as the spirits of the two sides clashed especially in military matters. Throughout the period the settlement was forced to practice a fort and blockhouse economy in which both military duties and farming chores were shared.[21]

The treaty signed at Fort Stanwix in 1768 not only stimulated activity on the tract, but it also rekindled interest in the Wyoming Valley by the Connecticut legislature, which ordered a search of all its charters to determine if its claims to western lands were valid. In response, a Crown adviser replied to Connecticut governor Benjamin Trumbull in words reminiscent of the seventeenth-century English attorney general: "the opinion that in general prevails . . . [in England] is, that all the Ancient Charters & Patents in the Colonies being Vague in their descriptions, drawn by Persons often unacquainted with the Geography of the Country, & Interfering frequently with each other, *must be evidenced by Actual Occupation . . . by early settlers.*" The Company hoped that its early colonization would help its charter requests. However, the general opinion in England seemed to be that Connecticut should not be directly involved in the case and that the dispute should be between the Susquehannah Company and the Penn family. Connecticut officially stayed out of this controversy. In 1770 the Privy Council ruled that the problem was a matter for the Pennsylvania courts. Finally, in 1771 the combined effect of the refusal of the British government to decide the matter, the efforts of the search committee, and the impact of a petition of 3,241 citizens in favor of official recognition caused the Connecticut Assembly to conclude "that the Lands west of the Delaware River, and

20. Warfle, *Connecticut's Western Colony,* 18–19, 22.

21. Boyd, ed., *Susquehannah Company Papers,* 4:vi–vii; John Penn to Thomas Penn, Mar. 10, 1770, 4:xii, 42–43. The area was under martial law for much of the early 1770s. At one point in 1770 the Pennsylvania forces captured the Connecticut settlement and imprisoned its leaders only to be defeated in a winter raid by the Paxton Boys and then lost again (ibid., 4:xxv).

in the Latitude of that Part of the Colony Eastward of the Province of New York, *are well Contained within the Boundaries & Descriptions of the Charter granted by King Charles 2d."* For the first time, Connecticut officially asserted its control of the Wyoming Valley. It did not actually define its relationship to the Company, however.[22]

The legislature was drawn into the search for recognition by this action, and it sought to shift official opinion in England as well and sent documents supporting its claim there in 1772. They were approved in writing by prominent English attorneys, including two solicitors general who denied the later claims of New York and Pennsylvania. To add further support, Connecticut passed an act in 1773 that asserted its claim and indicated its intention to meet with the Penns to make a settlement. Unfortunately, even though the meeting took place, it resolved nothing.[23]

The uncertain situations in England and with the Penns compelled the colony to move beyond mere recognition of the lands of the Wyoming Valley. In 1774 the legislature, under heavy lobbying pressure from Company investors, incorporated the Susquehannah Company lands into a huge township called Westmoreland. Over the next year opposition to the Company and its speculative purposes grew in Connecticut, but could not reverse support for the Company.[24]

As these legal maneuvers were taking place, settlement prospects were improving because of a series of events. Beginning in 1771, the title to the land was implicitly accepted by the Privy Council. The first band of settlers marched to the Wyoming and opened it for those who followed by ousting some resident Pennsylvanians. By the following year 1,922 settlers occupied Company lands. These inhabitants were not yet recognized by

22. Nutting, "Charter and Crown," 87–88; Boyd, ed., *Susquehannah Company Papers,* 4:27 (emphasis added); Nutting, "Charter and Crown," 88–89; and Warfle, *Connecticut's Western Colony,* 25. The Company was pleased for two reasons: first, because the Penns would be forced to attempt an enactment suit in Pennsylvania courts; and second, the Company had kept the colony of Connecticut out of the case. Boyd, ed., *Susquehannah Company Papers,* 4:215 (emphasis added).

23. Warfle suggests their opinions were biased by the high fees they received for them and that privately they expressed their disagreement with Connecticut's claim (*Connecticut's Western Colony,* 31). Robert J. Taylor, ed., *Susquehannah Company Papers,* 5:xxxii–xxxiv, 229–45, see esp. 240–45, where the argument is summarized. Nutting, "Charter and Crown," 91. Interestingly, the Company drafted two petitions to be presented to the Assembly in 1773. The proposed petition, which was never presented, included some elements of its successor in Ohio. "Twelve towns [would be established], each twenty miles across, arranged in a double row which together would be formed into a county 120 miles wide" (Warfle, *Connecticut's Western Colony,* 30). This plan had a more varied northern border and much smaller townships.

24. The area was specified as the land between the west shore of the Delaware River and a line fifteen miles west of the Susquehannah River. In May 1775 the limit was extended to the Fort Stanwix line, and the township was attached to Litchfield County in Connecticut (Taylor, ed., *Susquehannah Company Papers,* 5:269). The resultant tract is exactly the same size as the Western Reserve (ibid., 6:320). Gerlach, "Firmness and Prudence," 66. A pamphlet written by William Smith of Pennsylvania, *An Examination of the Connecticut Claim, to the Lands in Pennsylvania,* argued that the western border of Connecticut proceeded northwest from the coast rather than straight west. The long essay provided ammunition for conservatives to attempt to overthrow Governor Trumbull. A meeting was called at Middletown in March 1774 in order to draw up an anti-Susquehannah petition as a way of gaining support. Benjamin Trumbull responded with his own pro-Company pamphlet, and the print war was on. In the election the pro-Company forces won handily (Warfle, *Connecticut's Western Colony,* 32–37).

the legislature, and therefore in 1772 they created their own system of local government controlled by laws paralleling those of Connecticut.[25]

Pennsylvanians, called Pennamites, were not encouraged by these actions. A band of armed Pennamites, acting as representatives of the Pennsylvania government, attempted unsuccessfully to drive out the Yankee settlers. Their failure left Connecticut settlers in firm control and prompted the Connecticut legislature to upgrade the Company lands from a township to a new county. In 1776 Westmoreland County was created with all governmental apparatus, including justices of the peace, county courts, and a militia.

Finally, the Susquehannah Company and the State of Connecticut had won—or so it appeared. Settlers continued to enter the area and boosted the population to at least 3,000 by 1778. Unfortunately, the area was exposed to British troops and their Indian allies. A combined force attacked in July 1778 as part of the British war effort, killing at least 150 men and causing many who avoided death to flee the area. The Wyoming Valley residents remained destitute and fearful for several years even though no further British attacks occurred. Throughout the Revolutionary War, at the request of nationalists, the conflict between the two states subsided because of this outside threat.[26]

However, the conflict over the importance of the land continued. In Connecticut, a series of pamphlets appeared. Benjamin Trumbull, author of the most extensive pamphlet, said that since the state owned the land in the Wyoming Valley, it should benefit from further sales. He defended the large sums spent to fight for the area and asked, "Will a tract of country which might be sold for some hundred thousand sterling and make a public fund sufficient annually to pay all our publick expences to the end of time, enrich our college and support all the schools in the colony utterly ruin it?" Clearly, Trumbull thought the tract would be a valuable source of income and that it could cut taxes and support schools. The suggested school fund was not acted on immediately but would become a reality in the 1790s. The promise of eliminating taxes forever in Connecticut, unfortunately, would not.[27]

THE ARTICLES OF CONFEDERATION AND THE TRENTON DECISION

After 1775 the fight for control of the territory took place on several fronts. First, the legal battle between Connecticut and Pennsylvania shifted. In 1776 the Privy Council postponed its decision on which colony owned the land until "those colonies return to their Allegiance." Consequently, the focal point moved to the Continental Congress. Here Pennsylvania quickly pressed its claims as soon as both states ratified the Articles of Confederation.

25. Warfle, *Connecticut's Western Colony*, 29.

26. Taylor, ed., *Susquehannah Company Papers*, 7:xv–xvii, 59–62. Claims submitted for damages totaled 38,308 pounds, according to a petition submitted in 1780 (ibid., xviin11, 62n3). C. Collier, *Sherman's Connecticut*, 77; Boyd, "Connecticut's Experiment," 64.

27. Taylor, ed., *Susquehannah Company Papers*, 6:109.

Since the Articles had not been accepted by enough states to implement them, Connecticut began what would be a series of maneuvers to forestall a final decision.[28]

The Articles themselves were in trouble at the time, because a number of so-called landless states who had no claims to western lands refused to ratify the document until all states gave up their rights to territory in the west. Connecticut did agree to give up its claims *west* of the Susquehannah Company lands if the territory it relinquished was divided up into New England–style townships. Significantly, it also acknowledged the Mississippi River as the western boundary of the ceded lands, since the Treaty of Paris that ended the French and Indian War set the river as the western border of English North America. Thus ended the south sea and western ocean claims of Connecticut.[29]

Other major states, including Virginia, New York, and Massachusetts, claimed western lands but agreed to cede those lands north of the Ohio River as long as they could reserve some tracts there. For its part, the national government promised to use the lands for the benefit of all states, reimburse them for some expenses incurred in war, and allow new states to be formed in the area. Finally, in 1781, Maryland ratified the Articles and they became law. At the time, four states, including Connecticut, had ceded lands with various qualifications. Congress continued to insist that Connecticut and Massachusetts relinquish their claims. Connecticut remained firm hoping acceptance of Virginia's cession and the admission of Vermont as a separate state, where many former Connecticut residents lived, would enhance its chances of retaining the Wyoming Valley.[30]

While this hope was not realized, a resolution of the matter did take place. The ninth article of the Articles of Confederation provided a mechanism for solving disputes between two states, and Pennsylvania asked that it be used to solve the Wyoming Valley problem. Congress agreed and set June 1782 as the trial date. Connecticut continually tried to delay the proceedings, but the trial began in November 1782 at Trenton, New Jersey. The arguments took several weeks with each side claiming the validity of its charter and the weakness of the rival claim. The tribunal, much to the chagrin of Connecticut, was dominated by men from states with no western claims. It rendered its decision on December 30, 1782. The unanimous ruling included no explanation and read: "the State of Connecticut has no right to the lands in Controversy . . . the Jurisdiction . . . of all the Territory . . . now claimed by the State of Connecticut, do of right belong to the State of Pennsylvania."[31]

On one hand, the trial was a triumph for republican government because "two pow-

28. Ibid., 7:24.

29. Ibid., 63–66; see also Robert Taylor, "Trial at Trenton," *William and Mary Quarterly* 3d ser., 26 (Oct. 1969): 526–28.

30. Gerlach, "Firmness and Prudence," 68. See Merrill Jensen, "The Cession of the Old Northwest," *Mississippi Valley Historical Review* 23 (1936): 27–48. Interestingly, Maryland always exempted lands bought from the Indians before the Revolutionary War, since many of its prominent citizens were involved in land companies that had purchased land in the 1750s and 1760s. Merrill Jensen, "The Creation of the National Domain," *Mississippi Valley Historical Review* 26 [1939–40]: 323–42. Gerlach, "Firmness and Prudence," 68.

31. Julian P. Boyd, ed., *The Papers of Thomas Jefferson* (Princeton: Princeton Univ. Press, 1952), 6:476–77. See the long, detailed editorial note entitled "The Connecticut-Pennsylvania Territorial Dispute" (ibid., 474–87). Taylor, ed., *Susquehannah Company Papers*, 7:xxii–xxxiii, summarizes the debate. For the decree, see ibid., 247–49.

erful and populous states, sovereign and independent (except as members of the federal union) [were] contending for a tract of country equal in extent and superior to some European kingdoms. Instead of recurring to arms . . . they submit[ted] to the arbitration of judges mutually chosen from indifferent states." On the other hand, Connecticut had clearly lost the battle for jurisdiction over the Wyoming Valley. Only individual land claims of each settler remained unresolved.[32]

An anonymous verse added to the minutes of the Connecticut legislature just after the Trenton decision summarized the mood: "Annihilated and out of Sight; / If what the Court have done is right."[33]

"Firmness and Prudence"

Seemingly, Connecticut had lost its long-running battle for western lands, but in reality the quest was only momentarily stymied. The state reacted to the Trenton decision, which it thought unfair, by revoking its cession of western lands previously submitted to Congress but not yet accepted. In January 1784, Connecticut ceded its claims to the nation, again "excepting and reserving to this State for the Use of this State, and to satisfy the Officers and Privates of the Connecticut Line of the Continental Army the Lands to which they are entitled by the Resolve of Congress, all the Territory and Lands situate and Lying between the . . . Western Bounds of Pennsylvania and [a] . . . Line to be drawn at one hundred and twenty Miles distance there from."[34]

Here was the final formulation of the tract. It would be begin at the Pennsylvania line and continue west 120 miles, like Connecticut, and it would conform to the sixty mile width of both the parent state and the Indian deed of 1755. If successful, Connecticut had "reserved" these lands and named the area at the same time.[35]

In the words of one incredulous member of Congress, "Connecticut having failed in her attempts to cut one degree out of the State of Pennsylvania, has just entered her claim to the Same degree Westward of Pennsylvania." So rather than acquiescing to the Trenton decision Connecticut requested a new grant similar to the Susquehannah Company tract beyond the border of Pennsylvania. Not surprisingly, Congress refused to accept the provisions.[36]

32. Christopher Collier, *Connecticut in the Continental Congress* (Chester, Conn.: Pequot Press, 1973), 54. See Boyd, ed., *Papers of Thomas Jefferson*, 6:482–85.

33. Leonard Labaree, ed., *The Public Records of the State of Connecticut, for the Years 1783 and 1784* (Hartford: State of Connecticut, 1943), http://olc1.ohiolink.edu/record=b197338015:11.

34. See a series of letters printed in the *Hartford Courant* in January 1785 entitled "The Claims of Connecticut to Lands west of the Delaware, deduced from authentic Records and fairly stated" (Jan. 4, 11, 18, 25 and Feb. 1, 8, 15). These letters discussed not only the patent and boundary disputes but also the plight of the Wyoming settlers. Gerlach, "Firmness and Prudence," 68–75; Taylor, ed., *Susquehannah Company Papers*, 7:xxxv, 355.

35. Webb, "Connecticut Land Company," 146–47.

36. Hugh Williamson to the governor of North Carolina, Sept. 30, 1784, Edmund Burnett, ed., *Letters of Members of the Continental Congress* (Washington, D.C.: Carnegie Institution of Washington, 1921–36), 7:596.

Connecticut was not powerless, however. Pressure was mounting to open lands north of the Ohio River for settlement, and by 1785 Virginia, New York, and Massachusetts had ceded their claims. Congress, ignoring Connecticut, passed a Land Ordinance that provided a plan for dividing the territory and shunned Connecticut's claims because the western lands in question were already ceded by Virginia and because Congress had already provided lands for all soldiers. Undaunted but somewhat conciliatory, the Connecticut Assembly passed a new resolution that still claimed the tract but gave all land west of it to Congress. As the stalemate dragged on, one optimistic Connecticut representative commented, "If Connecticut proceeds in the affair with firmness and prudence, she may yet retain the Boundary she has proposed," because Congress wanted to sell the lands as soon as possible.[37]

A number of complex issues were present in the ensuing debates. First, the plight of the Susquehannah settlers provided a crucial bargaining chip used by the Connecticut delegation to gain a western reserve. Residents were especially vulnerable because they did not have title to the Wyoming land they occupied. After the Trenton decision, the victorious Pennsylvanians began to harass the Connecticut settlers. Their leader was arrested and imprisoned, some frightened residents were forced to sign unfavorable leases, and Pennsylvania authorities "dispossessed a number of familys tumbled their Goods and Every thing out of doors and by force drove them from the buildings." These actions evoked outcries in Connecticut and appeals to the federal government that threatened the Trenton decision.[38]

On the national level, the Wyoming settlers lost another battle when Congress rescinded an order to set up a court to determine private land rights there. The repeal of September 1785 gave the Pennsylvania legislature control over land rights and worsened the outlook for those on Susquehannah Company land.[39]

The Pennsylvania legislature, conciliatory in the afterglow of its successful fights, began in 1785 to pass laws designed to placate the Connecticut settlers. It coupled an amnesty act for some who had violated Pennsylvania law with an act to allow local elections that would permit some settlers to hold office. Also, a separate county, Luzerne, was created for the Wyoming area. Ultimately, the Pennsylvania assembly reversed the rhetoric of a decade and confirmed the titles of Connecticut settlers in March 1787. The act caused a violent reaction by some of the Connecticut people, and rumors abounded

---

37. C. Collier, *Connecticut in the Continental Congress*, 70–71.

38. See petition of Nov. 11, 1783, Taylor, ed., *Susquehannah Company Papers*, 7:320–24, 8:xv–xxii. Obadiah Gore to William Judd, Nov. 21, 1783, ibid., 7:330–34. The testimony of Peter Obersheimer given in April 1784, when he was a member of the Pennsylvania militia sent to the Wyoming Valley, acknowledges the inhumane treatment. Prisoners from Connecticut who were arrested were held in several taverns "for twenty four Hours, without Witles or thrinck." When he asked why, he was told "Demmn the yenckees, Let them Dye thay Do not Deserve no Better" (ibid., 395). See *Hartford Courant*, July 18, 1785, for a series of resolutions passed by the proprietors of the Susquehannah Company that stated that the Company "would take all proper measures to defend [its property] and our settlers."

39. Boyd, ed., *Papers of Thomas Jefferson*, 6:484–85.

that they intended to establish a separate state. Of course, the rumors remained just that. Unfortunately, from this point on the settlers were gradually abandoned by powerful groups of political leaders in both Connecticut and Pennsylvania.[40]

COLLUSION

In Congress another major shift occurred as the two quarreling states struck a bargain. Roger Sherman, the Connecticut delegate who was "as cunning as the Devil" in political matters, approached Pennsylvania for help in obtaining a reserve. Sherman probably used the treatment of the Wyoming settlers and the fear that the lands requested by Connecticut would impinge on the western border of Pennsylvania to obtain that state's support. An agreement was reached that one member of Congress said "was nothing but a State juggle contrived by old Roger Sherman to get a side wind confirmation to [land in the west which] they had no right to." Connecticut, for its part, would "use Means to induce these [land] Companies to relinquish their Pretentions to such Claims" in exchange for land farther west. Pennsylvania agreed to protect the actual settlers, to treat them with justice, to preserve their private rights, and to support "the implied Right of Connecticut to the 120 Miles not ceded [to Congress] . . . [so] that Connecticut may find Means from that Source to quiet her Companies with respect to Western Lands." Notice in this explanation compensation for military service is not mentioned but compensation to land speculators is. Understandably, the agreement was confidential: "these Things being understood rather than expressed, may be differently conceived of by different Minds." If they were successful, Pennsylvania was assured that the Trenton decision would stand and the disputed Susquehannah Company lands in Pennsylvania would be free of controversy and Connecticut would receive a tract further west.[41]

What remained was the implementation of the plan. The two states who "agreed to meet each other on the ground of reciprocal Confidence and Generosity" joined to support each others' causes in 1786. Said one Pennsylvania member of Congress, "[the

40. Warfle, *Connecticut's Western Colony*, 42–44. Successful Pennsylvania claimants would receive lands elsewhere in the state. The act was repealed in 1790. The difficulties continued when the Company granted lands in the mid-1790s. In 1799 a compromise act passed that forced Connecticut settlers in the seventeen original townships to pay for lands. In the long run the Connecticut contingent obtained title to much of the land and dominated county politics (ibid., 47–48). Reportedly these leaders were also land speculators who might benefit from these changes.

41. Jeremiah Wadsworth to Rufus King, Hartford, June 3, 1787, Charles R. King, ed., *Life and Correspondence of Rufus King* (New York: G. P. Putnam's Sons, 1894), 1:221. Grayson continued, "Some of the States particularly Pansylvany, voted for them on the same principle that the powers of Europe give money to the Algerines [the notorious pirates of the Mediterranean]." Earlier in the same letter, Grayson acknowledged that some states criticized Virginia for not supporting Connecticut's request for western lands since Virginia reserved some lands within its ceded tract. He did not find the argument compelling and Virginia voted against Connecticut consistently (William Grayson to James Madison, May 28, 1786, Burnett, ed., *Letters*, 8:373). Charles Pettit to Jeremiah Wadsworth, May 27, 1786, Burnett, ed., *Letters*, 8:369.

agreements] were not unperceived by Congress and their Desire of promoting Peace and Harmony induced them to acquiesce in the Views of the two States." Other states thought acquiescence was important for a number of reasons summarized in a letter from William Grayson to George Washington: "the tranquility of the Union [would result]: the procuring of a clear title to the residue of the Continental lands: the forming a barrier agt. [against] the British as well as the Indians: the appreciating the value of the adjacent territory and facilitating the settlement thereof." Furthermore, as James Monroe wrote to Richard Henry Lee, "we have been inform'd that [Connecticut] and Pena. are on the point of variance with respect to wiomin, and that this [reserve] is necessary to satisfy the Susquehannah and Delaware companies of Connecticut, who create this mischief.... We are also assur'd that unless we accept this cession, Connecticut will open an office for the whole degree claim'd by her to the Mississippi River." Many of these concerns were real enough to find support in Congress. Finally, on May 26, 1786, it agreed to the cession by a vote of ten to two. The following September Connecticut deeded to the nation the territory not included in its reserve.[42]

The persistence of Connecticut paid off. What began as a real need for new lands over thirty years before by a colony ended in ownership of truly western lands by a new state. Moreover, the tract was virtually the same size and was at the same longitude as the Susquehannah Company lands, thus confirming the physical similarity of the two efforts by Connecticut. It does appear that the plight of the settlers on the Susquehannah Company lands convinced some of the need for a reserve, but by far the most important reason for the compromise was the persistence of Connecticut and the land hunger of settlers and speculators. In the final analysis, the Company and its settlers were abandoned for lands that would benefit the state and a group of investors.

EARLY STATE OWNERSHIP

In the story of the sale of the tract, it is interesting to note that many involved in the Susquehannah Company were not involved in subsequent developments. Apparently, the effort to obtain a grant from the federal government was not really to compensate the investors in the Susquehannah Company but to provide land speculators with further investment opportunities. Also, it had been nearly thirty-five years since the Company was formed and many of the original investors were no longer concerned.

Initially, Connecticut expected to administer the lands and to dispose of them quickly, but numerous obstacles prolonged the actual distribution for nearly a decade.

The Continental Congress discussed the Western Reserve in several sessions in 1786.

42. Burnett, ed., *Letters,* 8:369. It was assumed that settlement would take place quickly (ibid., 373). May 24, 1786, ibid., 365–66; Gerlach, "Firmness and Prudence," 73; C. Collier, *Connecticut in the Continental Congress,* 72–73.

Fortunately, there was little likelihood of a reversal since the Connecticut claim had been tacitly acknowledged in the Land Ordinance of 1785. The survey of the Old Northwest required in the document placed the northern line of survey forty miles south of Connecticut's western claims, thereby acknowledging that the state owned the land farther north.[43]

The debate over the distribution of the lands in the General Assembly of Connecticut supported the notion that it was to pay soldiers. However, an early proposal from a special western lands committee of the Assembly favored speculators. It set the minimum size of a tract at 5,000 acres and the price at 50 cents per acre, payable in either federal or state paper. Agrarian interests replaced the plan with one that allowed smaller lot sizes and divided the tract into townships six miles by six miles, payable in state money or specie. A further provision established the method of surveying the eastern portion of the Reserve. Six tiers of townships would be laid out parallel to the western border of Pennsylvania, and the tiers were to be numbered; the first tier bordered Pennsylvania. Similarly, each township was numbered south to north in each tier or range; the southernmost was designated number one. With the apparatus in place, it appeared in October 1786 that the lands of the Western Reserve would be sold if not to soldiers at least to small farmers. Such was not to be the case, however.[44]

CONSTITUTIONAL CONVENTION

There was still one more threat to the grant of land itself. In spring and summer of 1787, the Constitutional Convention met. As it became clear that a new government was about to be formed, it also became clear that any previous agreements could be negated. In the convention, James Madison, still riled by the confirmation of the grant to Connecticut, complained that the tract had been "dealt out to Cont. to bribe her acquiesence" to the Trenton decision. Pennsylvania continued to support Connecticut partially to quell the militaristic passions of the Wyoming settlers.[45]

In the convention itself, Connecticut interests wished to preserve the Reserve at all costs. Its delegates, remembering the Trenton decision all too well, apparently wanted to change the body that decided land disputes between states. Instead of the special body

43. Webb, "Connecticut Land Company," 147.

44. The proposal included clear instructions to surveyors to lay out townships from the Pennsylvania line to the Cuyahoga River, but the fees allowed proved to be a burden and the surveys were not completed. Other provisions reserved 500 acres in each township for support of schools and 500 for support of gospel ministry, and 240 acres were to be given to the first minister to settle in the town. Compatibility with the United States was guaranteed in the following clause: "Measures not inconsistent with the principles of the confederation of the United States shall from Time to Time be taken . . . [by the General Assembly to preserve peace and good order] untill this State shall resign its Jurisdiction of the Same and Government be settled amongst them upon Republican principles"(Labaree, ed., *Public Records,* 6:238; for problems with the fees, see 357). Webb, "Connecticut Land Company," 148.

45. C. Collier, *Sherman's Connecticut,* 259. Collier cites no source for this assertion.

invoked by the Articles of Confederation, Connecticut wanted either Congress or the legislative branch with equal representation to adjudicate. There it could align itself with landless states and have a better chance of success.[46]

Connecticut succeeded in changing the mechanism for solving land disputes between states and in keeping its reserve. Historians differ on how this was accomplished in the Constitutional Convention. According to one interpretation, Connecticut, perhaps remembering its previous success with Pennsylvania, made a deal with South Carolina. The pact exchanged Connecticut's support for the perpetuation of the slave trade and a prohibition on export duties for agricultural products for South Carolina's support of the Western Reserve.[47]

In the absence of direct proof of this agreement, most historians believe the compromise did not involve the Western Reserve. In the words of Luther Martin, delegate from Maryland, "I found the *eastern* States, notwithstanding their *aversion to slavery,* were very willing to indulge the southern States, at least with a temporary liberty to prosecute the *slave-trade,* provided the southern States would in their turn, gratify them, by laying *no restrictions on navigation acts.*" Connecticut also worked to preserve, in the words of Connecticut delegate Roger Sherman, "the claims of particular states." Whenever the issue of lands reserved by individual states was discussed, Sherman and his fellow delegates spoke for these rights and were able to preserve them. Consequently, the new government allowed the bargain between Pennsylvania and Connecticut to stand. The new government would not meddle with the compromises reached by the Confederation Congress.[48]

46. Forrest McDonald, *The Formation of the American Republic, 1776–1790* (Baltimore: Penguin Books, 1965), 176–77.

47. Richard Barry, *Mr. Rutledge of South Carolina* (New York: Duell, Sloan, and Pearce, 1942), 330–35, suggests some agreement over the slave trade and the navigation acts provisions; but McDonald, *Formation of the American Republic* (176–77 and nn 298–99), infers from vague evidence the deal protecting the Reserve was activated when the issue of land disputes came to the floor of the convention. Most historians think the Northern states allowed slavery in exchange for federal regulation of foreign trade. Max Farrand, ed., *The Records of the Federal Convention of 1787,* rev. ed. (New Haven: Yale Univ. Press, 1966), 2:449. See also C. Collier, *Sherman's Connecticut,* 204–5, 259, 270–71. For a confirming view, see James H. Hutson, "Riddles of the Federal Constitutional Convention," *William and Mary Quarterly,* 3d ser., 44 (July 1987): 415–16. Hutson could find no proof that the dinner meeting between Sherman and Rutledge ever took place and argues that since Congress had agreed to the creation of the Reserve in May 1786, it was unlikely it would be overturned.

48. Farrand, ed., *Records of the Federal Convention,* 2:462–63, 465. Apparently, the bargain rankled some well into the 1790s. A correspondent to William Lane indicated that Mr. Livingstone had proposed a resolution into the House of Representatives to inquire into the title of the Connecticut Reserve. It was in response to a Connecticut plan to have debtor states pay their balances and was not intended to be anything but an annoyance (Philadelphia, Feb. 10, 1797, box 14, William G. Lane Papers, Yale University Manuscripts Collections, New Haven, Conn.).

CONNECTICUT: LAND SALE

Seemingly, the only remaining impediment was to secure Indian title so that the lands in the Reserve could be efficiently surveyed and quickly dispensed. As early as 1787 a letter in the *Hartford Courant* criticized the comptroller of Connecticut for not expediting the sale of the state's western lands by accepting continental currency. In fact, many prospective investors had switched to the Ohio Company and its settlements at Marietta, which accepted federal money. In 1788 the committee appointed to oversee western lands employed Gen. Samuel Parsons to make a treaty with the Indians and to survey the area. He reported little progress with the Indians.[49]

There was continued interest in the lands throughout the period. The state did grant two portions of the tract before it decided to sell the rest at one time. A tract was sold to Parsons apparently to pay him for his services. Also, the state fulfilled one of its promises to the national government when it agreed to compensate those whose property was destroyed by British attacks on towns along the Connecticut coast during the Revolutionary War. The half-million-acre tract in the westernmost portion of the Reserve, later called the Firelands, was distributed to those "sufferers" with proven claims.[50]

In the meantime the Assembly formed a committee to receive bids on the remainder of the tract from "any person or persons, company or companies." Despite this gesture, the legislature hesitated to sell the Reserve. After Elijah Austin offered to buy the entire tract for $325,000 in October 1791, the committee for western lands was instructed not to sell because the Indians were threatening, and the price of lands in both western New York and in the Congress lands in Ohio was much lower than the state hoped to obtain for its land. A notice in the *Hartford Courant* the same month expressed the fear that the Assembly would, in trying to wait for a rise in value, hold the land "till the monied men have vested their money in others lands or enterprises, and then a few designing men will have an opportunity of purchasing these lands *cheap*." In contrast, "Farmer" proposed to have each town subscribe to a fund that would buy the lands to keep them from "the land jobbers or speculators . . . [in order to] diffuse the benefit" to state residents.[51]

The next year a committee was appointed to receive offers, which began to filter in by October. Gradually, the bidders raised their offers to $500,000 in 1793 and then to George Kirkland's bid of $1 million in 1794. Just as the patience of Connecticut was rewarded

---

49. See letter by "Detector" from the *Litchfield Weekly Monitor,* which was reprinted in the *Hartford Courant,* Dec. 3, 1787; Committee Report, Nov. 27, 1788, doc. 210, ser. 1, Western Lands, Connecticut Archives, Connecticut State Library, Hartford.

50. The land was especially valuable because it contained a source of salt. This parcel was the only part of the Reserve sold by the state of Connecticut to an individual. See Nov. 21, 1791, doc. 20, ser. 2, Western Lands, Connecticut Archives; Henry Barnard, *History of the School Fund of Connecticut* (Hartford, Conn., 1853; reissued 1931), 12.

51. Barnard, *History of the School Fund,* 12–13; doc. 20, ser. 2, Western Lands, Connecticut Archives. Royal Flint made another offer for $350,000 at the same time (ibid., 20). *Hartford Courant,* Oct. 24, 1791. A "Freeman" argues against the farmer saying that the proposal would turn honest people into land jobbers and that the group would be so unwieldy that it would never succeed (ibid., July 29, 1793).

with the land grant, the three-year wait had more than tripled the price of the land. Finally in May 1795 the legislature established $1 million as the minimum bid set for the Reserve. The Indian title, however, remained unsolved in the early 1790s.[52]

CONNECTICUT: THE DISPUTE OVER THE USE OF THE PROCEEDS

Unfortunately, a more volatile and perplexing problem also emerged. The beneficiaries of the funds generated by the sale had to be determined. As early as 1774 mention was made of using the proceeds to pay state debts and to fund education in some way. This suggestion was apparently ignored when, in October 1791, the lower house of the Assembly discussed a bill to give the proceeds of the sale to local religious societies to pay their ministers. The discussion continued into the next session but reached no conclusion on the distribution of proceeds.[53]

In the intervening period the Assembly in 1793 passed the controversial Appropriations Act, which repeated the essence of the 1791 bill. It said the proceeds from the sale of the land should go to the "use and benefit of the various ecclesiastical will check societies, churches, or congregations . . . to them to be applied to the support of their respective ministers, or preachers of the gospel and schools of education."[54]

There was considerable opposition to the bill that passed the lower house by the relatively slim margin of 83 in favor and 70 opposed. The debate also focused a seething undercurrent of opinion against the established church in the state and against the Federalist political party that supported it. In fact, some thought the clergy pressured the assembly into passing the act to give them financial support and enhance their declining prestige.[55]

A debate in the public press of unparalleled magnitude focused on the funds but quickly pitted those interested in more general reform against those who wanted to preserve the status quo. A letter that appeared in most major Connecticut newspapers summarized the fears of many even though it defended the bill. It stated that "much has been said about [the fund's] being a trick of the old standing order. . . . there has been a good deal said about the dissenters (so called) being shaved (as they term it) out of the money. . . . Some say it will make the preachers too independent." Some in favor of the bill argued privately that "the hell of Democracy had been opened upon us in this State lately . . . and . . . the Appropriation has been the torch."

"Aristides" commented that the bill would help compensate for the "unavoidable effects of the late war in producing a relaxation in the principles and practice of moral-

---

52. Two New Yorkers, John Livingston and Elihu Chauncey, offered $350,000, and Austin raised his offer to $356,000. See ser. 2, Western Lands, Connecticut Archives docs. 26, 29, 37, 41, 46.

53. Taylor, ed., *Susquehannah Company Papers,* 6:109; Barnard, *History of the School Fund,* 12.

54. Barnard, *History of the School Fund,* 14.

55. Ibid. See James R. Beasley, "Emerging Republicanism and the Standing Order: The Appropriation Act Controversy in Connecticut, 1793–1795," *William and Mary Quarterly,* 3d ser., 29 (Oct. 1972): 587–610, esp. 590.

ity," but it would only assist in paying for more preaching and schooling and not make it any better "or more attended to." Another correspondent chided the religious purposes of those in the debate: "If a religion whose purposes are universal love and harmony, is to be supported and promoted by a means which will blow sparks of faction and party spirit into violent flame, it is to me a new way of promoting religion. Much better would it be for the state of Connecticut that their western lands should be sunk by an earthquake, and form a part of the adjoining lake, than that they should be transported hither for a bone of contention." Other supporters of the bill pointed to the "40 to 50 vacant parishes in this state . . . [to which] it must appear that religion has decayed, is decaying, and wants support."[56]

This intense public debate, which continued through the winter of 1793–94, led the lower house to the repeal of the act granting the proceeds to churches in May 1794. As the debate continued until the next session in October 1794, a compromise was offered that would grant the income from the sales to local school districts or the ministry at the discretion of a majority of the voters in the district.[57]

Moses Cleaveland, soon to be a leader in the development of the Western Reserve, favored repeal. He was convinced that the tract would continue to rise in value if the state held on to it. In addition, he was part of a group of Congregationalists who attacked current religious leaders as too snobbish and too conservative because they supported the standing order and the Federalist party. More significantly, Cleaveland feared the clergy would become "a separate order of men. . . . contrary to the public good and to the principles of republicanism." While he was not "hostile to the clergy: they are useful men in their place [he cautioned that] . . . when they deviate from their proper line of duty, and assume that which belongs to the province of others they are hurtful."[58]

Many others agreed with Cleaveland and resented the clergy's fiscal and political selfishness. Some objected to the appropriations bill for it did not promise support to religious groups such as Quakers and Jews, who did not have ministers and, thus, would not benefit from the sale of the lands. Mr. Payne commented that the clergy are "materially interested . . . ; for they know, that if the appropriation should take place, a large part

56. Beasley effectively argues that Federalists wanted to link the funds to the churches not so much for the financial benefit, which would probably have been small, but for the control it would give the clergy over church and school funds for the foreseeable future. This was especially enticing in an era of declining prominence for the Standing Order (ibid., 609). Barnard, *History of the School Fund*, 15; Timothy Dwight to Oliver Wolcott Jr., Oct. 26, 1794, Oliver Wolcott Jr. Papers, Connecticut Historical Society, cited in Bonnie B. Collier, "The Ohio Western Reserve: Its Influence of Political Parties in Connecticut in the Late Eighteenth Century," *Connecticut Review* 1 (Nov. 1975), 58; Barnard, *History of the School Fund*, 16; *Hartford Courant*, May 19, 5, 1794.

57. The vote was 109 for repeal and 58 against. The upper house did not agree with the repeal but did suspend the sale of the land (Barnard, *History of the School Fund*, 24). For part of the debate in the *Hartford Courant*, see May 26 and June 2, 1794. Beasley, "Appropriation Act Controversy," 590.

58. Edmund Morgan, *The Gentle Puritan: Life of Ezra Stiles, 1727–1795* (New Haven: Yale Univ. Press, 1965), 414–15. Morgan includes Cleaveland in a list of opponents to the Federalists who began meeting in 1791 and were called by opponents the Nocturnal Society of the Stelligeri. B. Collier, "The Ohio Western Reserve," 54; Barnard, *History of the School Fund*, 30.

of their salaries will become sure and permanent, and the people not realizing it and seemingly less burdened, will feel more willing to enlarge their pay; of course they will become more independent of the people." Payne followed with the telling point that seemed to be on the minds of many residents: "The influence of the clergy has been gradually declining for half a century; and had its fatal stab when the famous act passed known by the name of the conscience bill. Fifty years ago no office either civil or military could be obtained, unless the candidate bowed to the shrine of superstition, and yielded tamely to the yoke of ecclesiastical tyranny, the established religion of this State, but happily for the people of this State at present no such, at least very few such unjust opinions, and practices are now among us."[59]

Another undercurrent in the debate was the power of the upper house, the Council of Assistants, which vetoed the repeal twice. It was a symbol of aristocratic power since its members were elected with virtually no opposition. The aristocracy should be attacked according to one fledgling republican representative. His appeal was heard in the lower house, which turned out some who voted for appropriations to the clergy and replaced them with supporters of repeal. The fight was carried on within Congregationalism by those who feared the establishment of an intolerant clerical hierarchy rather than by members of dissenting sects, since they were too small and disorganized to have any impact.[60]

Another realistic fear motivated opponents. Many felt the clergy controlled the choice of teachers and, therefore, controlled the school system. This needed to be changed. Opposition leaders sought established school districts led by elected councils. Significantly, such a system was enacted in May 1794 in the midst of the appropriations controversy.[61]

Perhaps the most convincing discussion concentrated on the disparity between the ability of the local societies and local schools. As one representative pointed out, "ecclesiastical societies [should] not apply the school money." The problem was that, on the one hand, the societies were beholden to a specific sect while, on the other hand, school funds were for all residents regardless of religious affiliation. The debate continued through 1794 and 1795.[62]

Clearly, the debate convinced many legislators that the schools should be independent of the clergy and should receive the proceeds of the sale of the Western Reserve. Consequently, the final act passed in May 1795 sent all the funds from the sale of the western lands to a "perpetual fund . . . to the support of schools in the several societies constituted" for that purpose. Further provisions allowed each school society to give money to the ecclesiastical societies if it chose to do so.[63]

59. Beasley, "Appropriation Act Controversy," 606–7. Moreover, he continued, how could all groups even those not currently in existence, be guaranteed support. Barnard, *History of the School Fund*, 31, 43–44.

60. Beasley, "Appropriation Act Controversy," 596–97. Collier argues that as early as 1792 the Council feared attacks by young men ("The Ohio Western Reserve," 55). Beasley, "Appropriation Act Controversy," 596. According to Beasley, four of the leaders of the opposition became leading Republicans in Connecticut after 1800, and this was the training ground for the beginning of that party (ibid., 598–99).

61. Beasley, "Appropriation Act Controversy," 604–5.

62. Barnard, *History of the School Fund*, 49–50. The clergy were defended as faithful, diligent workers who were not well paid. See, for example, *Hartford Courant*, June 30, Dec. 22, 1794, Feb. 2, 9, Mar. 2, 1795.

63. Barnard, *History of the School Fund*, 60, 61. The vote was 94 in favor and 52 against.

The long debate was over. On the surface the outcome seemed a simple choice, but the controversy signaled the deteriorating power of the standing order that failed to shore up its declining position in the state. That it failed and that a separate set of school committees was established to further remove the funds from ministerial interference signaled a major loss for the standing order. It also suggested that many Connecticut residents might want to leave the state to avoid the dwindling but still powerful ruling elite.

SALE

Surprisingly, this successful internal revolt did not immediately spawn either a shift in Connecticut politics or a further challenge to the power of the Congregational establishment. It seems that many opponents of the standing order in the Appropriations Act debates became allies and business partners "deeply engaged in the land speculation" in the Connecticut Land Company. Speculation ran so high in some Connecticut towns that "many respectable farmers [in Suffield had] to mortgage their Farms to the state to secure the Debts which they contracted for the Connecticut Western Reserve."[64]

There was an undercurrent in the debates against selling the lands quickly. Several problems compelled legislators to ignore the advice. First, the "slender" title to the Reserve was not guaranteed by the United States government. Moreover, the Indian title was not yet extinguished. Third, there was a real threat that western Pennsylvanians might move into the area and claim it by possession (thus echoing the tactics used successfully by the Susquehannah Land Company).[65]

With these factors in mind, the legislature set $1 million in specie as the minimum acceptable amount for the tract and appointed a committee to proceed with the sale. By August 1795 there were seven offers from inside and outside the state. Over several days the committee noticed "that the State companies had . . . put an end to all further competition," at which time another offer arrived from Massachusetts and the state companies agreed to consummate the deal in the face of renewed competition. The Connecticut Land Company, as it was called, agreed to pay $1,200,000 for the tract. An analysis of some of the investors shows that at least six of the forty-eight members of the Company were active in the appropriation controversy on the side of repeal.[66]

64. B. Collier, "The Ohio Western Reserve," 53. Collier disagrees that this early Republican movement started with the Appropriations Act. She sees its roots three years earlier in the Certificate debate that made it more difficult for dissenting sects to obtain state funds (ibid., 57n39). She further argues that this setback for Republicanism in Connecticut allowed Federalists to control the state until 1817. Alexander King to Orestes King, May 9, 1801, Suffield misc., Connecticut Historical Society cited in B. Collier, "The Ohio Western Reserve," 60.

65. See "Caius," *Hartford Courant,* Feb. 2, 1795.

66. Part of the attempt to ensure that state investors received the grant included the tactics of one of the most prominent speculators in Connecticut, Gideon Granger Jr. He wrote to Ephraim Kirby in June 1795: "You Know that [Aaron] Austin is one of the Comtte and [Uriel] Holmes is his Son in law. We wish you to draw Holmes to our interest" by offering Holmes "a some Share with You" to influence Austin "Indirectly." See B. Collier, "The Ohio Western Reserve," 54, 64–65. Barnard defends the school fund by stating that in 1850, out of a population of 309,978, only 526 adults could not read (*History of the School Fund,* 70). B. Collier, "The

The state's "firmness and prudence" resulted in a four-fold improvement in the price of the tract. It also ensured that most of the leading families in the state were shareholders. Clearly, while the proceeds would go to schools, the state avoided an opportunity to sell the land itself with no intervening parties. The venture held great promise both for the land speculators and for residents who wanted to settle the lands. In this way, Connecticut was able to perpetuate the goals of the Susquehannah Company formulated more than forty years earlier.

Ohio Western Reserve," 60. The investors who favored repeal were Pierpont Edwards, $60,000; William Judd, $16,256; Ephraim Kirby, $20,000; Elisha Hyde, $28,700; Moses Cleaveland, $32,600; Gideon Granger, $40,000; and perhaps Luther Loomis, $22,159. While this essay offers many insights, B. Collier does not prove that the majority of the investors were Republicans, since she only mentions six names specifically. Further, her claim that speculation diverted the Republicans from forming a more substantive effort against the establishment is interesting but unproven.

The Political Economy of Nullification
Ohio and the Bank of the United States, 1818–1824

KEVIN M. GANNON

Between twelve and one o'clock on the afternoon of September 17, 1819, a wagon pulled up in front of the Chillicothe Office of Discount and Deposit, one of the two branch offices of the Bank of the United States in Ohio. Dismounting from the wagon, John Harper and his companions James McCollister and Thomas Orr burst into the bank's lobby. McCollister and Orr, "in a ruffian-like manner," quickly jumped the counter and made their way to the bank's vault. The bank's cashier, Abraham Claypoole, attempted to block McCollister and Orr and protect the vault, but was "forcibly prevented" from doing so by Harper, who had roughly "intruded himself behind the counter." Claypoole remonstrated with the men and repeatedly tried to detain them, but he was again "forcibly repulsed" as Harper and his companions made off with more than $120,000 from the bank's vault. Frustrated in their efforts to apprehend the "ruffians," Claypoole and the bank's president, William Creighton, could only give a deposition of the afternoon's events to Chillicothe's mayor and hurriedly write the central office of the Bank of the United States for further instructions.[1]

The events of the seventeenth would have been sensational enough if they were a simple bank robbery. But this episode was much more complex. Harper and his cohorts were not mere "ruffians"; they were state officials operating under a commission from the Auditor of Ohio. Their confrontation with Claypoole and the forcible removal of funds from the Chillicothe branch's vault were actually efforts to collect a tax—a levy mandated by Ohio's legislature with the intent of driving the branch offices of the Bank of the United States out of the state altogether. In collecting the tax, Ohio's leadership firmly asserted what

---

1. A. G. Claypoole to William H. Crawford, Sept. 17 and 25, 1819, *American State Papers, Finance* (Washington, D.C., 1858), 4:903–4.

Ohio History, Vol. 114 © 2007 by The Kent State University Press

it saw as the state's inviolable sovereignty against the perceived abuse of federal powers represented by the Bank. In addition, the day's proceedings were in direct defiance of the United States Supreme Court's ruling in the case of *McCulloch v. Maryland*, handed down earlier that year, which held that taxation of the Bank or any of its branches was outside the purview of a state's powers. Ohio's decision to ignore the ruling and proceed with its attempts to tax the Bank out of existence represented an intensification of a larger struggle against not only the Bank but against what Ohioans saw as the corrupt and despotic national authority that lay behind the its actions. With its defiance of that national authority, and espousal of states' rights ideology and nullification, Ohio's battle against the Bank of the United States became a larger conflict over the locus of sovereignty. The leadership of Ohio's anti-Bank forces was determined to preserve a particular vision of the ideal polity, a vision that it saw as fundamentally threatened by the operations of the national Bank within the state. In their use of the ideals of states' rights and nullification, Ohioans tapped into a wider tradition in antebellum political culture—a tradition that sought to preserve republican virtues against the forces of corruption and arbitrary despotism and which placed the idea of Union distinctly second to this preservation.[2]

Ohio had not always been a hotbed of anti-Bank sentiment. In fact, the years immediately following the War of 1812 were a period of heady economic prosperity for the state—prosperity that owed a large part of its existence to a rapid expansion of banking. Ohio was caught up in an economic boom experienced to some degree by most of the country after the war's conclusion in 1815. A continuing agricultural surplus that fed a high European demand, as well as the proliferation of salable land and easy credit, however, made Ohio a singular example of economic growth. Financing this boom was a rapidly expanding armada of state-chartered banks. Before the War of 1812, there were four of these state-sanctioned banks operating in Ohio, with a total capitalization of just under $900,000. At war's end, their numbers had increased to twelve, capitalized at almost a $1.5 million. Testifying to the strength and momentum of this growth, the ensuing year saw the number of state-chartered banks increase to twenty-one and their capitalization to more than $2 million. Additionally, numerous "banks" were operating in Ohio during this period without the state's permission, functioning essentially as paper money mills and cash dispensaries. Ohio's banks, legal and otherwise, played an important role in the economic growth of a region short on specie, as they provided the two items most in demand dur-

2. On political economy in the early republic, see Drew McCoy, *The Elusive Republic: Political Economy in Jeffersonian America* (Chapel Hill: Univ. of North Carolina Press, 1980), and Joyce O. Appleby, *Capitalism and a New Social Order: The Republican Vision of the 1790s* (New York: New York Univ. Press, 1984). For states' rights thought and its relation to the idea of Union, see Kenneth Stampp, "The Concept of a Perpetual Union," *Journal of American History* 65 (June 1979): 5–33. Examining the idea of Union as only the means to an end is Paul C. Nagle, *One Nation Indivisible: The Union in American Thought, 1776–1861* (New York: Oxford Univ. Press, 1964), 13–31. For the persistence of localism and the difficulties in the creation of an overarching nationalism (and, by extension, national authority), see John Murrin, "A Roof without Walls: The Dilemma of American National Identity," in Richard Beeman et al., eds., *Beyond Confederation: Origins of the Constitution and American National Identity* (Chapel Hill: Univ. of North Carolina Press, 1987), 333–48.

ing the postwar boom: currency and credit. Because the banks were able (and certainly willing) to supply these commodities, the exponential growth in agricultural production and land sales that lay at the root of Ohio's prosperity—and the immigration that growth attracted—was possible.[3]

This high degree of economic expansion and seemingly boundless prosperity meant that Ohio—despite its predominantly Jeffersonian political culture—possessed a climate quite congenial to banks during this period. The enthusiasm for ready cash and a functioning medium of exchange allowed earlier suspicions of banks to be significantly curtailed. This relaxed attitude extended to the newly created Second Bank of the United States as well. Chartered in 1816 after the financial debacles of the War of 1812, and supported by most of the hegemonic National Republican party, the Bank of the United States helped to meet the demand for currency in states, like Ohio, that needed it to facilitate expansion through liberal credit policies. Under its first president, William Jones, the Bank contributed to the rapid expansion of credit in Ohio, and indeed the entire West, while providing little in the way of active direction for the national economy. Such was the enthusiasm for Bank-fueled prosperity that, by 1817, Ohioans had mounted a serious effort to persuade the Bank of the United States to open a branch office within the state.[4]

The location of a branch office, known formally as an Office of Discount and Deposit, was a matter of great interest for Ohio's economic elite. With the postwar boom in Ohio came a new class of leaders, a set of regional elites that dominated both the politics and economy of their particular area; in fact, one of the great ironies of this period of apparent prosperity was that inequalities in wealth among Ohioans actually increased to a significant degree. The reasons these cadres of wealthy regional leaders supported the extension of the national Bank's business into Ohio were twofold. First, it made good business sense. The rapid expansion of unchartered ("wildcat") banks and the shaky currency they produced threatened the stability of the state-chartered banks, which were the preserve of Ohio's economic elites. Bringing an Office of Discount and Deposit to the state, they hoped, would help to regulate the economy, prevent "the promiscuous circulation of unauthorized bank paper," and lend "a more stable and solid appearance" to Ohio's "money system." But there were more fundamental reasons for the economic leadership of Ohio to

3. Andrew R. L. Cayton, The *Frontier Republic: Ideology and Politics in the Ohio Country, 1780–1825* (Kent, Ohio: Kent State Univ. Press, 1986), 110–18; C. C. Huntington, "A History of Banking and Currency in Ohio before the Civil War," *Ohio Archaeological and Historical Society Publications* 24 (1915): 285–87; John D. Aiello, "Ohio's War upon the Bank of the United States: 1817–1824" (Ph.D. diss., Ohio State University, 1972), 1–2; Ernest L. Bogart, "Taxation of the Second Bank of the United States by Ohio," *American Historical Review* 17 (June 1912): 312–13.

4. Huntington, "Banking and Currency in Ohio," 282–84; Cayton, *Frontier Republic*, 115–16; Ralph C. H. Catterall, *The Second Bank of the United States* (Chicago: Univ. of Chicago Press, 1903), 27–35. For earlier Republican accommodation with commercialism and banking, see Cathy Matson, "Capitalizing Hope: Economic Thought and the Early National Economy," *Journal of the Early Republic* 16 (Summer 1996): 273–91, esp. 283–85. On these issues after the War of 1812, see Richard E. Ellis, "The Market Revolution and the Transformation of American Politics, 1801–1837," in Melvyn Stokes and Stephen Conway, eds., *The Market Revolution in America: Social, Political, and Religious Expressions, 1800–1880* (Charlottesville: Univ. of Virginia Press, 1996), 150–56; and Lance Banning, *The Jeffersonian Persuasion: Evolution of a Party Ideology* (Ithaca, N.Y.: Cornell Univ. Press, 1978), 298–302.

petition the Bank for a branch office. Not only did the spread of wildcat banking portend economic instability, but the social transformation these banks represented posed a serious threat as well. The state-chartered banks were controlled by Ohio's de facto gentry; the wildcat banks were not. In order to maintain what they saw as their proper position of economic and political leadership, the state's elites desired an end to the proliferation of unchartered banks and the economic leveling those institutions promised.[5]

The proposed branch office of the national Bank became an object of a heated rivalry between the gentries of Chillicothe, the state's original capital, and Ohio's preeminent commercial city, Cincinnati. Lobbying for an Office of Discount and Deposit in Cincinnati were such figures as prominent lawyer and future president William Henry Harrison; Chillicothe's boosters included Governor Thomas Worthington and Duncan McArthur, the Speaker of Ohio's House of Representatives. The competition became so intense that Worthington's efforts to personally lobby William Jones for a branch office at Chillicothe brought a deluge of criticism from Cincinnati's advocates, who accused Worthington of abusing his office. The *Cincinnati Western Spy* asserted that Worthington had "descended to the grade of a mere pettifogging intriguer for the pecuniary or commercial interests of his own particular section of the state." Rather than fulfilling his obligations as governor, the *Western Spy* declared, Worthington had become "an avowed agent of sectional interests." Despite Worthington's initial efforts, the Bank decided to award an Office of Discount and Deposit to Cincinnati, scheduled to open in January 1817. But Worthington persisted, pulling all available strings in the national financial establishment, and his second effort was rewarded by the opening of a branch office in Chillicothe the following October.[6]

Ohio thus occupied a unique position among the states by the end of 1817, with two Offices of Discount and Deposit within its borders. The hopes of Ohio's economic leadership for stability would remain unrealized, however. Under William Jones, the Bank of the United States pursued a policy similar to that of Ohio's state banks, chartered or not—one that emphasized a liberal extension of credit and a casual approach to administration and oversight. In effect, the branch offices of the Bank remained virtually autonomous, and they took full advantage, becoming major contributors to the heavy flow of currency and credit in the state's postwar fiscal euphoria. Given that the national pattern for the exchange of bank notes generally flowed from the South and West to the North and East, what this meant was that notes rarely—if at all—circulated back West. Thus, the western branch offices could essentially issue paper currency without restriction. In Ohio this is precisely what occurred, and the Bank's branch offices made the state's supply of paper

5. Cayton, *Frontier Republic,* 118–20; Ellis, "Market Revolution and the Transformation of American Politics," 162–63; "The United States Bank," in *The Muskingum Messenger,* May 30, 1816, quoted in Cayton, *Frontier Republic,* 119.

6. Aiello, "Ohio's War upon the BUS," 7; Cayton, *Frontier Republic,* 120–24; *Western Spy* (Cincinnati), Nov. 15, 1816, quoted in Alfred B. Sears, *Thomas Worthington: Father of Ohio Statehood* (Columbus: Ohio State Univ. Press, 1958), 201; William T. Utter, *The Frontier State: 1803–1825,* vol. 2, *A History of the State of Ohio,* ed. Carl Wittke (Columbus: Ohio State Univ. Press, 1942), 276–78.

money all the more abundant; it was not uncommon to see more than thirty different varieties of bank paper trade hands in Ohio's major towns. Coupled with similar practices on the part of the state banks, Ohio's Offices of Discount and Deposit (with tacit consent from the Bank's administration) fueled an immense surge of speculation, credit extension, and inflation with their inexhaustible note issues throughout 1817 and 1818. While times were prosperous, few noticed the essentially shaky foundation of Ohio's economic expansion. Yet, the overextension of credit, rampant speculation, and glut of paper money placed Ohio and its banks (state and national) in a precarious position and made them extremely vulnerable to collapse.[7]

In the late summer of 1818, the collapse came. The United States' first serious economic depression hit first and hardest in Ohio and the other western areas that had enjoyed the highest degree of expansion and prosperity the previous three years. General causes for what became known as the Panic of 1819 included a decrease in the European demand for American agricultural products and the British decision to purchase cotton from its Indian colonies rather than the American South. Most significant for the U.S. banking system, though, was the decision on the part of most European nations to return to the gold standard, which precipitated a major specie drain in the United States as the chain of debts from state banks to the national Bank to European creditors came due. It quickly became evident that much of the prosperity of the postwar boom was illusory, built on a paper foundation of credit and bank notes that quickly lost value with the onset of hard times, the contraction of credit, and the demand for specie payments. Ohio's experience was no different, and the state's economic growth came to a grinding halt. Ohio entered the Panic of 1819 earlier than much of the country—by the summer of 1818, actually—and the resulting depression would not only leave the state with deep economic scars but profound cultural and ideological effects as well.[8]

Ohio's anti-Bank animus was born in the shocks of the Panic of 1819. The crisis that began for Ohioans in the summer of 1818 would resurrect latent concerns and fears about the powers—and the potential for their abuse—of national institutions, especially the Bank

7. Catterall, *Second BUS*, 27–39; Matson, "Capitalizing Hope," 285; Bray Hammond, *Banks and Politics in America from the Revolution to the Civil War* (Princeton: Princeton Univ. Press, 1957) 251–62; Huntington, "Banking and Currency in Ohio," 283–88.

8. Cayton, *Frontier Republic*, 126–28; Ellis, "The Market Revolution and the Transformation of American Politics," 163–64; Huntington, "Banking and Currency in Ohio," 285–88. The only book-length treatment of the Panic of 1819 is Murray Rothbard, *The Panic of 1819: Reactions and Policies* (New York: Columbia Univ. Press, 1962). See also Samuel Reznek, "The Depression of 1819–1822: A Social History," in Murray Rothbard, *Business Depressions and Financial Panics: Essays in American Business and Economic History* (Westport, Conn.: Greenwood Press, 1968), 51–72; Andrew R. L. Cayton, "The Fragmentation of a 'Great Family': The Panic of 1819 and the Rise of the Middling Interest in Boston, 1818–1822," *Journal of the Early Republic* 2 (Summer 1982): 143–67; Sarah Kidd, "'To be harassed by my Creditors is worse than Death': Cultural Implications of the Panic of 1819," *Maryland Historical Magazine* 95 (Summer 2000): 161–89. For the political transformations emerging out of the depression in Ohio, see Emil Pocock, "Popular Roots of Jacksonian Democracy: The Case of Dayton, Ohio, 1815–1830," *Journal of the Early Republic* 9 (Winter 1989): 489–515; Robert M. Blackson, "Pennsylvania Banks and the Panic of 1819: A Reinterpretation," *Journal of the Early Republic* 9 (Fall 1989): 335–58; Charles Sellers, *The Market Revolution: Jacksonian America, 1815–1846* (New York: Oxford Univ. Press, 1991), 103–71.

of the United States. As the perilous state of affairs became obvious to William Jones and the Bank's directors in early 1818, they decided to pursue a policy of rapid retrenchment and contraction to replenish the Bank's dangerously low supply of specie. For Ohio, this policy was both drastic and unexpected. After all, the Bank had been an active participant in issuing currency and extending the credit that fueled the speculation occurring to such an extent across the state. In the process, much of the debt held by Ohio citizens, corporations, and even municipalities had been transferred to the Bank of the United States. The consequences of this fact would become evident in July 1818. On the twentieth, the Bank ordered its Cincinnati branch to pursue a stringent policy of debt collection by collecting outstanding balances at the staggering rate of 20 percent a month. This sudden reversal of Bank policy—from easy credit to draconian retrenchment—stunned the financial leadership of Cincinnati. In a letter to Jones, the presidents of several prominent Cincinnati banks protested the terms of the Bank's recollection policy and expressed doubts that any institution in the area could meet them. Jones, however, refused to reconsider, and a brusque reply to the remonstrance of the Cincinnati bankers left no doubt of his unwillingness to recant the order of the twentieth. An earlier letter to Secretary of the Treasury William Crawford explains the attitude behind Jones's dismissal of the claims of Cincinnati's banking community. "He must be a sturdy debtor, indeed," Jones scoffed, "who boldly withholds both principle and interest, and defends it as a matter of right." In a second order to the Cincinnati office, Jones ordered the cashier not to accept any bank notes from the Cincinnati banks as payment on their outstanding debts.[9]

Jones's commitment to a policy of contraction was a desperate move to bring the Bank back from the edge of disaster. In Cincinnati, however, disaster was unavoidable. Faced with impossible demands from the Office of Discount and Deposit, the leading banks of Cincinnati suspended specie payment on November 5. After this surrender, the state banking system of Ohio underwent a spectacular collapse. By January 1819, only two or three banks in the whole state had not suspended specie payments. In addition, the Bank's policy of contraction meant that specie left Ohio at an unprecedented rate, leaving in its wake assorted worthless bank paper and rapidly falling prices. In this predominantly agricultural state, low prices meant a severe financial crisis for a large portion of the population. By 1820, farm prices barely covered transportation expenses, while real estate became unsalable. The only real estate transactions that occurred with any regularity were foreclosures by the Cincinnati Office of Discount and Deposit. Such was the degree of previous credit-financed land speculation that the Bank of the United States, through these foreclosures for debt, owned a significant portion of Cincinnati by 1821. By the end of 1818, Ohio had entered the worst economic crisis of its short history—a crisis produced in the long term by an increasing involvement and interdependence in a wider market economy over which individual Ohioans had little control. But the immediate cause of the panic in

9. Huntington, "Banking and Currency in Ohio," 291–92; Utter, *Frontier State,* 278–85; Jones to Crawford, June 23, 1818, *American State Papers, Finance,* vol. 4; Bogart, "Taxation of the Second BUS," 316–19.

Ohio was not nearly so subtle, and there was little doubt among the citizens of Ohio about who was to blame for it. Describing the suspension of specie payments by Cincinnati banks, the *Liberty Hall and Cincinnati Gazette* declared that "this policy was forced upon them by the hostile attitude assumed by the bank of the United States." Heedless of the consequences for Ohio, the Bank's directors thought only of their institution's safety and their own financial gain. "It seems the directors of the town banks had a lesson of humility to learn before they approached the august presence of their High Mightinesses [the national Bank's directors], and because they did not uncover their heads and humbly pray for relief, the whole country is to be visited with a signal vengeance," the paper seethed. "This is the most pitiful pretext for distressing a whole community that was ever invented by an arbitrary power," was the flat declaration of *Liberty Hall*'s editor.[10]

Liberty Hall's denunciation of the national Bank was no isolated tantrum. Jones's policy of contraction, and its continuation by his successor as president of the national Bank, Langdon Cheves, became the focus of Ohioans' wrath. An interpretation of the panic as the Bank's doing rapidly evolved, beginning in Cincinnati and quickly spreading throughout the state. Many Ohioans would have agreed with the latter-day observation of William Gouge, the trenchant critic of the national Bank, that during the early months of the panic, "the Bank was saved, and the people were ruined." Others in Ohio put it more bluntly. The Bank of the United States was "a monster of iniquity," according to the *Cleaveland Register*, "brought into existence under the administration of a short sighted chief magistrate, by a corrupt congress, who trampled on the constitution they had sworn to support in order to gratify their ambition for wealth." This hostile rhetoric, however, was more than idle ranting; it was evidence of a deeper ideological reality in Ohio that would have serious consequences for the national Bank. The onset of the panic and the Bank's seeming culpability loosed a wider antiaristocratic impulse that placed the Bank at the center of a malevolent conspiracy aimed squarely at the republican liberties of the nation. With its roots in both Ohio's Jeffersonian political culture and the current context of economic distress, this impulse quickly made itself a prominent feature in Ohio's political discourse during the panic.[11]

The idea of a conspiracy fomented by a small, aristocratic element of society and aimed overtly at the liberties of the people was a recurring theme in the political culture of the early American republic. Based largely on the Enlightenment ideal of rational self-determination,

10. *Liberty Hall and Cincinnati Gazette*, Nov. 11, 1818; *Niles' Weekly Register*, Jan. 9, 1819 (Hezekiah Niles was a strenuous critic of banks, especially the Bank of the United States, and devoted large amounts of column space to assertions that the Bank precipitated the panic.); Huntington, "Banking and Currency in Ohio," 297–300; Utter, *Frontier State*, 290–94; Cayton, *Frontier Republic*, 126–28; Aiello, "Ohio's War upon the BUS," 20–21; *Liberty Hall and Cincinnati Gazette*, Nov. 10, 1818, quoted in Utter, *Frontier State*, 288.

11. William Gouge, *A Short History of Paper Money and Banking in the United States* (Philadelphia: T. W. Ustick, 1833), 110; *Cleaveland Register*, Dec. 29, 1818, quoted in Cayton, *Frontier Republic*, 130. Edwin Perkins argues that Jones had actually gotten the situation under relative control, that it was Langdon Cheves's "inappropriate" policies for the current economic climate and his fixation on accumulating large reserves of specie that exacerbated the panic's effects and prolonged its course by creating a significant, but artificial, contraction ("Langdon Cheves and the Panic of 1819: A Reassessment," *Journal of Economic History* 44 [June 1984]: 455–61 [quoted at 456–57].)

this understanding of politics assumed that consciously made decisions were the explanation for political actions. Human agency and its intentions were the primary focus of political understanding; that is, political events had very human, and thus eminently traceable, causes. For the context of Ohio, then, the Bank's actions may have been ostensibly geared toward fiscal goals, but the larger reality pointed to something far more sinister. Why else would the Bank's policies change so suddenly? Why did the western states suffer under the contraction and not the North or East? Why did the Bank's directors so sharply dismiss the concerns of the local banks? These questions tangled with other pertinent issues for Ohioans, most notably the regional elites' domination of the state's political and economic affairs. The end of the postwar boom brought a critical reassessment of the role played by the Ohio "gentry" and its institutions—especially the United States Bank. There was an intimate connection between these elites and the Bank's branch offices; the list of each office's directors overlapped with the leadership of the state government to a significant degree. For example, Governor Worthington was also on the board of directors for the Chillicothe Office of Discount and Deposit, a distinction he shared with House Speaker Duncan McArthur, while Congressman William Henry Harrison was one of the directors of the Cincinnati branch. The detrimental effects of the Bank's policies on the state's financial institutions, coupled with its role in the onset of the depression, only served to heighten suspicion toward the national Bank and its Ohio proponents. Given the circumstances in which they found themselves as the depression worsened, Ohioans increasingly saw the Bank of the United States as the primary vehicle by which a small class of aristocratic, corrupt men sought to undermine the very basis of liberty in the state.[12]

There had first been stirrings of this sentiment almost immediately after the branch offices had opened in Cincinnati and Chillicothe. In December 1817, concerns that the Offices of Discount and Deposit, controlled by a distant national authority, would curtail the business of the more familiar state banks, and thus assume financial hegemony over Ohio's farmers and merchants, prompted legislative action. On the thirteenth, Ohio's General Assembly created a joint committee to investigate the possibility of taxing the Bank's branches and thus ensuring a modicum of accountability. There was ample precedent for taxing financial institutions in Ohio. State banks had been taxed to raise the necessary revenue to pay off Ohio's debt from the War of 1812. In addition, the legislature had passed laws against the activities of both wildcat and out-of-state banks, whose notes had flooded the state and threatened to drive the notes of Ohio's chartered banks out of circulation.

12. See Ellis, "The Market Revolution and the Transformation of American Politics," 163–65. The classic study of the idea of conspiracy in American political culture is Richards Hofstadter, "The Paranoid Style in American Politics," in *The Paranoid Style of American Politics and Other Essays* (New York: Knopf, 1965). On the ideas of rational and individual motivations in politics, see Gordon Wood, "Rhetoric and Reality in the American Revolution," *William and Mary Quarterly*, 3d series, 23 (Jan. 1966): 3–32. Wood takes his analysis further in "Conspiracy and the Paranoid Style: Causality and Deceit in the Eighteenth Century," *William and Mary Quarterly*, 3d series, 39 (July 1982): 401–44, which argues convincingly that the idea of "malevolent conspiracy" was one of the most common frameworks in which Americans of this period interpreted political events.

In its 1815–16 session, the General Assembly passed an act that imposed a $1,000 fine on agents of banks not chartered by the state and denied those institutions access to the state's courts and other legal machinery.[13] Thus, Ohio's government had shown a willingness to both regulate and levy taxes on financial institutions for either revenue or the protection of the state-chartered banks.

Despite this tradition, however, the joint committee reported that taxation of the branches of the United States Bank—though legal—would be ill-advised, as "it would still be impolitic in the legislature of this state being one of the youngest and most highly favored in the Union to be among the first to contravene the acts of the general government." This air of caution expressed by the committee did not reflect the feelings of the entire legislature, though, and the report was promptly reversed by a thirty-seven to twenty-two vote in the House of Representatives—a more accurate reflection of popular sentiment in Ohio. On January 19, 1818, the House adopted a substitute report, drawn up by prominent Cincinnati lawyer and editor Charles Hammond, which declared both that the state had a right to tax branches of the national Bank, and that it was "expedient" to do so at that time. The branch offices were "unquestionably a proper subject of taxation," the Assembly declared. The state banks paid taxes, and the charter of the Offices of Discount and Deposit did not specifically exempt them from coming under the same provisions. Most significantly, however, the report argued that "these branches must very seriously affect the operations of the state banks" as well as the state's economic well-being. "The capital introduced into the country through these branches, is directly calculated to wither our agriculture and cramp our manufacturers."[14]

By its allusion to the "direct calculations" of the branch offices' transactions, the seeds of a conspiratorial interpretation of the Bank's operations were evident in this substitute document. But even more remarkable was the fundamental logic that underlay the report, as it made sweeping declarations on the nature of federal-state sovereignty. The report left no doubt where Ohio would stand on this issue: "The states that compose the American Union are independent sovereign states," the legislature asserted. Though conceding both the constitutional limitations upon a state's right of taxation and the power of Congress to charter a bank, the report refused to let the two mingle. "The law establishing this bank, attempts not to confer upon the stock of the company any exemption from taxation, either by the state or by the United States" was the committee's unqualified declaration. The report heaped scorn on the argument that the Bank was immune from taxation by virtue of its federal charter. If that was true, the legislature argued, "congress may extend

---

13. Bogart, "Taxation of the Second BUS," 313–15; Ohio, General Assembly, *Acts of a General Nature* (Columbus, 1820), 18: 218–23. The office at Chillicothe was not scheduled to open until January 1818, but the national Bank had already approved the branch's location, and the board of directors was in place—thus, any legislative action, it was assumed, would apply to the Chillicothe office as well as that of Cincinnati.

14. Ohio, General Assembly, House of Representatives, *Journal of the House of Representatives, 1817–1818* (Columbus, 1818), 144, 307–15; Huntington, "Banking and Currency in Ohio," 314–15; Aiello, "Ohio's War upon the BUS," 36–37; Bogart, "Taxation of the Second BUS," 315.

this prohibition at pleasure. They have only to incorporate a company to merchandise and manufacture and become a partner in the trade, and the funds and the business are at once privileged from the profane touch of state legislation." This would lead toward the consolidation of political and economic power at the federal level at the expense of the state's sovereignty, the report warned. According to the legislature, the Bank—if unchecked—would control public finance, monopolize commerce, and ruin the operations of the state's institutions, both financial and political.[15]

Given the prevalence of these sentiments, the provision asserting the constitutional right of taxation passed overwhelmingly, by a vote of forty-eight to twelve, while the "expediency" provision was also approved by a large margin. On the heels of the report's approval, a bill was introduced to levy a tax on the capital of the Bank of the United States' operations in Ohio. All the momentum seemed to be on the side of those who advocated taxing the national Bank, but extensive lobbying efforts by the directors of both the Cincinnati and Chillicothe branches—including Speaker of the House Duncan McArthur—prevented the final passage of the bill. This lobbying, combined with a significant number of legislators still hesitant at taking such a serious step as challenging the sovereignty of the federal government, was enough to postpone consideration until the next meeting of the legislature, scheduled for December 1818.[16]

When the legislature reconvened at the end of the year, however, this tentative climate had undergone a complete transformation. The national Bank's contraction policy implemented in July and the resulting financial collapse made the Bank and its relationship to Ohio central issues in the fall elections of 1818. The events of the summer focused opposition to the Bank of the United States so dramatically that the state government was essentially remade over the issue. Worthington was ousted as governor, McArthur lost his bid for reelection to the House of Representatives, and virtually every candidate identified with the Bank of the United States was defeated. Prominent critics of the Bank, such as Charles Hammond, were easily elected. The new governor was Ethan Allen Brown, who was a vocal leader of the state's anti-Bank politicians.[17]

The legislative session that began in December was marked from the outset by a new breed of overt hostility to the Bank of the United States. On December 15, the House voted to form a committee charged with investigating the Bank of the United States and strategies for taxing its branches and regulating its activities in Ohio. The committee was stacked with anti-Bank men, including its chair, Charles Hammond. Governor Brown implicitly encouraged these activities in his first address to the General Assembly on the

---

15. Ohio, *House Journal (1817–1818)*, 307; Huntington, "Banking and Currency in Ohio," 315–16.

16. Ohio, *House Journal (1817–1818)*, 360; Bogart, "Taxation of the Second BUS," 314–15; Aiello, "Ohio's War upon the BUS," 35–40.

17. Aiello, "Ohio's War upon the BUS," 43–45; Utter, *Frontier State*, 299–301. It is ironic that, given his vehement opposition to the national Bank, Brown as a young man had embarked upon his career by becoming a student, and then a paid assistant, in the New York City law office of Alexander Hamilton (John S. Still, "The Life of Ethan Allen Brown: Governor of Ohio" [Ph.D. diss., Ohio State University, 1951], 6–7).

sixteenth. Addressing the question of the Bank's taxation, Brown declared that since "the state banks are subjected to the imposition of taxes, or their equivalent, there appears no evident reason why these branches [the Offices of Discount and Deposit] should be exempt." This would, according to Brown, "be a partiality, unjust to the local banks" as well as an infringement on Ohio's sovereign power of taxation within its own borders. Already fortified by Brown's support, the committee's intentions were further bolstered by the taxation of the Bank by other states in 1818 and early 1819. The legislatures of Maryland, Tennessee, Georgia, North Carolina, and Kentucky had all levied taxes—ranging from $5,000 to $60,000 per branch—on the offices of the Bank within their states. In addition, the new western states of Illinois and Indiana enacted constitutional provisions forbidding the existence of banks chartered outside their borders.[18]

The legislature perhaps hoped that merely establishing this investigative committee would be enough of a threat to drive the Bank of the United States out of Ohio, but there was little opposition to actually levying a tax should this more subtle threat prove insufficient. The committee made its report to the General Assembly on January 19, 1819, and placed the blame for the economic crisis that beset Ohio squarely at the feet of the national Bank. According to the committee, its investigation of all banking operations in the state led "inevitably to the conclusion, that the establishment and management of the branches of the United States bank within this state, have very largely conduced to the present embarrassment of the circulating medium, and have had a direct effect in producing the recent suspension of specie payments by the State banks." The committee concluded that the only recourse left for Ohio to protect itself was to drive the Bank out of the state. To this end, the report recommended a tax of $50,000 on any unauthorized (non–state chartered) financial institution in Ohio if they persisted in their operations past a certain date and reported a bill—drafted by Hammond—into the legislature to accomplish this objective.[19]

"An Act to levy and collect a tax from all banks and individuals, and companies, and associations of individuals, that may transact banking business in this state, without being authorized to do so by the laws thereof" became law in Ohio on February 8, 1819. The act stipulated that a tax would be collected from any unauthorized financial institution

18. Brown's address is reprinted in Ohio, *House Journal (1818–1819)*, 90–103 (quoted at 92); Aiello, "Ohio's War upon the BUS," 44–51; Utter, *Frontier State*, 300–301; Hammond, *Banks and Politics in the United States*, 263–64; Catterall, *Second BUS*, 83–89; Huntington, "Banking and Currency in Ohio," 313–14. Kentucky's taxation of the BUS and the ensuing political imbroglio within the state are detailed in Sandra F. VanBurkleo, "'The Paws of Banks': The Origins and Significance of Kentucky's Decision to Tax Federal Bankers," *Journal of the Early Republic* 9 (Winter 1989): 457–87. The State of Pennsylvania also petitioned Congress to restrict the operations of the Bank of the United States to Washington, D.C., asserting that the institution threatened the sovereignty of the states. See Herman V. Ames, *State Documents on Federal Relations: The States and the United States* (Philadelphia: Univ. of Pennsylvania Press, 1900), 89–90.

19. Ohio, General Assembly, *Report of the Committee on the Subject of Levying a Tax on the Capital of the United States Bank, Employed in Ohio* (Columbus, 1818); Aiello, "Ohio's War upon the BUS," 45–51; Huntington, "Banking and Currency in Ohio," 300–301.

transacting business in the state as of September 1, 1819. The law's preamble made it very clear precisely what "unauthorized institutions" the legislature had in mind: "Whereas the president and directors of the Bank of the United States, have established two offices of discount and deposit, in this state, at which they transact banking business by loaning money, and issuing bills in violation of the laws of this state," those offices "should be subject to the payment of a tax for the support of government." This tax, to be collected every September 15 from banks falling under the provisions of the act, was $50,000 per office. The Auditor of Ohio was authorized to commission "any person whom he may appoint" to collect the tax from "the Bank of the United States, or individual, company or association, from whom the same may be due." Should the Bank refuse payment, the Auditor's agent was directed to collect the required amount from its "goods, chattels, rights and credits." Anticipating stiff resistance from the officers of the Bank's branches, the law enjoined the agent to exert every effort to collect the tax. To this end, the act declared "that the person entering such banks, after demand and refusal of the payment of the tax . . . if he cannot find in the banking room any money, bank notes, goods, chattels or other property . . . it shall and may be lawful, and it is hereby made the duty of such person, to go into each and any other room or vault of the banking house, and every closet, chest, box or drawer in such banking house to open and search; and any money, bank notes, or other goods and chattels" were to be collected as the required tax. Should any further resistance be encountered, the offending parties were subject to legal penalties. The Auditor was to deposit the funds in the state treasury, save a 2 percent commission for the collecting agent. The law was remarkable not only for the extraordinarily high tax but for its overtly aggressive provisions regarding the tax's collection. The prohibitively high tax made it obvious that Ohio's political leadership was determined to employ one of the most significant of the state's sovereign powers to completely rid the state of the Bank, despite the fact that it was a federally chartered institution. The battle lines had been drawn, as Ohio had vigorously asserted its sovereignty in the face of what many the state's citizens saw as a corrupt agency that represented a conscious design against their liberties and well-being.[20]

What was already a high-stakes conflict became more so in March 1819 with the delivery of the United States Supreme Court's opinion in the case of *McCulloch v. Maryland*. The case revolved around the same sort of taxation policy, as the state of Maryland had levied a tax on the Baltimore branch of the Bank of the United States. Maryland's intentions were similar to those of Ohio, in that the primary aim of its tax was to drive the Bank out of the state. It quickly became clear, though, that the sovereignty issues involved would give the case much larger ramifications than those merely affecting banking matters. Thus, the case attracted not only a great deal of attention but formidable legal talent as well. Appearing for the Bank were Daniel Webster, one of the preeminent political figures of antebellum America, and Attorney General William Wirt and renowned lawyer William Pinkney. Joseph Hopkinson, Walter Jones, and the distinguished Luther Martin

20. Ohio, *Acts of a General Nature*, 18:179–87.

argued the case for Maryland. In their attempt to deny the Bank's right of exemption from taxes, the lawyers for Maryland claimed that the Bank was essentially a private corporation (only 20 percent of its directors were appointed by the government; the rest were privately elected) and thus was not entitled to infringe upon the sovereignty of a particular state. This sovereignty was defined, Hopkinson argued, by the power of taxation. Since the Constitution did not totally prohibit the states from levying taxes, they enjoyed "concurrent sovereignty" with the federal government in these matters and thus had the right to tax a private institution—such as the Bank—operating within their borders. Webster answered this argument for the Bank by arguing that the "unlimited power to tax" was "a power to destroy." There was no disputing that Congress had the power to charter a national bank, Webster argued. The states, therefore, had no power to tax such an institution, as such an action would "destroy" an instrument of federal sovereignty. This, Webster concluded, would fly in the face of the Constitution, as it was "the supreme law of the land and controls all state legislation and their constitutions." Should the states be allowed to tax the Bank—the creation of federal sovereignty—"the bank . . . must depend on the discretion of the State governments for its existence." In Webster's view, the consequences would be "inevitable": the disintegration of the federal government into a quibbling mass of "sovereign" states. The justices agreed. On March 7, 1819, Chief Justice John Marshall ruled for the Court in favor of the national Bank. Not only did the opinion declare Maryland's taxation of the Bank of the United States unconstitutional, it was also a sweeping assertion of federal sovereignty. In finding for the Bank, Marshall argued that the federal government possessed a wide latitude of implied powers, including the power to charter a bank. The sovereignty of a state, he continued, could not interfere in any way with the federal government's exercise of those powers without subverting the entire basis of the constitutional framework. Thus, the *McCulloch* decision struck deeply against the ideas of states' rights while vigorously asserting a doctrine of federal sovereignty and supremacy. It was the Court's judgment "that the states have no power, by taxation or otherwise, to retard, impede, burden, or in any manner control, the operations of the constitutional laws enacted by congress to carry into execution the powers vested in the general government."[21]

The reaction to the *McCulloch* decision from state-sovereignty advocates was one of furious denunciation. The *Niles' Weekly Register* proclaimed that the Court had decreed "a total prostration of the state rights" and "that we may as well inter, at once, the form of a constitution of which the spirit has been murdered." Judge Spencer Roane of Virginia, writing as "Hampden" in the *Richmond Enquirer,* published a series of essays attacking Marshall's opinion as an unconstitutional usurpation of power. The *McCulloch* decision

---

21. *United States Reports* 4 Wheaton (1819), quoted at 316, 327, 436; G. Edward White, *The Marshall Court and Cultural Change, 1815–1835,* abr. ed. (New York: Oxford Univ. Press, 1991), 542–44; Herbert A. Johnson, *The Chief Justiceship of John Marshall, 1801–1835* (Columbia: Univ. of South Carolina Press, 1997), 73–74, 140–44; For a vivid description of the both sides' arguments, see Robert Remini, *Daniel Webster: The Man and His Time* (New York: Norton, 1997), 164–67. For a thorough analysis of the Court's opinion, see White, *The Marshall Court,* 543–52; Johnson, *John Marshall,* 144–47.

was fundamentally flawed, according to Roane, because "the court had no power to adjudicate away the reserved rights of a sovereign member of the confederacy, and vest them in the general government."[22]

The reaction in Ohio was even more vehement. James Wilson (grandfather of future president Woodrow Wilson), the fiery editor of the *Western Herald and Steubenville Gazette,* summed up the Court's decision as "The United States Bank, EVERY THING!! The Sovereignty of the States, NOTHING!!" The *McCulloch* decision, according to Wilson, posed a serious threat to Ohio's sovereignty. "If the U.S. Bank is permitted to tax us without our consent," he argued, "to locate branches among us without our consent—and said branches to be free from taxation for state purposes—we had better, instead of calling a convention to amend our constitution, call a convention to offer it up, unconditionally, to the general government, and return to the territorial days." More understated, but just as firm in its opposition, was the *Liberty Hall and Cincinnati Gazette*'s observation that "it is apparent that great dissatisfaction prevails respecting this decision." Hinting at Ohio's determination in its battle against the Bank, the editor declared, "we should not be surprised if the court should be called upon to revise it by the perseverance of some of the states in asserting their claim to the right of taxation." Charles Hammond expressed a prevalent view among Ohioans, arguing that the *McCulloch* case smacked of collusion between the Bank and the higher levels of the federal government. Hammond denied the decision's applicability to Ohio and its decision to tax the branch offices in Chillicothe and Cincinnati. "If . . . the country must be prostrated at the feet of an overbearing stock-jobbing aristocracy, I most earnestly wish that all may be satisfied that the outrage is warranted by the Constitution," a proposition that he seriously doubted. "Should the reasoning of the Court fail in giving this general satisfaction, I hope the freemen of Ohio feel enough of the spirit of independence to afford the Judges an opportunity of reviewing their opinion," Hammond urged. "It is time enough to succumb," he concluded, "when the Western states have been heard, and when their rights have been decided upon in a case where they are themselves parties." Most of Ohio's anti-Bank forces refused to consider the *McCulloch* decision as having any bearing on the tax law scheduled to go into effect in September. Some of them, however, foresaw more serious consequences stemming from the Court's doctrines. An anonymous correspondent to Wilson's *Western Herald* wrote that "as soon as the decision of the supreme court appeared, I thought I could discern in it, a disposition to prostrate the state sovereignties—I have now no doubt on the subject." Wilson editorialized that the time was right to hearken back to "the intrepid and pure old democratic party of 1798 and 1800." By invoking the states' rights "principles of '98," Wilson testified to the continuing strength of these ideals in Ohio's political culture. An anonymous author, writing as "Dion," revealed an even more potent strain of resistance in Ohio by predicting disunion should the consolidating measures of the federal government continue at the

22. *Niles' Weekly Register,* Mar. 13, May 22, 1819; Roane quoted in Gerald Gunther, ed., *John Marshall's Defense of* McCulloch v. Maryland (Palo Alto, Calif.: Stanford Univ. Press, 1969), 111.

expense of the western states. The idea, "however delicate to handle, must sometimes be publicly discussed," he declared.[23]

Behind the scenes, however, there was some question among the leaders of the struggle against the Bank on how best to proceed. Writing to Hammond, Governor Brown argued that too many states were opposed to the *McCulloch* decision for Congress not to act, and if Ohio persevered in its efforts to tax the Bank, it might have the day in court that Hammond and others demanded. For his part, Brown declared, he was still committed to the taxation policy. Furthermore, the political and economic climate of Ohio in early 1819 virtually guaranteed that the Court's dictum would not sway many of the anti-Bank politicians from their course. The economic crisis was rapidly intensifying as foreclosures were increasing exponentially, prices approached their nadir, and specie flew out of the state with increasing speed. The Bank of the United States became even less worthy of respect in the eyes of Ohioans when James McCulloch, the cashier of the Bank's Baltimore branch and central figure in the Bank's defense of its operations in the *McCulloch* case, was revealed as a participant in a scheme of embezzlement and fraud involving hundreds of thousands of dollars.[24] These factors combined with the larger constitutional issues employed by Hammond, Brown, and others against the *McCulloch* decision to ensure that Ohio's plans to tax the national Bank out of the state would continue—even if that meant outright defiance of one or more branches of the federal government.

A standoff ensued for the subsequent few months, as the Offices of Discount and Deposit, taking their cue from the *McCulloch* decision, continued their operations, while the state legislature had no intention of repealing the taxation law and the Auditor still considered it his obligation to collect the tax on the appointed date. September first came and went, and the branch offices remained open. It was not until the eleventh that the Bank officials realized that the state was in earnest and attempted to stop the imminent collection. That day, the state Auditor, Ralph Osborn, was notified by lawyers representing the branch offices that they intended to apply for an injunction within the next three days at the United States Circuit Court at Chillicothe to enjoin the state from proceeding with the collection of the tax. On September 15 Osborn was served with a copy of the petition in chancery applying for this injunction, as well as a subpoena to appear the following January. But, technically, these papers did not constitute an injunction. Osborn doubted he could be enjoined in the first place, as he believed that action would place the Offices of Discount and Deposit in violation of the February taxation act. Proceeding with his duties under the law, he commissioned John L. Harper as the agent to collect the tax. To

23. *Western Herald and Steubenville Gazette*, Mar. 20, May 22, 1819; *Liberty Hall and Cincinnati Gazette*, Apr. 6, 13, 1819; *Chillicothe Supporter*, Mar. 3, 1819; *Liberty Hall and Cincinnati Gazette*, Apr. 6, 1819; Aiello, "Ohio's War upon the BUS," 66–67; Utter, *Frontier State*, 303. For an examination of Ohio's Jeffersonian political tradition, see Cayton, *Frontier Republic*, esp. 68–80.

24. Aiello, "Ohio's War upon the BUS," 70–71; Catterall, *Second BUS*, 42–50; Hammond, *Banks and Politics in the United States*, 268–72. For representative editorials on the specie drain and the perceived culpability of the BUS, see *Western Herald and Steubenville Gazette*, June 26, Sept. 4, 1819.

hedge his bets, however, Osborn submitted the papers he had been served to Ohio's secretary of state, Jeremiah McClane, who in turn submitted them to various state attorneys for their opinions in the matter. The answer was not long in coming. The attorneys denied that the papers constituted a proper injunction; therefore, Osborn—and, by extension, Ohio—was free to proceed legally in the collection of the tax.[25]

This was the path that brought Harper, McCollister, and Orr into the Chillicothe Office of Discount and Deposit on September 17. Their confrontation with the office's unfortunate cashier, while perhaps excessively rough, was eminently legal under the provisions of the February statute. Successful in their endeavors to collect the tax, Harper and his companions deposited the funds taken from the Chillicothe branch office in the state-chartered Bank of Chillicothe overnight, with the intention of moving them to the state treasury at Columbus the next day. While doing this on September 18, Harper, eight miles outside of Columbus, was served with an injunction proscribing collection of the tax. Having already collected the tax, Harper ignored the order and proceeded to deposit the funds in the state's repositories in Columbus. Osborn was also served with an injunction, but, since the tax monies were already safely ensconced in the state treasury, he claimed the matter was now out of his power and thus the injunction was moot. For their part, Bank officials could only fulminate against the "outrage" visited upon them by the State of Ohio. Writing to William Crawford, the Bank's president, Langdon Cheves, was furious. "The outrage . . . can be rarely paralleled under a Government of laws," he seethed, "and, if sanctioned by the higher authorities of the State, strikes at the vitals of the Constitution." Former governor Worthington also criticized the state's actions. "I view the transaction in the most odious light," he declared, "and from my very soul I detest it . . . I am ashamed it has happened in Ohio."[26]

25. Aiello, "Ohio's War upon the BUS," 71–72; Utter, *Frontier State,* 304–5; Bogart, "Ohio's Taxation of the Second BUS," 323–24. Various pro-Bank historians (see John Bach McMaster, *History of the People of the United States . . .* [New York: Appleton, 1883–1913], 4:498, and William Graham Sumner, *History of Banking in the United States* [New York: H. Holt, 1896], 153) have argued that Osborn defied a federal injunction in pursuing the collection of the tax from the branch offices, but this was not the case. While Osborn was indeed served with extensive paperwork, none of it fulfilled the requirements for a legal injunction per se. The papers served on Osborn are appended to his report to the General Assembly; see Ohio, *House Journal (1819–1820),* 44–67.

26. Abraham Claypoole's reports to Langdon Cheves and William Crawford represent the most detailed account of the events in the Chillicothe office. See *American State Papers, Finance,* 4:903–6, 910; Aiello, "Ohio's War upon the BUS," 72–74; Bogart, "Taxation of the Second BUS," 324; Cheves to Crawford, Sept. 30, 1819, *American State Papers, Finance,* 4: 905. (The letter is all the more interesting in light of Cheves's stance as a determined nullifier in South Carolina's confrontation with the Jackson administration some dozen years later [a point also noted by Catterall, *Second BUS,* 90n.]); Worthington to Cheves, n.d., excerpted in *American State Papers, Finance,* 4:905–6. Bray Hammond, in *Banks and Politics in America* (268), uses the letter as evidence that Ohio's government was divided on the issue of taxing the Bank's branch offices. In his eagerness to disparage Ohio's actions, however, Hammond mistakenly asserts that Worthington was governor at the time the tax was collected and this letter was written, when he had in fact left office almost a full year before. Thus, Hammond's insinuation that Ohio's legislature acted alone is in error, as it obviously enjoyed the full support of Governor Brown. A similar error is contained in Huntington, "Banking and Currency in Ohio," 320–21. See Still, "Life of Ethan Allen Brown," 79–80.

But these were the sentiments of a decided minority. A survey of newspaper reaction to the actions of the state officials finds very little criticism, compared with a high degree of support. The *Ohio Monitor* asked, "Could our confidence possibly have been stronger than it was, that the state of Ohio exercised more than her legitimate right of sovereignty in collecting a tax from the U.S. branches, in this state?" The *Liberty Hall and Cincinnati Gazette* editorialized that the Bank had no right to resist the laws of Ohio: "When a monied institution, with a capital of thirty-five millions, acquires so great an ascendancy in the public mind as to put on the garb of inviolability and be identified with the interest and safety of the community, it is time to enquire, whether it is not already subjecting our minds to a domination which . . . will be irresistible." All the state had done, the editorial continued, was to protect its liberties and the liberties of its citizens against a corrupt outside power, bolstered by the *McCulloch* decision—which the paper termed "a judicial usurpation, which had . . . become a precedent for the total extinguishment of state rights." The threat to Ohio's state rights was clear: "If the general government can create a monied institution, in the very bosom of the states, paramount to their laws, then indeed is state sovereignty a mere name, 'full of sound and fury, signifying nothing.'" A letter from "Civis" in James Wilson's *Western Herald and Steubenville Gazette* put the issue in concise terms: "The question is, shall the state recede from maintaining its own right against an association of shavers and paper dealers, because they are named 'the Bank of the United States,' and because a decision of the supreme court has been held in their favor, upon a partial and hasty view of the subject?" For his own part, "Civis" thought not. "The reasons of the court, in support of their opinion, have been published: they are not satisfactory," he declared. As for Ohio's course, "Civis" asserted that "she acts as an independent state should always act."[27]

Further encouragement came from word that the Bank of the United States would soon close its Office of Discount and Deposit in Cincinnati, effective October 1820. Ostensibly, the closing was because Cheves felt that there were too many branch offices, but given Ohio's anti-Bank activities, there were certainly other factors at work as well. The Bank's leadership, though, was unwilling to concede the point any further. The national Bank swiftly filed suit against Ralph Osborn, John Harper, and Harper's assistants to recover the funds taken from the Chillicothe office. Chief Justice John Marshall also served a permanent injunction on the state officials of Ohio, forbidding the use of the funds extracted from the Chillicothe branch. Harper and Thomas Orr were arrested by a deputy marshal for trespass and imprisoned for several months (until freed on a technicality in their Circuit Court trial of January 1820). In addition, Harper and Osborn were also served with papers requiring them to appear in the United States Circuit Court to explain their disregard of the injunctions served them after the tax was collected.[28]

27. *Ohio Monitor,* reprinted in the *Hamilton Gazette and Miami Register,* Dec. 14, 1819; *Liberty Hall and Cincinnati Gazette,* Oct. 5, 1819; "Civis," *Western Herald and Steubenville Gazette,* Oct. 2, 1819.

28. Aiello, "Ohio's War upon the BUS," 75–93; Bogart, "Taxation of the Second BUS," 324–25; G. A. Worth to William Crawford, Oct. 7, 1820, in *American State Papers, Finance,* 4:943; Huntington, "Banking and Currency in Ohio," 319–21.

The case was continued until the Circuit Court's next session the following September, when it was heard by Justice Thomas Todd. In the meantime, the Bank had retained the legal services of Henry Clay, the powerful Kentucky senator and future presidential candidate. Arguing for the Ohio officials was none other than Charles Hammond, who by now had become the most visible of Ohio's anti-Bank leaders. The Bank already had two favorable injunctions granted—one against any future collection of the Bank tax by Ohio officials and the other ordering the return of the funds deposited in the state treasury. But Hammond was able to strike a significant blow of his own for the state. After Clay had presented evidence of trespass against the Ohio agents for their actions at the Chillicothe office, Hammond argued against its admissibility, and his objection was upheld by Justice Todd. As one observer recounted, "Mr. Clay took snuff with both hands, seemed quite bewildered and at the mercy of his opponent." Hammond took advantage of this opening and declared that "the object of his client was, not to gain a technical triumph, but to try the right" of the larger issues involved in the case, even though this technicality could have caused the case to be dismissed then and there. Therefore, he declared, he would agree "to an amendment which would raise the actual question—let a verdict pass by consent & take the case on Bill of exceptions to the S.C. of the U.S."[29] In short, Hammond had accomplished precisely what he wanted: by an appeal to the larger issues of sovereignty involved in the cases against Osborn and Harper, he guaranteed Ohio its day in the highest court in the nation, where it could challenge the *McCulloch* decision.

The battle between Ohio and the national Bank dominated the political as well as legal discourse in the state during this period. Coming right on the heels of the state's collection of the tax, the 1819 elections were rife with rhetoric that defined how far most Ohioans were prepared to go in their assertions of states' rights and their challenge to federal sovereignty. Samuel Swearingen and Richard Douglas, two candidates for the state legislature, introduced a "Declaration of Independence against the United States Bank," to general approbation. Modeled after the 1776 Declaration of Independence, the document charged the Bank with offenses comparable to the depredations of George III, such as its "having quartered large bodies of armed brokers" among the citizens of Ohio. Thus, they concluded, "all connection between the people and the branch banks ought to be dissolved" and, flatly defying the Supreme Court's assertions of national authority in the *McCulloch* decision, argued "that as a free and independent state we have full power to levy a tax upon all banks within our jurisdiction of whatever denomination and by whomever established." Arguing the "evident truth" that Ohio, and every other state, possessed inviolable traits of sovereignty, Swearingen and Douglas declared (following the original Declaration's Lockean logic) "that whenever any act of the general government becomes destructive of this principle, it is the right of the people of the individual states to oppose it in a constitutional way, and if possible, to alter or abolish it." So militant was this spirit

29. Clement L. Martzolff, ed., "The Autobiography of Thomas Ewing," *Ohio Archaeological and Historical Society Publications* 22 (1913): 171–72; Huntington, "Banking and Currency in Ohio," 320.

of resistance that even William Henry Harrison was forced to renounce his past service as a director of the Cincinnati branch office and climb aboard the anti-Bank bandwagon. To bolster his campaign for the state senate, Harrison declared he was now an enemy of all banks, in particular the Bank of the United States, "which may be converted into an immense political engine to strengthen the arm of the general government and which may at some future day be used to oppress and break down state governments." The court battles and the continuation of the economic crisis into 1820 only served to heighten the enmity of Ohioans toward the national Bank. That fall, anti-Bank candidates, including Ethan A. Brown and Charles Hammond, again marched to overwhelming electoral victories.[30]

Anti-Bank sentiment reached new heights in December 1820 with the convening of the General Assembly and its immediate consideration of Ralph Osborn's report on the proceedings of the previous year, submitted on December 5. The report was referred to a joint committee, which reported back to the General Assembly one week later. The report of the joint committee (largely the work of Hammond) was the fullest expression yet of the lengths to which Ohio had gone to resist incursions on its sovereignty. The actions of the Bank, the committee asserted, were "to every substantial purpose, a process against the State." The only reason state officials were named as defendants was "to evade the provisions of the Constitution," namely the Eleventh Amendment, which protected states from being named as parties in lawsuits. The report then addressed the Supreme Court's assertions embodied in the McCulloch decision: "The committee are aware of the doctrine, that the Federal Courts are Exclusively vested with jurisdiction to declare, in the last resort, the true interpretation of the Constitution of the United States. To this doctrine, in the latitude contended for, they can never give their assent." Claiming the ultimate authority to interpret Constitutional provisions (in this case, the Eleventh Amendment's denial of Supreme Court jurisdiction in suits involving a state as a party), the committee essentially nullified the McCulloch decision. Nullification—the idea that the states, as the original parties to the Constitution, could judge for themselves the constitutionality of federal measures and "nullify" them should they violate the terms of that framework—was the most powerful assertion of state sovereignty short of secession.[31]

Nullification exists in the historiography of the early republic as a largely Southern phenomenon, concerned with the sectional implications of certain federal legislation. This emphasis derives from the most famous instance of the doctrine's use, South Carolina's nullification of the tariff laws of 1828 and 1832 and the ensuing crisis these actions produced between the state and President Andrew Jackson's administration. But the rather mechanistic

30. Swearingen and Douglas's "Declaration of Independence" was reprinted throughout the state; see, for example, *Western Herald and Steubenville Gazette,* Oct. 30, 1819; Huntington, "Banking and Currency in Ohio," 321; Aiello, "Ohio's War upon the BUS," 93.

31. Ohio, General Assembly, Joint Select Committee on the Bank of the United States, *Report of the Joint Committee of Both Houses of the General Assembly of Ohio, on the Communication of the Auditor of the State upon the Subject of the Proceedings of the Bank of the United States, against the Officers of State, in the United States' Circuit Court,* cited in Ohio, *House Journal (1819–1820),* 98–132. The report is also excerpted in Ames, *State Documents on Federal Relations,* 94–101; Ohio, *House Journal (1819–1820),* 100–106 (quoted at 106).

association of the idea of nullification with a state's invalidation of specific federal legislation, as expressed by South Carolina's premier theorist on the subject, John C. Calhoun, obscures the larger meaning and appeal the concept held for Americans throughout the Union during the years of the early republic. Understood in this context, nullification assumes a larger ideological dimension. Based on the states' rights assumption that the Union created by the Constitution was really a "compact" among separate and sovereign states, nullification meant that should any party to this arrangement—namely, the federal government—violate the terms of the constitutional compact, the states were free to exercise their rights as parties to that compact and nullify actions that violated the arrangement. The same justification that Calhoun would later use to rationalize South Carolina's nullification of federal tariff legislation was applied by Ohio to nullify not a specific piece of legislation but a larger pattern of federal intrusion on what Ohioans saw as their state's sovereign liberties. The Bank's declarations of immunity from taxation and the Supreme Court's *McCulloch* decision were both actions that "the people of this state," according to James Wilson, "so long as they determine to protect their rights, cannot recognize as correct." Ohio's use of nullification testified to both the seriousness of the sovereignty question involved in the battle with the Bank and the vehemence with which Ohio's political leadership was prepared to defend the state's liberties against the encroachments of what it saw as a consolidated and corrupt national authority.[32]

To bolster its argument concerning the rights of individual states versus the expansive view of federal sovereignty embodied by the Bank, the committee turned to the Virginia and Kentucky Resolutions of 1798—authored by James Madison and Thomas Jefferson, respectively, and perhaps the most assertive expressions of states' rights ideology in the history of the young republic. Referring to the Resolutions (and Madison's supporting Report of 1800) as "the true text-book of republican principles," the committee argued that "the question, whether the Federal Courts are the sole expositors of the Constitution of the United States in the last resort," had "been decided against the pretension of the federal judges" by the Jeffersonian triumph in the election of 1800. Backed by this solidly "republican" tradition, the state thus had a "duty . . . from which it cannot shrink without dishonor" against "the encroaching pretensions" of the federal courts. Addressing the *McCulloch* decision, the committee was "not satisfied that it is a correct one." The *McCulloch* case was nothing more, the committee argued, than a test case, reeking of collusion between the Bank and the Supreme Court, contrived from the beginning. "This

---

32. [John C. Calhoun,] "Exposition and Protest," in *Union and Liberty: The Political Philosophy of John C. Calhoun,* ed. Ross M. Lence (Indianapolis: Liberty Fund, 1992), 311–65. *Western Herald and Steubenville Gazette,* Oct. 16, 1819. For the persistence of states' rights thought, its relationship to the idea of nullification, and its wide applicability during the antebellum period, see Stampp, "The Concept of a Perpetual Union"; Forrest McDonald, *States' Rights and the Union: Imperium in Imperio* (Lawrence: Univ. Press of Kansas, 2000). The two most thorough treatments of the South Carolina nullification crisis are William Freehling, *Prelude to Civil War: The Nullification Controversy in South Carolina, 1816–1836* (New York: Oxford Univ. Press, 1965), and Richard E. Ellis, *The Union at Risk: Jacksonian Democracy, States' Rights and the Nullification Crisis* (New York: Oxford Univ. Press, 1987).

decision served to prop [the Bank's] sinking credit," the report contended. "It is truly an alarming circumstance, if it be in the power of an aspiring corporation, and an unknown and obscure individual [James McCulloch], thus to elicit opinions, compromitting the vital interests of the states that compose the American Union." It did not necessarily follow, however, that acquiescence was required in the decisions of the Court; in fact, the committee asserted that there were "cases in which the decisions of the tribunal have been followed by no effective consequences." Therefore, the report argued, "in great questions of political rights and political powers a decision of the Supreme Court of the United States is not conclusive of the rights decided by it," and this was precisely the case with the Court's opinion in the *McCulloch* case.[33]

Having effectively nullified both the Court's decision and the authority by which it claimed jurisdiction, the committee proceeded to recommend several measures and resolutions. It urged the Assembly to adopt further legislation that would prevent the Bank from attempting to reassert its sovereignty in Ohio—specifically, the report advocated a law withdrawing legal protection to the Bank within the state, essentially rendering it an outlaw. Then came the resolutions, all of them vigorous declarations of state sovereignty. One resolution declared that the members of the General Assembly "do recognize and approve the doctrines" of the Virginia and Kentucky Resolutions and considered them "recognized and adopted by a majority of the American people." Another resolution denied the Circuit Court's assertions of federal sovereignty, based on the committee's interpretation of the Eleventh Amendment. The committee also advanced resolutions reaffirming Ohio's right to tax "any private corporation of trade incorporated by the Congress of the United States" and operating within the state, especially the branches of the national Bank. Capping off the assertions of Ohio's sovereignty was a resolution denying the validity of "the doctrine that the political rights of the separate States, may be settled and determined in the Supreme Court of the United States, so as to conclude and bind them, in cases contrived between individuals, and where they are no one of them parties direct." Here was the rationale behind Ohio's rejection of the *McCulloch* decision and the idea that the federal courts could decide this question of state sovereignty.[34]

The resolutions proffered and actions recommended by the committee were the culminating expression of the larger vision of political economy that underlay Ohio's nullification of the *McCulloch* decision and the provisions of the Bank's federal charter. The blame

---

33. Ohio, *House Journal (1819–1820)*, 109–13 (quoted at 112); Jonathan Elliot, ed., *The Debates in the Several State Conventions, on the Adoption of the Federal Constitution* (Washington, D.C.: privately printed, 1836), 4:566ff.

34. Ibid., 129–32. Governor Brown forwarded copies of the report and resolutions to Jefferson, Madison, and New Yorkers DeWitt Clinton and John Jay. Clinton and especially Jefferson approved of Ohio's course. Jefferson wrote Brown that he thought the Supreme Court was leading the federal government away from what he saw as the true principles of the Constitution: "the Judiciary is the dangerous corps of sappers and miners—because they are in place for life and beyond responsibility" (Jefferson to Brown, Feb. 21, 1821, quoted in Still, "The Life of Ethan Allen Brown," 88–89). Aiello, "Ohio's War upon the BUS," 97–98.

for the severe dislocations of the Panic of 1819 was placed directly on the Bank of the United States, particularly with regard to the conduct of its two branch offices in Ohio. By the end of 1819, the Bank represented for most Ohioans the embodiment of a corrupt, aristocratic bastion of privilege, conspiring against the interests and well-being of the republic by its abuse of power. The fact that the Bank wielded its authority from distant offices in Philadelphia made it seem that the rights and interests of Ohio's citizens were merely obstacles to be trampled over in its quest for wealth and dominance. One of Governor Brown's correspondents decried this perceived attitude on the part of the Bank's directors, "that this institution will show the states that they are but secondary in magnitude." Indeed, the arbitrary policies of the Bank, as it sought to protect its own financial health, had become for Ohioans the root cause of the current depression. The *Liberty Hall and Cincinnati Gazette* attacked the Bank as "a monied aristocracy at Philadelphia . . . vested with power" by the federal government, an institution that, "by a simple order from its cashier," could "blight the prospects of any district of the country which either its interest or its caprice may select as suitable prey."[35] Faced with an economic collapse they saw as triggered by the distant authority of the Bank of the United States, most Ohioans viewed the political and economic powers of the Bank as fundamentally interrelated and framed their critique of the institution accordingly. It is here that the nexus between ideology and interest—between the political and material—became the driving force behind Ohio's actions. Far from being mutually exclusive, the political tactics and economic concerns of Ohio's anti-Bank leadership worked hand in hand to frame what would become the strategy of nullification. To them, the Bank represented a corrupt force, sanctioned by federal privilege, that posed a fundamental threat to both the liberties and livelihoods of the people of Ohio. Given this vision of political economy, the mutually reinforcing nature of Ohio's ideologically and materially based attacks on the Bank becomes evident.

The resolutions proffered by the joint committee received an overwhelming endorsement from the General Assembly. Acting on the committee's recommendations, the legislature passed "an act to withdraw from the Bank of the United States the protection and aid of the laws of this state, in certain cases," on January 29, 1821. The law offered the national Bank a choice: pay a 4 percent annual tax on its dividends in Ohio or be denied the use of any of the state's legal mechanisms, a prohibition that would bring the business of the branch offices to a complete halt. In early February, the General Assembly offered a compromise of sorts, passing an act stipulating that the so-called "outlaw" act of January 29 would be suspended, provided the Bank agree to submit to the same taxation as a state-chartered bank and drop the suits currently pending against the state's officials. The Bank refused to budge, however, and another standoff over taxation ensued. This time, though, the federal courts would have none of it, and an injunction was served against the state of Ohio forbidding the collection of any new tax. By its refusal to either suspend the opera-

35. Philemon Beecher to Ethan Allen Brown, Jan. 1, 1819, microfilm, reel 1, Ethan Allen Brown Papers, Ohio Historical Society, Columbus; *Liberty Hall and Cincinnati Gazette,* Nov. 17, 1818.

tions of its branches in Ohio or to drop the lawsuits against Osborn and other state offic-ers, the Bank enabled the "outlaw" act to become effective in September 1821. Denied the use of any part of Ohio's legal apparatus, the Bank's branches were in many cases unable to transact even the most basic business. The "outlaw" act thus became the mechanism by which the state nullified the Bank's federal charter. Not only had Ohio persisted in its nul-lification of the *McCulloch* decision, it seemed determined to persist in its denial of federal jurisdiction over the offices of the Bank within its borders.[36]

The matter was then resumed in the courts, with the Circuit Court rendering a deci-sion in the Bank's favor on September 5, 1821, upholding the permanent injunction against Ohio's collecting taxes from the Bank's branches and ordering the return of the funds removed from the Chillicothe office two years before. There was resistance to the deci-sion, however, as the office of State Treasurer had changed hands since the initial collec-tion of the tax. The new Treasurer renounced any responsibility for the funds but also refused their return. As a result, he was arrested, and a federal marshal seized the keys to the Treasury's vault and removed the funds, returning them to the Bank officials—an interesting evocation of the events of two years previous. The reaction was not as vehe-ment throughout the state as it was for the earlier actions of the Bank and decisions of the Circuit Court. This was perhaps due to the fact that the suit against Ralph Osborn was still scheduled to be heard by the Supreme Court—indeed, Governor Brown, in his 1821 message to the General Assembly, held out the hope that the Court, in this instance, would recognize Ohio's position as legitimate and reconsider the *McCulloch* decision.[37]

The case of *Osborn v. Bank of the United States* did not come onto the Court's docket until the 1824 term. In the meantime, the situation between Ohio and the Bank of the United States was one of uneasy détente. But the attitude of most Ohioans, and certainly the political leadership of the state, had changed little. The Bank was still seen as a some-what sinister entity—powerful, corrupt, and dangerous. The Circuit Court's injunction meant that it still paid no taxes, continually exacerbating the resentment of Ohioans. Dis-content toward this situation meant continued support for the "outlaw" act; if the Bank was to enjoy such a high degree of control over the state's economic landscape, without sharing in the tax burden, then there was little desire to extend the state's legal protection to either "persons or property" associated with the Bank.[38]

When *Osborn v. Bank of the United States* finally came before the Supreme Court in early 1824, it signaled the final installment of more than five years of conflict between Ohio and the federal government over the proper locus of sovereignty. Arguing for Ohio were both Ethan A. Brown and Charles Hammond, as well as John Harper and John Wright. The Bank, as it did in 1819, retained Daniel Webster and William Wirt and added Henry Clay

36. Ohio, General Assembly, *Acts Passed at the First Session of the Nineteenth General Assembly . . .* (Colum-bus, 1821), 108–10; Huntington, "Banking and Currency in Ohio," 325–26; Aiello, "Ohio's War upon the BUS," 98–101.

37. Aiello, "Ohio's War upon the BUS," 102–4.

38. Huntington, "Banking and Currency in Ohio," 326.

and John Sergeant to its counsel. Hammond, as lead counsel for Ohio, based the state's argument on the Eleventh Amendment, declaring that "the state of Ohio is, in fact, the sole defendant in this cause," and therefore the Court had no jurisdiction. Hammond also urged the Court to "reconsider" the McCulloch decision, as it infringed on Ohio's sovereign right of taxation. "The question," Hammond argued, "whether the Bank of the United States . . . is exempt by the constitution of the Union, from the taxing power of the state, depends upon the nature and character of the institution." The Bank, Hammond asserted, was a private corporation and thus not entitled to the constitutional protections it claimed to enjoy. Preventing Ohio from taxing a private corporation operating within its borders was, Hammond contended, a fundamental violation of its sovereignty. "If . . . for a consideration of money the government of the nation can exclude . . . subjects from the taxing power of the states, and appropriate them to itself, the equal rights of both supposed to be secured by the Constitution, are annihilated." This was perhaps the most salient point Ohio could make—that the Bank was essentially a private corporation, therefore subject to state powers of taxation, and that Ohio could not be a defendant in the suit brought by because of the Eleventh Amendment. Hammond was so convinced of the truth in his argument that he had it published in pamphlet form, a copy of which made it into the hands of Chief Justice Marshall, who privately complimented the skill and logic Hammond exhibited.[39]

Despite these private sentiments, Marshall and a majority of the Court ruled for the Bank on March 19. In an opinion that reaffirmed the essential tenets of the *McCulloch* decision, despite Hammond's urgings to the contrary, the Court denied the validity of Ohio's jurisdictional argument by declaring that since the state was not a party of record in the case, the Eleventh Amendment did not apply. Again asserting the constitutional right of Congress to charter the national Bank, the Court once again denied the right of the states to tax the institution or any of its branches. In almost every aspect, the *Osborn* decision signaled a repudiation of Ohio's anti-Bank activities, despite Hammond's lingering conviction that the Court did not satisfactorily address his jurisdictional arguments.[40]

After the Court's decision, the anti-Bank activity in Ohio waned to the point of nonexistence. Indeed, the *Osborn* decision passed without comment in most of the state's newspapers. Historians examining the conflict point to this seeming acquiescence in the

39. *United States Reports* 9 Wheaton (1824), quoted at 756, 765, 795; Charles Hammond, *The State of the Case and Argument for the Appellants, in the Case of the Bank of the United States, versus the Auditor and Treasurer of the State of Ohio, and Others, in the Supreme Court of the United States* (Cincinnati: privately printed, 1823), 79–80; Aiello, "Ohio's War upon the BUS," 112. Hammond had also published a pamphlet attacking the Supreme Court's erosion of states' rights claims in the 1821 case of *Cohens v. Virginia,* where he denied the Court's authority in such matters. The Constitution, Hammond argued, was the "supreme" law of the land, "but the supremacy of the law and the supremacy of the government are not the same thing . . . there are certain subjects upon which the states alone can prescribe the law," therefore the "supremacy" of the federal government was not an established fact. The Union, according to Hammond, "was never created to coerce the states" (*Review of the Opinion of the Supreme Court of the United States, in the Case of Cohens vs. Virginia . . .* [Steubenville, Ohio: James Wilson, 1821]; a letter was appended by Ethan Allen Brown).

40. 9 Wheaton 738–899; Johnson, *John Marshall,* 157–61; White, *The Marshall Court,* 524–35; Aiello, "Ohio's War upon the BUS," 120.

Court's decision as proof that Ohio's political leadership employed states' rights argu-ments and the doctrine of nullification only out of convenience—that these served the economic needs of Ohioans in a period of crisis and were easily abandoned with the re-turn of good times. But this interpretation creates an artificial separation between ideol-ogy and interest, assuming that political ideas only resonate in times of acute economic distress. States' rights and nullification sentiment in Ohio was helped, but not spawned, by the fact that the Bank was seen as bringing about the Panic of 1819. The reaction to *Os-born* was muted, but not because Ohio had abandoned its position. In fact, the course of events over the previous few years had served to validate the state's stance—a crucial point ignored in many treatments of the controversy. The Cincinnati Office of Discount and Deposit had closed in October 1820. The Chillicothe branch's activities were significantly reduced, to the point where it only exchanged BUS notes, and it would be closed as well by the end of 1825. By shutting the doors of its chief Ohio branch office in the midst of the state's assault on its authority, the Bank essentially gave in to Ohio's demands. The "outlaw" act was repealed in early 1826, but only because it represented a moot point. The Court's decision in 1824 seemed to deny Ohio's rights under the Eleventh Amendment, but Marshall's opinion took refuge in the narrow logic of "party of record" doctrine, meaning that it was only because Osborn's name appeared at the head of the proceedings that the case did not fall under the amendment's provisions. Hammond's larger argument about Ohio's immunity from suits by the Bank remained unanswered. In the important, essen-tial aspects of the case, Ohio's states' rights position remained largely intact. In the eyes of Hammond and the state's other leaders, only by applying tortured definitions of "public" corporations and jurisdictional issues could the Supreme Court have its way in upholding the *McCulloch* decision. The larger point about the nature of the relationship between the states and the federal government was not addressed and would continue to be open to debate throughout the subsequent decades. In essence, Ohio's use of nullification worked: it accomplished the express purpose of asserting the state's sovereign rights by removing the Bank from its borders, even if other factors had aided the process.[41]

The Supreme Court, in the *Osborn* case, further built on the extension and nationaliza-tion of federal sovereignty—an extension that ran from *Martin v. Hunter's Lessee* (1816),

41. A representative statement of the "convenience" argument is Patricia L. Franz, "Ohio v. the Bank: An Historical Examination of *Osborn v. The Bank of the United States*," *Journal of Supreme Court History* 23 (Jan. 1999): 112–37. Franz argues that "the 'non-reaction' to the decision in Ohio during a period when the economy appeared to be on the rebound lends strong support to the argument that the primary concern of the legisla-ture, and others involved in the taxation, had been the Bank's impact on the state's economy." If the Eleventh Amendment/states' rights issue "had been the primary concern," the Court's ruling, according to Franz, "would have drawn howls of protest" (131). This interpretation is echoed in, among other works, Bray Hammond, *Banks and Politics in America*, 268. Marion A. Brown takes a contrary position, arguing that republican values were "the driving force for the anger and frustration over the incursion of an alien force into Ohio" and that states' rights theory played an important role in the actions of Ohio's government—though Brown does not explore the idea of nullification as expressed by Ohio's leadership (Brown, *The Second Bank of the United States and Ohio (1803–1860): A Collision of Interests*, Studies in American History, Vol. 22 [Lewiston, N.Y.: Edwin Mel-len Press, 1998], quoted at 121); Catterall, *Second BUS*, 398; Aiello, "Ohio's War upon the BUS," 122.

to the *McCulloch* decision, through *Cohens v. Virginia* (1821), *Osborn,* and *Planters' Bank v. Georgia* (1824).[42] Yet Ohio's expressions of state sovereignty and nullification were far from repudiated. The ideas remained hotly contested issues and would reappear regularly throughout the United States during antebellum period. The clash between Ohio and the national Bank was therefore not an isolated event; it was, rather, part of a larger strain of American political culture in the early national period that emphasized state sovereignty and the protection of republican liberties against corrupt, hostile, and aristocratic combinations. The idioms of conspiracy and causation in which Ohioans couched their anti-Bank protests testified to the strength of these ideas in the early American republic and placed Ohio's anti-Bank activities firmly within established political traditions. Far from representing a simple economic conflict between "haves" and "have-nots," Ohio's crusade against the Bank of the United States was a crucial episode at the intersection of politics and economics that served to define and articulate an alternative political discourse to the emergent nationalism represented by the second Bank of the United States and the Marshall Court. Understanding the struggle between Ohio and the Bank in this larger context, then, points toward a more nuanced and accurate understanding of the dynamic and contested relationship between individual states and the federal government in an era during which such concepts as "Union" and "nationalism" were still very much open questions.

---

42. For an analysis of the tradition of sovereignty created by the Marshall Court in these decisions, see White, *The Marshall Court,* 485–594.

Explaining John Sherman
Leader of the Second American Revolution

Marc Egnal

Explaining John Sherman has an importance that goes beyond the activities of one midwestern politician. Although his older brother, Civil War general William Tecumseh Sherman, is better known today, John had a far greater impact on nineteenth-century America. His public career stretched from the late 1840s to the end of the century. No single figure was more important in shaping the policies of the early Republican Party or in laying the basis for the broad set of changes called the "Second American Revolution." Thus, explaining John Sherman sheds light on the direction of the party he helped establish, as well as the creation of the modern industrial state.[1]

The arc of Sherman's career suggests the central role he played during a half-century in politics, and the respect his colleagues accorded him. Sherman entered politics as a Whig but, angered by the Kansas-Nebraska Act, became a founder of the Republican Party. Elected to Congress from Ohio in 1854, he soon stood out for his legislative skills and clear sense of purpose. Passing over more senior members, the Speaker in 1856 chose Sherman and

Versions of this essay were presented at meetings of the Organization of American Historians, March 2004, and the British Association of American Studies, April 2004. For their valuable comments, I'd like to thank Peter A. Coclanis, Daniel W. Crofts, Jane E. Flaherty, Michael F. Holt, James L. Hutson, Heather Cox Richardson, and Michael A. Ross.

1. Surprisingly, there is no modern biography of John Sherman. Two older works, Theodore Burton, *John Sherman* (Boston: Houghton, Mifflin, 1906), and Winfield S. Kerr, *John Sherman: His Life and Public Services,* 2 vols. (Boston: Sherman, French, 1907), are badly out of date. On the Second American Revolution see Charles A. Beard and Mary R. Beard, *The Rise of American Civilization,* 2 vols. (New York: Macmillan, 1927, 1930), 1:628–724, 2:3–121; Marc Egnal, "The Beards Were Right: Parties in the North, 1840–1860," *Civil War History* 47 (Mar. 2001): 30–56.

Ohio History, Vol. 114 © 2007 by The Kent State University Press

two other lawmakers to investigate conditions in Kansas. With Sherman doing most of the work, the committee produced a 1,300-page report that excoriated the proslavery forces and provided an extraordinary source of information for Republican partisans inside and outside Congress. In the ensuing debates, Sherman distinguished himself by his passionate opposition to the spread of slavery and the clarity of his vision for the economy. When the thirty-sixth Congress convened in December 1859, Sherman was the overwhelming choice of the Republicans for Speaker. But the Ohioan had inadvertently signed a memorial endorsing Hinton Rowan Helper's abolitionist tract and on a series of ballots fell three votes short of a majority. After two months of fruitless divisions, Sherman withdrew. He became chairman of the Ways and Means Committee (the second most important position in the House) and helped guide the Morrill tariff through Congress.

Republicans agreed that had Sherman remained in the House after secession, they would have elected him Speaker. However, in 1861 the Ohio legislature elevated Sherman to the Senate, providing him with a new forum for his views and a new base of power. He took the lead in pushing through legislation for the National Banking System, income tax, and the new greenback currency. During Reconstruction he was a strong supporter of the Fourteenth Amendment and helped author the Reconstruction Act of 1867. Sherman continued to shape financial policy, and was largely responsible for demonetizing silver—the so-called "Crime of 1873." He then helped partially reverse that decision, securing the Bland-Allison Act of 1878 and the Sherman Silver Purchase Act of 1890. His antimonopoly sentiments were embodied in the Sherman Anti-Trust Act of 1890. He served as secretary of the treasury under President Hayes and secretary of state under William McKinley. Sherman did not achieve all his goals, and in the age of the spoilsmen and all-powerful monopolies he was often out of step with his party. But no single Republican was more influential during the second half of the nineteenth century.[2]

What motivated this man? Was Sherman driven by a concern for the fate of African Americans? The short answer is no; however, it is important to elaborate on that answer. After all, a significant group of Republicans were reformers before they became politicians. These individuals, including Charles Sumner, George Julian, Charles Francis Adams, and Salmon Chase, had long histories of opposing slavery and campaigning for the rights of free blacks. Sherman was not in that coterie.[3]

"I am no Abolitionist," Sherman announced in 1856. "I have always been a conserva-

2. John Sherman, *Recollections of Forty Years in the House, Senate and Cabinet: An Autobiography*, 2 vols. (Chicago: Werner Co., 1895), 1:110–250; Roger D. Bridges, "John Sherman and the Impeachment of Andrew Johnson," *Ohio History* 82 (Autumn 1973): 176–91; "John Sherman," *American National Biography*, ed. John A. Garraty and Mark C. Carnes, 24 vols. (New York: Oxford Univ. Press, 1999); Jeanette Paddock Nichols, "John Sherman: A Study in Inflation," *The Mississippi Valley Historical Review*, 21 (Sep. 1934): 181–94; William E. Gienapp, *The Origins of the Republican Party, 1852–1856* (New York: Oxford Univ. Press, 1987), 295–97, 351–52.

3. Eric Foner, *Free Soil, Free Labor, Free Men: The Ideology of the Republican Party Before the Civil War* (New York: Oxford Univ. Press, 1970), 103–48.

tive Whig. I was willing to stand by all the compromises—of 1850 and all." The Kansas-Nebraska Act jarred Sherman loose from his old political moorings and made him among the first to join the Republican Party. But before the war his goal was preserving the West for free settlers, not addressing the injustices of slavery. He emphatically rejected abolition. During the debate over the speakership, he stated: "Allow me to say, once for all, (and I have said it five times on this floor,) that I am opposed to any interference whatever by the people of the free States with the relations of master and slave in the slave States." This outlook, Sherman noted, was one he shared with the majority of Republicans. He observed in 1856: "The great mass of the Republican party never held to any sentiment that affects or impairs the constitutional rights of the South. It [the Party] is made up in a great measure of the conservative elements of the northern States—men of property, men of education, the farmers, mechanics, and laborers." Sherman even opposed abolition in the District of Columbia, a position favored by many of the New Englanders who had settled in Ohio's Western Reserve, where Sherman's congressional district lay. As late as the secession crisis he was willing to guarantee the South's "peculiar institution," stating, "Very well; let the Constitution be so amended. . . . I prefer such an amendment, as it will save us forever, I trust, from answering the oft-repeated assertion that we intend to interfere with slavery in the States."[4]

War changed Sherman's outlook, making him an advocate of emancipation. But his change of heart reflected his passionate determination to defeat the rebels, not a concern for the plight of the African Americans. "I will now say," he remarked in July 1861, "and the Senator may make the most of it, that rather than see one single foot of this country of ours torn from the national domain by traitors, I will myself see slaves set free; but at the same time I utterly disclaim any purpose of that kind." He underscored this approach, remarking in April 1862: "The proposition is simply that if, after sixty days, this rebellion is not subdued, or it shall degenerate into a guerilla warfare, and our loyal armies shall be driven from that country by the climate, rather than allow this rebellion to succeed, I would arm the slaves of the rebels without hesitation."[5]

Sherman favored gradual rather than immediate emancipation, particularly when the slaves belonged to loyal masters in the border states. "I believe that a system of gradual emancipation, easily adopted, would be wiser and better than any system of immediate emancipation," he stated in 1863 in discussing Missouri slaves. "You must prepare these people for a time, at least, to enjoy their liberty and take care of themselves. . . . I should be willing to . . . provide, say at the end of twenty years—any reasonable period—to pay for the slaves that are then living in the State of Missouri." Moreover, for Sherman the aftermath of slavery would never be equality. "I do not believe that the whites and the blacks will ever mingle together on terms of equality," he remarked in 1862. "My notions

4. Jan. 16, 1856, *Congressional Globe*, 34th Cong., 1st sess., 246 (hereafter *CG*, 34.1); Dec. 8, 1856, Dec. 6, 1859, Jan. 18, 1861, *CG*, 34.3, Appendix, 85, 36.1, 21, 36.2, 454.; Sherman, *Recollections of Forty Years*, 1:103–4;

5. July 18, 1861, Apr. 23, 1862, *CG*, 37.1, 190, 37.2, 1784.

on that subject have been defined often enough. I think the law of caste is the law of God; you cannot change it. The whites and the blacks will always be separate, or where they are brought together, one will be inferior to the other."[6]

Still, it is important to note that Sherman consistently condemned slavery, even during the years when he vowed not to disturb the institution in the South. "The history of civilized nations in the past," he observed in 1856, "the experience of the present age, the theory of our Government, and the natural teachings of the human heart, condemn the institution of master and slave as being injurious to the master, and a crime against the slave." His comments were hardly the ringing tones of Sumner or other antislavery advocates; however, they were far removed from the moral indifference of Stephen A. Douglas and many Northern Democrats.[7]

Slavery and the fate of African Americans were subordinate issues for Sherman. They never stood at the top of Sherman's agenda. "I had hoped that the slavery question would not have been thrust upon us during this session," Sherman remarked when Congress reconvened in December 1856. "The party with which I have the honor to act was willing to devote the short time until the close of this Congress to other pressing subjects which demand our legislative care; but this President and his supporters here are not content with this course." Perhaps Sherman's wish to avoid the slavery issue was naive, but such avowals were often repeated, underscoring his priorities. "I did not believe the slavery question would come up at all during this session," he noted in January 1860. "I came here with the expectation that we would have a business session . . . that we would analyze the causes of the increased expenditures of the Government, and the proper measures of redress and retrenchment. . . . And, but for the unfortunate affair of Brown at Harper's Ferry, I did not believe there would be any feeling on the subject."[8]

During the war Sherman made unmistakable his conviction that economic legislation was far more important than measures dealing with African Americans. Sherman's impassioned plea in 1863 for the National Banking Act reflects this sentiment:

The establishment of a national currency, and of this system, as the best that has been yet devised, appears to me all important. It is more important than the loss of a battle. In comparison with this, the fate of three million negroes held as slaves in the southern States is utterly insignificant. I would see them slaves for life as their fathers were before them, if only we could maintain our nationality. I would see them free, disenthralled, enfranchised, on their way to the country from which they came, or settled in our own land in a climate to which they are adapted, or transported anywhere else, rather than to see our nationality overthrown. I regard all those questions as entirely subordinate to this.[9]

6. July 9, 1862, Jan. 30, 1863, *CG*, 37.2, 3199, 37.3, 613.
7. Dec. 8, 1856, *CG*, 34.3, Appendix, 86.
8. Dec. 8, 1856, Jan. 20, 1860, *CG*, 34.3, Appendix, 85, 36.1, Appendix, 85.
9. Feb. 10, 1863, *CG*, 37.3, 845.

If concern for African Americans was never his principal motive, what explains John Sherman? This essay argues that Sherman was driven by a vision of economic growth strongly rooted in the needs of the Great Lakes economy.

Understanding Sherman and, more broadly, the Second American Revolution demands an examination of the nature of growth during the second half of the nineteenth century. Between 1850 and 1900 the United States became the leading industrial power in the world. Manufacturing increased twelve-fold, with over 80 percent of this output coming from a broad industrial belt that stretched from New England to the Great Lakes states. Within this area, however, growth was uneven. The Lake region grew most rapidly, while New England and the seaboard expanded more slowly. Figures for the states are suggestive, even if two states (New York and Pennsylvania) spanned these regions. Most striking was the relative decline of New England and the rise of the Midwest. In 1850 New England accounted for 27 percent of U.S. industrial output, while six midwestern states (Ohio, Illinois, Indiana, Wisconsin, Michigan, and Minnesota) produced only 12 percent of the total. Fifty years later these percentages were nearly reversed. In 1900 the midwestern states produced 27 percent of the nation's industrial value, while New England had dropped to 18 percent. New York had also declined, from 23 to 17 percent of the total, while Pennsylvania held its own, dipping only slightly from 15 to 14 of the total (thanks to thriving industries west of the Appalachians). Within the Midwest the most rapid growth came in the area near the Lakes; the districts near the Ohio River lagged far behind.[10]

Sherman spoke for the new, thriving Lake economy. The district he represented in the House bordered Lake Erie and included counties in Ohio's Western Reserve, where his family had first settled early in the century. In the years before the Civil War these regional loyalties shaped Sherman's approach to the issue he considered most important: government finances. Sherman argued that balancing the books, not slavery, should be the top priority for lawmakers. A first encounter with Sherman's speeches might suggest he was driven by an abstract belief in limited government. "Retrenchment and reform are now matters of imperative necessity," he announced in 1858, reiterating a theme he often sounded. "It is not the mere cry of demagogues, but a problem demanding the attention and worthy [of] the highest ability of the Representatives of the people. No party is fit to govern this country which cannot solve it." In May 1860 he affirmed: "The idea that a national debt is a national blessing is an absurd one, which should never have been tolerated; and I believe that no respectable political party proposes that the Government should go on as it has for three years past on the public credit." Closely scrutinizing a variety of bills, Sherman labored to cut government outlays while urging lawmakers to adopt a new tariff that would raise revenues.[11]

10. Data for manufacturing is from the published U.S. census, accessed online at http://fisher.lib.virginia.edu/collections/stats/histcensus/index.html, date of access, Nov. 16, 2006. On change in the Midwest, see Nicole Etcheson, *The Emerging Midwest: Upland Southerners and the Political Culture of the Old Northwest, 1787–1861* (Bloomington: Indiana Univ. Press, 1995); and Allan R. Pred, *The Spatial Dynamics of U.S. Urban-Industrial Growth, 1800–1914: Interpretative and Theoretical Essays* (Cambridge, Mass.: M.I.T. Press, 1966).

11. Apr. 6, May 27, June 8, 1858, Jan. 12, 1859, May 7, 1860, *CG*, 35.1, 1499–500, 2430–33, 2807, 35.2, 335–38, 36.1,

But there was nothing abstract about Sherman's approach to finances. The spending he so condemned flowed from the cronyism of James Buchanan's administration. "It is in vain to look to executive officers for reform," he observed in 1858. "Their power and influence depend upon executive patronage, and while we grant they will squander." The outlays he censored were often Southern, such as the construction of the Charleston and New Orleans custom houses.[12]

At the same time, Sherman backed projects that fit with his vision of national development. "I am willing to appropriate any amount necessary to aid in building a Pacific railroad," he noted in 1860, adding, "as we on this [Republican] side always favored it, we certainly should, in framing a revenue law, look to this new charge upon the public Treasury." Most significantly, Sherman supported spending money on the Lakes. Since the 1840s commerce on these inland seas had soared, as goods moved east on the Lakes to Buffalo, across the Erie Canal, and then to New York. The problem the region faced was that the Lakes had no natural harbors, and required expensive, continuous dredging operations to cut through sandbars and keep commerce flowing. In the fifteen years before the Civil War, federal money came in dribs and drabs, often blocked by Southern votes and the vetoes of Democratic presidents.[13]

Sherman introduced bills for Lake improvements, and was outraged when these measures were not approved. He remarked in 1858:

The rivers and harbors of the West in vain demand improvement. While millions are expended in your coast surveys and Atlantic defense, you scruple over a comparatively small sum, absolutely necessary to keep from destruction improvements already commenced in the lake harbors. If, while gentlemen are lavish in the public money, they would vote $1,500,000 to the protection and commerce of the great and growing power in the Northwest, it would show some kind of justice and liberality. But, sir, the region of the country which will in a short time control the destinies of this nation; which now, in its almost infancy, feeds your artisans and sailors, and in time of war furnishes sturdy defenders of your national honor, has appealed in vain for ordinary repairs of their harbors. . . . Time will soon cure this evil; and we who come from the West will have the power to legislate for ourselves, as the Atlantic and Gulf coast has done in times past.[14]

Support for the Morrill tariff, which was rejected in 1860 but adopted in 1861, again reflected Sherman's regional loyalties. Sherman had opposed the Tariff of 1857 for two

---

1946–47; Howell Cobb to Sherman, Dec. 15, 1857, microfilm, the Papers John Sherman, Library of Congress, Washington, D.C.

12. May 27, 1858, *CG*, 35.1, 2430–36.

13. May 7, 1860, *CG*, 36.1, 1947; Egnal, "The Beards Were Right," 45–56.

14. Jan. 18, May 27, 1858, *CG*, 35.1, 326, 2431; Howell Cobb to Sherman, Jan. 5, 1858, Sherman Papers.

reasons: it failed to provide sufficient revenue and it favored manufacturers over farmers. The Morrill tariff addressed both concerns. "The tariff of 1857 is the manufacturers' bill," he told the House in 1860. "But the present bill is more beneficial to the agricultural interest than the tariff of 1857." Sherman (and many midwestern Republicans) had voted against the 1857 act; he now led the campaign for the new revenue measure, which protected wool and flaxseed growers as well as eastern manufacturers. The Morrill tariff was a measure Sherman long remained proud of. "I have participated in framing many tariff bills," he observed in his memoirs published in 1895, "but have never succeeded in securing one that I entirely approved. The Morrill tariff bill came nearer than any other to meeting the double requirement of providing ample revenue for the support of the government and of rendering the proper protection to home industries."[15]

With secession and the war, Sherman along with his fellow Republicans strode confidently onto a new stage. No longer were they an opposition party; they were the incumbents shaping the course of American development. Sherman continued to speak for the Lake economy, and now was able to implement tax, banking, and currency policies that fostered its growth. "Like every other Senator, I endeavored to protect the interests of my constituents," he explained to the House in 1866. But while serving his constituents, Sherman also emerged as an outspoken proponent of a strong central government. Sherman felt what was good for his midwestern state (and particularly the region around the Lakes) was good for the country. "Although representing an interior State chiefly engaged in agriculture," he remarked in 1865, "yet I have always felt that the prosperity of our industry and section finally inured to the benefit of the whole nation and every part." Significantly, during the 1860s and 1870s the policies demanded by the Lake region coincided with the goal of creating a strong, national government.[16]

Sherman's advocacy of an income tax illustrates this interweaving of the national and the local. Few measures expanded the power of the central government more than the Revenue Act of 1861. Washington now had the right to inquire into every person's earnings. Sherman preferred this new tax to the many excises and levies Congress adopted. In 1864 he remarked, "I believe that a simple law trebling the income tax or raising it to ten percent., (not a very high war income tax,) a tax of about twenty per cent. on manufactures, would be far better than this complex mammoth bill. . . . We could then dispense with all the insignificant and trifling taxes with which the bill abounds." Sherman pointed to the fairness of the measure, which excluded the less wealthy. "I endeavored," he remarked in 1866, "to relieve the great laboring masses of the people from as much of the burden of taxation as possible." But Sherman was also keenly aware that this tax fell on the Northeast far more than on the Midwest. "The income tax," he admitted, "is paid mainly by New York and New England, and no relief is given from that tax of five and

15. May 10, 1860, CG, 36.1, 2053; Sherman, Recollections of Forty Years, 1:188; Jane Flaherty, "Incidental Protection: An Examination of the Morrill Tariff," Essays in Economic and Business History 19 (2001): 103–18.

16. Feb. 27, 1865, July 6, 1866, CG, 38.2, 1139, 39.1, 3610.

ten per cent. But a small portion of it is paid in an agricultural community . . . so that not one in ten of the constituents of my friend from Indiana [Senator Thomas Hendricks] and myself will pay any income tax."[17]

The Ohio senator's strong support for the National Banking Act of 1863 similarly conflated national and local goals. The measure that so delighted Sherman was designed to achieve several ends. It sold government bonds, which now became the mandated reserves for the national banks; it established a nationwide network of secure financial institutions; and it created a uniform national currency, providing an alternative to the notes circulated by the state banks. Sherman campaigned hard for the banking bill, praising the measure for its nationalism. He lauded the centralizing influence of the new system, contrasting it with the fragmentation inherent in the state banks with their separate notes of issue. "At present there is . . . a great diversity of interests," he observed. "The local banks have one interest, and the Government currency another. . . . But, sir, by the passage of this bill you will harmonize these interests; so that every stockholder, every mechanic, every laborer who holds one of these notes will be interested in the Government—not in a local bank, but in the Government of the United States—whose faith and credit and security he will be more anxious to uphold." He continued with a paean to a unified country: "There is a still higher motive for the passage of this bill. It will promote a sentiment of nationality. There can be no doubt of it. The policy of this country ought to be to make everything national as far as possible—to nationalize our country, so that we shall love our country. If we are dependent on the United States for a currency and a medium of exchange, we shall have a broader and a more generous nationality. . . . All private interests, all local interests, all banking interests, the interests of individuals, everything, should be subordinate now to the interests of the Government."[18]

The banking act was more than a triumph of nationalism; it was also a regional measure. The new system was demanded by the Midwest, not the Northeast where profitable, stable banks had long been engines of local growth. In January 1863 Sherman explained to his fellow senators the importance of restructuring the financial system in the North. "There is another objection to these local banks," he noted, "and it is one which we cannot disregard, and that is their unequal distribution among the States. In New England the circulation of the banks is now about $50,000,000, while in Ohio, a State with three fourths of the population of all New England, it is but $9,000,000. When you make the contrast with other States, it is still more marked. We, in the West, are now using the paper money of the New England and New York banks, and we are paying to the East the interest on $40,000,000, which we would much rather, in these times of difficulty, pay to the United States." A group of northeastern Republicans, led by Jacob Collamer

17. May 30, 1864, July 6, 1866, *CG*, 38.1, 2565, 39.1, 3610; Robert Stanley, *Dimensions of Law in the Service of Order: Origins of the Federal Income Tax, 1861–1913* (New York: Oxford Univ. Press, 1993), 15–23, 53–57, 96–99.

18. Leonard P. Curry, *Blueprint for Modern America: Nonmilitary Legislation of the First Civil War Congress* (Nashville, Tenn.: Vanderbilt Univ. Press, 1968), 197–206; Feb. 10, 1863, *CG*, 37.3, 843–44.

of Vermont, opposed Sherman and the bank bill. Despite their vigorous resistance, the measure became law in February 1863.[19]

For Sherman passage of the banking act was only the first step; completing this reform required that state bank notes be eliminated. He argued that two systems of circulating notes could not coexist. "I think the national banking system has been a grand and great success," he remarked, "and I would stake my reputation upon it; but it cannot undergo this system in competition with State banks that are now increasing their issue." Again his plans met with resistance. "I was entirely prepared," he noted in his memoirs, "not only to tax the circulation of state banks, but to tax such banks out of existence. But, while this feeling prevailed in the west, the opposite feeling prevailed in the New England and Middle States." Only in March 1865 did Sherman finally gain a prohibitive levy on state bank notes.[20]

Along with income tax and national banks, opposition to currency contraction was a third issue where Sherman brought together the interests of the Lake economy and a vision of national growth. The debate over contraction emerged during the first months of 1866. Eastern bankers favored drastically reducing the number of greenbacks in circulation, while western businessmen and Pennsylvania ironmasters advocated a slower pace of redemption. Westerners feared that Secretary of the Treasury Hugh McCulloch's plans to call in U.S. notes would check the rapid growth of their section. In the House vote of March 23, 1866, Republicans from New England and New York strongly backed contraction, while party members from the Midwest and Pennsylvania resisted the plan.[21]

Sherman tied his opposition to contraction to his strong belief in American growth. The Ohio Senator noted the gulf that divided him from Senator William Fessenden of Maine, an outspoken defender of McCulloch's policies. Sherman observed that Fessenden "interjects by saying we must look ahead. There is just the difference between him and me. I say the future for this country is hopeful, buoyant, joyous. We shall not have to beg of foreign nations, or even our own people, money within two or three years. Our national debt will be eagerly sought for, I have no doubt. I take a hopeful view of the future. I do not wish now to cripple the industry of the country by adopting the policy of the Secretary of the Treasury."[22]

19. Jan. 8, 1863, *CG*, 37.3, Appendix, 50; J. Medill to Sherman, Feb. 26, 1863, Sherman Papers; Curry, *Blueprint for Modern America*, 201–2; Heather Cox Richardson, *The Greatest Nation on Earth: Republican Economic Policies during the Civil War* (Cambridge, Mass.: Harvard Univ. Press, 1997), 80–91. In three articles that focus on this era, Glenn M. Linden documents the regional nature of voting on economic issues. See "'Radicals' and Economic Policies: The Senate, 1861–1873," *Journal of Southern History* 32 (May 1966): 189–99; "'Radicals' and Economic Policies: The House of Representatives, 1861–1873," *Civil War History* 13 (Mar. 1967): 51–65; "'Radical' Political and Economic Policies: The Senate, 1873–1877," ibid. 14 (Sep. 1968): 240–49.

20. Feb. 28, 1865, *CG*, 38.2, 1195; Sherman, *Recollections of Forty Years*, 1:284; Richardson, *Greatest Nation on Earth*, 84–102.

21. Robert P. Sharkey, *Money, Class, and Party: An Economic Study of Civil War and Reconstruction* (Baltimore: Johns Hopkins Univ. Press, 1967), 56–80.

22. Apr. 9, 1866, *CG*, 39.1, 1850; T. J. Porter to Sherman, Jan. 12, 1865, Sherman Papers.

Sherman's opposition to contraction must also be seen as part of the middle course he steered on currency questions—a policy that delighted his supporters in the Lake region. He adamantly opposed McCulloch's cautious approach, noting, "I am more hopeful than he is. He probably, like a good banker, as he is, wants a very large balance on hand. I have more confidence in the future, and am willing to trust the future." At the same time, Sherman loathed inflation. "No man of intelligence can reflect upon the present condition of public affairs," he remarked in 1864, "and especially the monetary affairs of this country, without feeling a sentiment of alarm. Every one will admit that the great evil of the times now is the inflation of paper money."[23]

The position Sherman staked out on the currency question reflected the constituency he served. He did not focus on the needs of the poor midwestern farmers. Those husbandmen, often resident in the Ohio Valley, adhered to the Democratic Party. They favored hard money before the Civil War and after the 1860s called for inflation. Rather Sherman represented the men and occasional woman on the make who took part in the Lake economy. These entrepreneurs wanted a steadily expanding currency that would facilitate their investments, but feared a flood of paper money that might disrupt their plans. The Ohio senator admirably served these successful farmers and businesspeople.[24]

John Sherman remained a powerful politician and an able representative of the Lake economy until his death in 1900. However, by the late 1860s Northern society and the Republican Party were changing, and so was Sherman's relationship to his party.

The rise of big business, the emergence of lawmakers who bowed to special interests, and the spread of corruption transformed the North and the Republican Party. In the years after the war the government spent, often with little or no oversight, vast sums on railroad building and other construction projects. By the 1870s the first trusts, which would dominate so many sectors of the economy, were emerging. The ensuing surge of corruption enraged and saddened many who had entered the Republican Party as reformers. Indiana congressman George Julian, who quit the Republican Party in 1872, remarked: "Our Civil Service was becoming a system of political prostitution. Roguery and plunder, born of the multiplied temptations which the war furnished, had stealthily crept into the management of public affairs. . . . While the issues of the war were retreating into the past the mercenary element of Republicanism had gradually secured the ascendancy, and completely appropriated the President."[25]

Sherman had not joined the Republicans as a reformer, and he did not leave the party as Julian, Sumner, and others did. Sherman had long viewed financial policies as a top priority, and he continued to focus on this area. He became chair of the Senate Finance

---

23. May 30, 1864, Apr. 9, 1866, *CG*, 38.1, 2563, 39.1, 1850.

24. On Democratic policies, see Irwin Unger, *The Greenback Era: A Social and Political History American Finance, 1865–1879* (Princeton: Princeton Univ. Press, 1964), 68–119.

25. George W. Julian, *Political Recollections, 1840 to 1872* (1884; rpt., New York: Negro Univ. Press, 1970), 330–31.

Committee in 1867, holding this post until 1877 when President Hayes appointed him secretary of the treasury. Much as he had done earlier, and to the delight of his constituents around the Lakes, Sherman steered a middle course between contraction and inflation. He charted a steady route despite strong winds that blew from silverites and gold bugs, greenbackers and conservative bankers. The coordinates that marked this path included the "Crime of 1873" which demonetized silver; the 1875 decision to keep $300 million of greenbacks in circulation; the Bland-Allison Act of 1878, which partially reversed the 1873 "Crime"; the resumption of specie payments in 1879; the Sherman Silver Purchase Act of 1890; and finally, the repeal of the Purchase Act, which had proved too inflationary. Sherman's course more resembled a ship tacking against contrary winds than a straight line. But the overall direction remained clear, and helped provide the growing nation with a stable but expanding money supply.[26]

Sherman bridled at the rampant corruption sweeping through his party. He supported civil service reform and resented the efforts of New York senator Roscoe Conkling and others to frustrate that reform. "It soon became manifest . . . ," Sherman observed, "that Senator Conkling intended to make a political contest against the policy of civil service reform inaugurated by President Hayes. . . . The motive of Mr. Conkling was hostility to President Hayes and his inborn desire to domineer." Sherman backed the appointment of the mugwump Theodore Roosevelt as collector of the port of New York, but was blocked by Conkling.[27]

The Ohio senator also distrusted monopolies and the power they exerted over the government. The Sherman Anti-Trust Act of 1890 was no aberration. It reflected Sherman's longstanding convictions. In 1866, for example, he had condemned the power of the Pennsylvania Central Railroad. "They compel the products of every portion of the West which reach Pittsburg to go over their road," he noted, "and they will not allow anybody else to build a railroad running from Pittsburg northwardly to get to New York or southwardly to get to Baltimore. They control, in a great measure, the legislation of Pennsylvania, and they lie right in the path of the commerce of this country." Sherman urged Congress to act, remarking, "It seems to me that since we have exercised some pretty strong powers, the time has arrived when, if we can, we should find in the Constitution some power to redress this evil."[28]

Sherman's reaction to the rise of big business makes clear that he wasn't simply a spokesman for the Lake economy; he was rather a defender of a Lake region characterized by the competitive enterprises that had flourished before the Civil War. In his memoirs he observed:

---

26. Nichols, "John Sherman," 185–88; Richard H. Timberlake Jr., "Repeal of Silver Monetization in the Late Nineteenth Century," *Journal of Money, Credit and Banking* 10 (Feb. 1978): 27–45; Allen Weinstein, "Was There a 'Crime of 1873'?: The Case of the Demonetized Dollar," *Journal of American History* 54 (Sep. 1967): 307–26.

27. Sherman, *Recollections of Forty Years*, 2:682.

28. May 29, 1866, *CG*, 39.1, 2872.

The tendency since the Civil War in every branch of industry has been to consolidate operations. To effect this, corporations have been created in most of the states and granted such liberal corporate powers, without respect to the nature of the business to be conducted, and with terms and privileges so favorable, that private enterprise without large capital cannot compete with them. Instead of small or moderate workshops, with a few hands, we now have great establishments with hundreds of employees, and all the capital of scores of stockholders under the control of a few men, and often of one man. . . . This power in the hands of a few is at this moment the disturbing element in many of our great industries.[29]

Opposition to monopolies led Sherman to criticize the high tariffs these industries secured. Sherman praised the Morrill tariff of 1861, but grew uneasy as rates increased. In 1865 he remarked: "I do not agree with my colleague that protection is now necessary. . . . We may hereafter with many commodities wish to invite foreign competition, as we do now with printing paper. Whenever the tendency in any manufacture is to monopoly or an unreasonable advance of prices, it may be politic to induce some competition." He particularly disliked duties that favored industry at the expense of agriculture. In his memoirs he reflected, "The real difficulty in our tariff laws is to avoid unequal and unjust discrimination in the objects of protection, made with a view to favor the productions of one state or section at the cost of another state or section. The dogma of some manufacturers, that raw materials should be admitted free of duty, is far more dangerous to the protective policy than the opposition of free traders." Sherman suggested that an impartial commission, rather than Congress, determine rates. He added, "Whenever the tendency of a monopoly is to prevent mutual competition, and to advance prices for any articles embraced in our tariff laws, the duty on the article should be at once reduced or repealed."[30]

Sherman also fought a rearguard battle to save the income tax. "By the terms of the then existing law it expired in 1872," he recollected in his memoirs. "I urged as strongly as I could its retention at least until the time expired, but it was repealed. I then believed, and now believe, that a moderate income tax, levied on all incomes above the sum of $1,000, or above a sum that will supply the ordinary wants of an average family in the United States with the necessaries of life, should be levied . . . according to the exigencies of the public service."[31]

John Sherman helped remake his world, but the results were not always the ones he had foreseen. He was an astute, respected politician and an outspoken nationalist. Above all, he was a spokesman for the Great Lakes region, the most rapidly growing part of the North. He helped lay the foundation for the development of this area by pushing for

---

29. Sherman, *Recollections of Forty Years*, 1:192.
30. Feb. 13, 1865, *CG*, 38.2, 774; Sherman, *Recollections of Forty Years*, 1:191–93.
31. Stanley, *Dimensions of Law*, 53–58; Sherman, *Recollections of Forty Years*, 1:307.

internal improvements: a sound national banking system, a secure currency that met the needs of entrepreneurs, moderate tariffs, and a tax structure that lifted the burden from the less wealthy citizens. Despite occasional setbacks, Sherman was extraordinarily successful in achieving his legislative goals. He was less successful in securing the country or even the region he wanted. The companies that came to dominate the Lake economy were not the small, entrepreneurial enterprises that Sherman so admired; they were the large corporations that controlled markets and corrupted lawmakers.

A review of John Sherman's career allows us to reflect on the causes of the Civil War and the Second American Revolution. If Sherman was representative of the early Republican Party, then the most prominent voices in this Northern party were not those of the reformers. Rather, the most influential leaders were individuals with a vision of economic development. While that vision demanded the West be the exclusive province of free labor, it regarded Southern slavery as a secondary issue that would be addressed by later generations. Studying Sherman also sheds light on the transformation of the United States. The Second American Revolution did not simply reflect the wishes of the North or the Republicans. Representatives of the Northeast often resisted these far-reaching changes. Explaining John Sherman suggests that this great Revolution was driven by the goals and representatives of the most rapidly growing area within the North: the Great Lakes region.[32]

---

32. These themes are elaborated in Egnal, "Beards Were Right," 30–56.

State Policies and the Public Response to Institutionalization

Caring for the Insane in Late-Nineteenth-Century Ohio

Deborah Marinski

In the late nineteenth century, the state government and public opinion in Ohio played an important part in the treatment and institutionalization of the insane. Asylum physicians and superintendents believed that the goal of recovery through the traditional methods of moral treatment were best supported in humanitarian institutions; therefore, they appealed to the state administration and the taxpayers for money to keep the daily routines functioning and to make necessary construction or supply changes. In order to legitimize their work inside the institution, they needed the open support of the public and to follow the recommendations of investigative boards, such as the Board of State Charities.

In Ohio, the Board of State Charities was first organized in 1867 by a legislative act that established the purpose for visiting and understanding the management and arrangements of state institutions. The first Board dissolved in 1872 but reorganized in 1875 to "investigate the whole system of public charities and correctional institutions of the State, examine into the condition and management thereof, especially of prisons, jails, infirmaries, public hospitals and asylums."[1] Members of the Board included politicians of political parties, reformers, physicians, and the state governor. They were charged with the responsibility of inspecting and making recommendations for the betterment of public institutions in construction, economy, and administration in order to provide the most up-to-date treatment for inmates and to satisfy the demands of the public. It is through the reports of this Board that the positive elements of Ohio's institutions are

---

1. "Eighth Annual Report of the Board of State Charities" (1883), 5, Ohio University Government Documents Department, Athens, Ohio (hereafter OU Government Documents); and Elliot Howard Gilkey, *The Ohio Hundred Year-Book: A Handbook of the Public Men and Public Institutions of Ohio from the Formation of the Northwest Territory to July 1, 1901* (Columbus, Ohio: Fred J. Heer, 1901), 353–54.

Ohio History, Vol. 114 © 2007 by The Kent State University Press

evident, as are the problems with treating the insane that led to new ideas for reform (including commitment procedures, state care, the role of the government and politics in institutionalization, hospital construction, and asylum management issues).

During the late nineteenth century, insane asylums became critical areas of discussion among superintendents, psychiatrists, state government officials, and the public because there was a constant need for institutions to treat and care for the insane throughout Ohio. As a report from the Dayton Insane Asylum shows, hospitals were continuously built and improved: "This is a most important and interesting field with plenty of room for advancement; and as Ohio is building one large asylum, and if she affords accommodations for all her insane, will soon be compelled to build another." The purpose of asylum building according to S. S. Schultz, superintendent of the Hospital for the Insane in Danville, Pennsylvania, was "to provide suitable, reasonable accommodation, and to do it so economically and at such a per capita outlay, that none who require it will need to suffer because there is not enough of it." Hospitals for the insane needed to be built, and they needed to be built in a cost-effective manner. During the late nineteenth century, asylum building in Ohio followed the cottage system (which utilized detached buildings) because of the accommodation of a greater number of patients, the lower building expenses, the lighter cost of daily functions, and the belief that this style best fit with moral, humane treatment.[2]

In Ohio the size and expenditures of insane institutions built on the cottage system were more economic and less extravagant than the traditional Kirkbride model. According to the eighth annual report of the Board of State Charities, the building of the Toledo Insane Asylum was a movement away from the "palaces" of the Kirkbride years toward a more cost-effective complex that would house a larger quantity of patients. This budget did not mean that the Toledo Insane Asylum would suffer from lack of funds or lower quality but would "gain rather than lose in all essential requirements." Increasing the size of the institution and the number of patients the hospital contained might lead one to believe that the fees of construction and maintenance would swell into the thousands; however, the Board of State Charities maintained that the per capita price at Toledo would be a quarter of the cost at the Columbus State Hospital. Also, "The new asylum will not only include and improve, as we believe, all that is best in the past, but it will do so at a cost so largely decreased as to demonstrate more fully than ever before the possibility, as well as the desirability, of State care for all the increasing number of the insane." In Ohio the Toledo hospital was the first built on the cottage plan, but according to a statement in the Columbus annual report, it was the hospital located in Massillon that was the culmination of positive economic factors and health care in one cottage-designed asylum: "it is

2. "Thirty-Second Annual Report of the Board of Trustees and Officers of the Dayton Asylum for the Insane" (1886), 7, Ward M. Canaday Center for Special Collections, Toledo, Ohio; S. S. Schultz, Superintendent of the Hospital for the Insane in Danville, Pennsylvania, "On Asylum Location, Construction and Sanitation," *American Journal of Insanity* 41 (Oct. 1884): 207; and W. W. Godding, "Aspects and Outlook of Insanity in America," *American Journal of Insanity* 47 (July 1890): 7–8.

the question of how well they are cared for, and from this point of view have arisen such institutions as Toledo, Gallipolis, and the now most perfect for the accomplishment of the object at which we aim, the new Massillon State Hospital."[3] The concerns for smart economics in the construction of the cottage-style insane asylums were only one part of the broader treatment of inmates, which was secondary to the appropriate care provided.

At both the old and new hospitals in Ohio, humane, moral treatment was the number one concern of the physicians and staff who played into the physical structure of asylums and the relationship between the doctors, state government, and public. The superintendent at Toledo exemplified this priority list, arguing, "Our first obligation, of course, is to the patients confined to our care" who needed food, clothing, shelter, and kind treatment so that "every effort is put forth, both medical and moral, for their betterment." The second concern at Toledo was to "the people whose philanthropy supports the institution."[4] W. W. Godding, superintendent of the Government Hospital for the Insane, wrote that hospital provisions "shall accomplish the largest result in the restoration to health in curable cases, the element of expense being here a subordinate one, and for the remainder, such comfortable provision at a moderate expenditure as shall insure safety to the community and humane care to the sufferer."[5] The cottage plan was considered essential to humane, moral treatment because of the economic and medical use of detached wards and buildings.

Insane asylums constructed on the cottage system supported the idea of segregating different types of insane patients (such as the curable, chronic, epileptic, criminal, or inebriate) at a more acceptable cost than constructing and staffing entirely independent institutions. The debate over the separation contributed to the rapid acceptance of institutions being built with a variety of buildings with diverse uses. Godding argued that "The requirement today is provision for all with reasonable expenditure in the construction of comfortable homes on flexible plans, varied to suit the particular class and condition of the insane for which they are intended."[6] In the traditional aggregate or Kirkbride brand institutions, the division of inmates could be modified by adding new buildings designed with the specific classifications in mind.[7] The psychiatrists, government, and public viewed cottage-style institutions as a means of providing the best, moral care of the insane patients and, throughout the late nineteenth century, as a means of addressing the issues of expenditure and lavishness.

3. "Annual Report, Board of State Charities" (1883), 10, 11, OU Government Documents; and "Sixty-First Annual Report of the Board of Trustees and Officers of the Columbus Asylum for the Insane" (1899), 17, Ohio Historical Society (hereafter OHS). The Massillon State Hospital was built on the cottage plan.

4. "Eleventh Annual Report of the Board of Trustees and Officers of the Toledo State Hospital" (1894), 8, Canaday Center.

5. W. W. Godding, "The State in the Care of Its Insane," *American Journal of Insanity* 46 (Jan. 1890): 314.

6. W. W. Godding, "Progress in Provision for the Insane, 1844–1884," *American Journal of Insanity* 41 (Oct. 1884): 145.

7. "Annual Report, Columbus" (1899), 17, OHS.

Various people had a voice in the construction, financial arrangements, and management of institutions for the insane in Ohio. The doctors and administrators had to run
the asylums and use their therapy knowledge to heal the mad patients; the government
appropriated funds for construction and daily operations; and the people paid for the
institutions through their taxes and philanthropic donations. Insane asylums in Ohio
had been constructed using "public moneys" appropriated by the state legislature. Once
received, the funds were dispersed by the superintendent and officers according to the
designated purpose. Through their "unhesitatingly appropriated" financial support of
institutions, society supported the work that insane asylums did for the inmates. According to a report by the Columbus Insane Asylum, the public viewed the "public institutions of the state as monuments to their generosity, and look with pride and pleasure
upon their beauties"; furthermore, "these institutions thus constructed and organized
have for many years enjoyed a large share of public confidence." Some reasons for this
confidence included the "benevolence and integrity" of trustees and superintendents,
high recovery rates, better health of others inmates, the architecture of the asylums, the
transfer of patients from jails and almshouses, the study of psychology and psychiatry,
and the constant construction of new institutions making more people familiar with the
institutions and their patients' treatments.[8] The growing awareness of insane asylums
led to foreign and domestic criticism.

The "organized condemnation" that came from the visibility of insane asylums
sparked accusations that American institutions were "unscientific and selfish in character." Many of these allegations and criticisms came from individuals from different
countries who considered the institutions within their own countries superior because
they were smaller and functioned more economically. Orpheus Everts, superintendent
of the Cincinnati Sanitarium, wrote an educational paper published in the *American
Journal of Insanity* titled "The American System of Public Provision for the Insane, and
Despotism in Lunatic Asylums," whereby he explained the other points of view, but
then refuted these positions and explained why American institutions were different
but not inferior. Those against American insane asylums viewed them as "too large, too
palatial, too expensively constructed; disagreeably monotonous in linear extension, an
offensively prison-like in aspect." Everts further argued, "That large hospital structures,
as compared with much smaller, are conspicuously economical, can not be denied. So
that, when considered in relation to territory, population, facilities for transportation
and other present and prospective circumstances, it can not well be said that American
hospitals for the insane are injudiciously capacious." According to Everts, insane hospitals "succored and sustained the helpless, and protected society from the dangerous,
yet irresponsible" and influenced public support of the institutions. Also, because of the

8. Orpheus Everts, "The American System of Public Provision for the Insane, and Despotism in Lunatic Asylums," *American Journal of Insanity* 38(Oct. 1881): 114–15; and "Forty-Third Annual Report of the Board of Trustees
and Officers of the Columbus Asylum for the Insane" (1881), 6, Canaday Center.

positive effect institutions had on the health of the insane, Everts maintained that "we can not conscientiously and intelligently say their cost, as a system, has been too great." Everts believed that large hospitals embraced all classes medically and financially unlike smaller, specialized hospitals; therefore, the cost and size of asylums was justified.[9]

Other condemnations about insane institutions stemmed from accusations of abuse, brutal punishment, and heroic medicine. Everts argued that, "More insane persons are ill-treated, injudiciously restrained, neglected and otherwise abused while among friends in the family relation, than suffer from similar treatment in the least reputable insane hospital in America, proportionately considered." The patients were provided a better environment in the institution than in the home. Furthermore, Everts explained that "a great source of error seriously affecting the hospital reputation lies hidden in the fact that the changed condition, circumstances, needs, sensibilities and propensities of the insane are forgotten by the outside world whenever hospital doors are closed upon them." The charges of brutality were often overblown by the press and "all the good that is daily done for these unfortunates—the weary watching day and night over the irritable insane, the thought, labor and money expended to ameliorate their sad condition—all this is forgotten, while one fatal accident is remembered against us as a sample of the daily routine of the institution." Everts maintained that cruelty was not a daily occurrence but was used as an accusation to discredit the institutionalization of insane individuals and the work of asylum physicians. The physicians and superintendents introduced methods to combat the claims of violence against patients.[10]

In order to contest public prejudice and charges of brutality some institutions allowed the public to visit.[11] Through open visitation the daily function of institutions and treatment of patients would be exposed to public inspection and opinion. According to the superintendent of the Cleveland Insane Asylum, it was when institutions were closed to the public that "very grave suspicions, based on the wildest imagination, are entertained in regard to the treatment of patients." In order to make the public see to positive elements of asylum life, at Cleveland the superintendent wrote:

> The less mystery—another name for ignorance—there is associated with an institution of this character, the better for all concerned. Let the public have a correct ideas of our architectural arrangements, and other facilities for treating and managing the insane, of our sanitary methods, and the means we possess for the promotion of their comfort, by a practical acquaintance with the same, and we shall soon find

9. Everts, "American System," 116–17, 119–20, 126, 128; and "Annual Report, Cleveland" (1882), 13, OHS.

10. Everts, "American System," 133, 129; "Thirty-Ninth Annual Report of the Board of Directors and Superintendent of the Longview Hospital" (1898), 10, Canaday Center; "Twenty-Eighth Annual Report of the Board of Trustees and Officers of the Cleveland Asylum for the Insane" (1882), 13, 17, OHS; and "Thirteenth Annual Report of the Board of State Charities" (1888), 18, OHS.

11. "Thirty-Eighth Annual Report of the Board of Directors and Superintendent of the Longview Hospital" (1897), 11, Canaday Center.

that much has been done to neutralize the traditional horrors of the ancient mad-house. What is needed by the public is light on these points, but light yields but little benefit when placed under a bushel. Let the public see us, and know us as we are, and the result can but be beneficial to it and to us.[12]

Public visits were to be monitored so as to not allow people to visit the institution solely "to see the crazy folks," which may disrupt the patients and employee performance. Appropriate guests included the family and friends of a committed inmate, members of the medical profession or charity organizations, pastors or church leaders, and government officials.[13] Allowing people to go into an asylum would show the physical, medical, and managerial aspects of institutional life.

The main argument against American insane asylums was the "unparalleled despotism" of management which critics argued resulted in greater physical abuse of patients. According to Everts this viewpoint was erroneous; hospitals simply could not be effectively governed and patients properly and swiftly treated under the proposed "aristocracy of hospital officials of various grades, who, appointed by American methods, would become either more despotic and irresponsible by combining in a common interest, or disastrously weak and inefficient by dissensions and antagonism."[14] Even though the political and personal issues of power and control would lead to an unfavorable healing environment and damage the moral and humanitarian treatment of insane patients, there was a demand for state control of institutions for these unfortunate members of society.

The insistence on state direction was based on the notion that the state had a duty and a responsibility to protect the less fortunate from themselves and the greater whole of society, while at the same time giving the insane, criminal, epileptic, or poor the essentials needed to better themselves and their situations.[15] State care was a crucial concern for the superintendents, physicians, inmates, and public for two interconnected reasons: it was the state's duty to ensure humanitarian care and therapy to the insane and also to protect society from these dejected elements of society and the threat of insanity. The superintendent of the Columbus Insane Asylum maintained that "it is the duty of the State, besides its laudable efforts in caring for these unfortunates when the victim of disease, to protect itself from the burden by preventing the development of as many cases as possible."[16] Superintendents of insane hospitals "have put themselves on record again and again as demanding that the State should make the best possible provision for every

12. "Twenty-Third Annual Report of the Board of Trustees and Officers of the Cleveland Asylum for the Insane" (1877), 22, OHS.

13. "Thirty-Fifth Annual Report of the Board of Trustees and Officers of the Cleveland Asylum for the Insane" (1888), 25, OHS; and "Seventeenth Annual Report of the Board of State Charities" (1892), 350–55, OU Government Documents.

14. Everts, "American System," 134.

15. "Twenty-Ninth Annual Report of the Board of Trustees and Officers of the Cleveland Asylum for the Insane" (1883), 33, OHS.

16. "Fifty-Fifth Annual Report of the Columbus Asylum for the Insane" (1893), 11–12, Canaday Center.

insane person within its jurisdiction, whatever the form of the disease, acute or chronic, curable or incurable."[17] Superintendents, as well as the public, considered state responsibility for the insane essential to providing humane, moral treatment and the protection of society as a whole.

The public reaction to insanity was to support the state government in its attempts to control the construction and function of insane asylums as a humanitarian answer to mental illness. The state government maintained that "the dictates of humanity demand that the insane shall be amply provided with everything which medical science has determined to be essential to the recovery of those who are recoverable, as well as for the proper care, comfort, and amelioration of those who remain unrecovered."[18] Society defended the government's role in institutional life as a means of preserving traditional ideals of humanity by arguing that "remedial treatment for a disease which renders a person incapable of self-direction and fulfilling his relations to society, comes within the legitimate scope of statutory enactment."[19] Because of the wave of social and medical demands for state care of the insane, a variety of lunacy laws were passed throughout the country.

Lunacy laws were intended to protect and serve society, establish the rights of the insane individual, and referred primarily to those acts dealing with commitment procedures and state provisions for the insane. While the social rights of the insane included "the right not to be meddled with and annoyed one jot more than is necessary, not to have a private misfortune made a matter of public discussion; not to be dragged before courts and juries with their superfluous inquiries into all the details of family life," the medical and moral rights of the insane were "the right of being protected against the danger of the disease and of being cured as speedily as possible."[20] Personal rights were not defined by central laws pertaining to all states of the union but determined on a state-by-state case.

Each state had the responsibility of making its own lunacy laws and providing care and treatment for the insane population; therefore, there was a wide diversity of laws dealing with commitment, organization, and management of institutions. In the 1890s there was a call for uniformity in commitment procedures; several different methods were utilized throughout the country, some of which were considered unfair, unscientific, and outdated. Stephen Smith wrote, "the methods of commitment in many States, now so defective, and so devoid of accuracy, and, in some instances, of humanity, would be greatly improved and brought more in harmony with the present state of knowledge of the insane and their proper care."[21] In his article, "Unification of the Laws of the States Relating to the Com-

17. Godding, "Progress in Provision," 134–35.

18. Carlos F. MacDonald, "State Care and State Maintenance for the Dependent Insane in the State of New York," *American Journal of Insanity* 53 (July 1896): 71.

19. John Charles Bucknill, "The Care of the Insane and Their Legal Control," *American Journal of Insanity* 37 (July 1880): 48–49.

20. "The Rights of the Insane," *American Journal of Insanity* 39 (Apr. 1883): 415–16, 430.

21. Stephen Smith, "Unification of the Laws of the States Relating to the Commitment of the Insane," *American Journal of Insanity* 49 (Oct. 1892): 158.

mitment of the Insane" (*American Journal of Insanity*), Smith described the multitude of commitment procedures utilized throughout the states and territories.

The first method of commitment was through the decision of the justice of the peace, who may or may not use the testimony of physicians, family members, or friends in his consideration. This process was practiced in five states and led to commitment without a trial. Smith wrote that this system "is in every respect inadequate and incompetent. On a justice of the peace, an inferior civil officer, is imposed the responsible duty of determining one of the most difficult questions in medical science." The justice was deemed "uninformed" about the causes, symptoms, and treatment of insanity and therefore should not have the power to consign a person to an institution.[22]

The second type of commitment came through the decision of a judge. (It was used in two territories and eighteen states, including Ohio.) This course was determined by a probate, county, circuit, or supreme court judge who had been elected by the people. According to Smith, the use of elected judges "marks an advance of public opinion in the direction of giving more character and more precision to the process." The variations of this practice included the use of patient or medical testimony. In several states the accused person would be summoned to court and judged without a professional medical examination, in essence, treated "like an ordinary offender." In other states the judge was required to visit the insane person in his private dwelling, which could influence the judge's decision but had "no practical value."[23]

A third way of committing a patient was through a trial with a jury of laymen, which was utilized in five states. Smith felt that "this method of procedure is essentially that adopted for minor criminals in police courts and has but one element that gives the patient any certainty of being dealt with judiciously. This is the requirement that he shall be examined by qualified physicians, and that their testimony shall form a necessary part of the procedure."[24] The failure to use physicians as part of the jury made commitment based on decision of laymen unmerited.

The fourth commitment procedure was a trial, but the jury was made up of both laymen and physicians. Three states employed this method, which Smith maintained, "though not very radical, still shows the trend of public thought in the direction of a scientific and clearly rational method of treating the insane." This process made sure that the accused person received a fair trial based on medical findings.[25]

The state of Delaware demonstrated the fifth form of commitment; however, its method was not much different than the decision by a judge. In Delaware the decision was made by the chancellor of the state after he had been personally petitioned by family,

---

22. Smith, "Unification of the Laws," 162. The five states that used the justice of the peace included Virginia, West Virginia, North Carolina, Tennessee, and Indiana.

23. Ibid., 162–66. The eighteen states were Louisiana, Florida, Rhode Island, Wisconsin, Oregon, Washington, Nevada, Michigan, Idaho, South Carolina, Missouri, New Jersey, California, Alabama, Arkansas, Ohio, Montana, and Massachusetts, and the two territories were Utah and Arizona.

24. Ibid., 166–67. The five states were Maryland, Mississippi, Colorado, Texas, and Wyoming.

25. Ibid., 168–69. The three states were Illinois, Kansas, and Minnesota.

friends, or a physician. Because of the power that one man without medical training had over the future of the person who was charged with insanity, this method was increasingly archaic and its application deteriorating.[26]

The sixth form of commitment was based on a commission that was appointed by a judge (a common practice when dealing with people below the poverty level). This route was used in five states, and Smith believed this system "not unlike that by a jury. It is entirely destitute of that accuracy which should characterize such proceedings, and is liable to subject the patient and friends to injudicious and disturbing treatment."[27] Because a judge appointed a commission to investigate claims of insanity that did not include medical professionals, the resulting verdict could be incorrect.

The seventh method was exercised in three states and one territory with resolutions made by the Commissioners of Insanity, who were a county based group that decided the matters on all cases of insanity. According to Smith, the members of this assembly had "high character" and superior qualifications because of the "permanency of the commission." Also, the "method of conducting the proceeding" was an important factor in determining the outcome of the investigations in a professional and medical way.[28]

By selecting the best points from various state laws, Smith proposed a merger of procedures centered on evaluations and certifications by trained physicians. Providing the most fair and honest practice of commitment through lunacy laws would "demand that care and treatment which will most certainly and effectually restore the curable to health and will best promote the well-being and usefulness of the incurable."[29] With the increasing emphasis placed on the role of the physician in commitment, there was another practice preferred by the family and friends of the insane: voluntary commitment.

Patients who willingly checked themselves into asylums could not be kept for more than a few days and were free to check themselves out of the institution. Voluntary commitment allowed patients and their families freedom from the public humiliation that often resulted from trials and verdicts and showed that hospital inmates were willing to seek the help of the physicians and institutions and would dispute the public prejudices against insane asylums that were "convincing the public that while the doors open freely inward they are as feely opened outward."[30] If done early enough, it also could give the patient a greater chance at recovery. In Ohio the idea of voluntary commitment supported the establishment of a temporary hospital where patients could receive immediate treatment without full commitment to a lunatic asylum.[31]

26. Ibid., 168, 169.

27. Ibid., 169–70. The five states were Rhode Island, Connecticut, New Mexico, Kentucky, Georgia. In Rhode Island this method was used only in certain cases but still without medical testimony.

28. Ibid., 170–72. Iowa, Maine, and Nebraska were the three states, and the Dakotas were the territory.

29. Stephen Smith, "Proposed Change of the Legal Status of the Insane, In Accordance with Our Present Knowledge of the Nature of Insanity, for the Purpose of Securing for Them More Rational and Efficient Treatment," *American Journal of Insanity* 50 (Jan. 1894): 331.

30. "Notes and Comments," *Journal of Insanity* 54 (July 1897): 147.

31. "Sixty-Third Annual Report of the Board of Trustees and Officers of the Columbus State Hospital" (1901), 14, OHS; and "Twenty-Seventh Annual Report of the Ohio Board of State Charities" (1902), 13, OU Government Documents.

The second area of commitment methods that lunacy laws dealt with was the organization, management, and funding of institutions. In his article "The Distribution and Care of the Insane in the United States," Judson B. Andrews provided a summary of the possible types of institutions and their organizational structures, which included "State, county, municipal, private and incorporate asylums." State institutions were managed by the board of trustees who reported to the state legislature. County and municipal asylums were responsible to the local officials who appointed a committee to manage the institutions. The incorporated asylums were private institutions that were held accountable by "hospital boards."[32] The medical community generally agreed that state institutions were better equipped, financially supported, and medically staffed than county or municipal institutions.

Andrews composed a second article titled "State versus County Care" in which he addressed the superiority of state care, something that was increasingly important in the late nineteenth century as an area of discussion among the medical community, state officials, and the public. According to Andrews there were three reasons why "State asylums and state care are superior to that furnished by the county," including better buildings, superior organization, and finer conduct within the asylum.[33] First, the structures that housed the patients were larger and allowed the segregation of the sexes and the classes of insanity in different wards; they had more modern heating, lighting, and ventilation; their location supported a superior water system and access to cities and transportation; and they had more acreage for farming, outside recreation, and for various shops and buildings for institutional supplies and self-sufficiency. Secondly, the organization and management was controlled by men of "high character, without pecuniary interest in the erection [of the building] or in furnishing supplies," who were not paid for their service as members of the board of managers. Also, the superintendent, assistant physicians, matrons, and stewards had more experience and higher education. Finally, the conduct of the institution was supported by qualified attendants, adequate food supplies, appropriate seasonal clothing, and suitable medical treatment through moral therapy.[34] Even with these reasons supporting state care there were some people defending county asylums.

Two arguments in favor of county care predominated: First, insane patients sent to state institutions were further separated from their friends and families who could not visit because they could not afford the travel expenses. Second, state asylums cost too much money for the state and taxpayers. According to Andrews, both of these reasons had little ground to stand on, arguing that several state asylums were located "with reference to ease of access from the district which it serves; while county asylums are located upon the county farms, which in many instances are removed from the main lines of

32. Judson B. Andrews, "The Distribution and Care of the Insane in the United States," *American Journal of Insanity 44* (Oct. 1887): 195.

33. Judson B. Andrews, "State Versus County Care," *American Journal of Insanity* 45 (Jan. 1889): 397.

34. Andrews, "State Versus County Care," 398–99.

travel, and are really more difficult to access." As for the higher cost of state asylums, Andrews contended that county asylums sent the more difficult and expensive cases to larger state institutions where they were provided a higher quality of care and treatment. Stephen Smith argued that "with the same character and quality of care, the counties with their small numbers are not able to keep their patients any more cheaply than the State institutions with their large numbers. If the State were willing to lower its standard of care to the county limit, it could certainly keep its patients as cheaply."[35] Another doctor echoed these sentiments, stating, "in every instance where local authorities have undertaken to establish and maintain an institution for the insane on a curative or hospital basis, like that of a State hospital, the standard of care has in nor respect equaled, even approximately, that which the poorest of the State institutions affords."[36] The insane patients who were sent to county institutions remained there until they could secure a place in a state institution where they would receive more humane, moral treatment.

In Ohio, state care prevailed over county care, but there was still a demand for proper provisions for any person who needed the aid of the state or county. The idea that "the state accepts the responsibility for maintenance of all its citizens who are unable to maintain themselves on the accepted minimum standard of living" was a traditional concept established in Ohio with the first "poor law" in 1790 (when Ohio was still part of the Northwest Territory). This law dominated lunacy legislation in Ohio through the early twentieth century; however, if there was not a place in the state system, counties were responsible for providing some level of care.[37] The second constitution of Ohio passed in 1851 declared that "institutions for the benefit of the insane, blind and deaf and dumb, shall always be fostered and supported by the state; and be subject to such regulations as may be prescribed by the General Assembly."[38] This law did not mention county care, which led to a humanitarian problem in the nineteenth century. Almshouses and prisons at the county level were considered barbaric, cruel, and inhumane establishments, which increased the demand for more state provisions and institutions. It was not until June 30, 1903, that the legislature passed a law stipulating care and treatment for all insane individuals in state institutions.[39]

Asylum management by doctors and government officials was of growing concern throughout the late nineteenth century, especially in Ohio. Joseph Workman, former su-

35. Ibid., 401–3.

36. MacDonald, "State Care and State Maintenance," 73; P. M. Wise, "State Care of the Insane," *American Journal of Insanity* 54 (Jan. 1898): 373–84; and "Twentieth Annual Report of the Board of State Charities" (1895), 8, OHS.

37. Aileen Elizabeth Kennedy, *The Ohio Poor Law and Its Administration* (Chicago: Univ. of Chicago Press, 1934), viii–24.

38. The Second Constitution of the State of Ohio, found in Gilkey, *The Ohio Hundred Year-Book*, 98.

39. "Thirtieth Annual Report of the Ohio Board of State Charities" (1905), 54; "Annual Report of the Ohio Board of State Charities" (1902), 11; "Sixteenth Annual Report of the Board of State Charities" (1891), 27–28, all found in OU Government Documents. "Transactions of the Thirty-Fifth Annual Meeting of the Ohio State Medical Society, 1880, 43, OHS; and "Address by Governor Asa Bushnell," *The Ohio Bulletin of Charities and Corrections* (1898), 3–5, OHS.

perintendent of the Toronto Asylum for the Insane, argued, "It is my belief that no small proportion of American asylums are too much governed, and that some of them have been sadly misgoverned." Several problems included the possession of power, "uncertainty of the tenure of office by superintendents," and "interference of the governors or trustees of asylums."[40] These issues were visible in the mismanagement of Ohio institutions that stemmed from the influence of political parties on appointments. H. C. Rutter, superintendent of the Athens Asylum for the Insane, wrote, "The asylums of Ohio have been made the football of political parties, and the accession to power of either political party in the State has too often been signalized by a complete change of administration."[41] The problem of political spoils and its institutions was a not only prevalent in Ohio. It was a national concern for asylum physicians and members of the Association of Superintendents, who saw several superintendents forced out because of spoils.

Dr. Godding wrote a brief statement about A. B. Richardson and his expulsion from his position because of the spoils system, attesting to the support Richardson had throughout the country and the negative impact of his dismissal on Ohio: "We have just lost Dr. Richardson in this way. No, it is not we but Ohio that has lost a man that she can ill afford to lose. When a good man is turned down in that way, he will still find work for humanity and do it with his might. Such a man is never lost. We shall hear from Dr. Richardson again."[42] Another nationally renowned physician from Ohio, Richard Gundry, who was superintendent of three different hospitals in Ohio throughout his career, was relieved of his leadership position "because his political affinities did not correspond with those of the newly elected governor." The partisanship and spoils system damaged Ohio's institutional security and effectiveness, giving the state a notorious reputation throughout the country.[43]

The practice of appointing men through their service to a political party—instead of their experience, education, and ability to control a massive institution filled with a particular group of people—led to a variety of institutional problems. Because of the threat of losing one's position with each election, superintendents and physicians could increase the number of recovered patients, attempt different therapy treatments, or cut back or increase spending to show their value to the current or new administration.[44] Godding expressed the concern he had for politicians controlling the medical atmosphere of the institution: "When a hospital for the insane becomes a part of the political spoils and its officers are appointed mainly with reference to their efficient services in

40. Joseph Workman, "Asylum Management," *American Journal of Insanity* 38 (July 1881): 5, 6–9; and "Transactions of the Thirty-Fifth Annual Meeting of the Ohio State Medical Society" (1880), 41, OHS.

41. "Review of State Annual Reports for Ohio," *American Journal of Insanity* 38 (July 1881): 91.

42. Godding, "Aspects and Outlook of Insanity," 8.

43. Richard Gundry Obituary, *American Journal of Insanity* 49 (Oct. 1892): 365; C. E. Wright, "Large or Small Hospital for the Insane—Which?" *American Journal of Insanity* 47 (July 1890): 43–51; "Annual Report, Board of State Charities" (1891), 9–13; and "Fourth Annual Report of the Board of State Charities" (1879), 16–21, OHS.

44. G. Alder Blumer, "The Commitment, Detention, Care and Treatment of the Insane in America," *American Journal of Insanity* 50 (Apr. 1894): 538–56.

the late campaign, and when at the next election these men are rotated out to give place to another set of political healers (heelers?), if possible worse than the first, what hope is there for the institutions or their unfortunate inmates? Ward politicians married to pot-house politicians and out of that union came forth lunatic doctors! Heaven save the mark, and God save their patients!" At the Athens Hospital for the Insane it was argued that "there may be science in politics, but politics and medical science can not be made into a successful mixture. The combination invariably leads to the sacrifice of the latter, for politics knows no interest paramount to its own." Another area of concern was that institutions would not receive adequate appropriations for improvement of old hospitals or for the construction of new hospitals. According to a report from the Cleveland Insane Asylum, politics failed to financially support institutions but "the reorganization, or tearing to pieces, of these institutions, as a rule, every two years, so far as their management is concerned, is what politics does do." Also, public opinion could be affected economically and socially by the appointment of inept men.[45]

The problems of political influence and the strain of financially sustaining the institutions led to weaker public confidence and less support of insane asylums. Several superintendents gave their opinions as to what should be done to improve the lagging relationship between asylum doctors and society, including defining the responsibility of the psychiatrist and spurring monetary support of the institutions. Godding argued that it was up to the professional organizations, like the National Conference of Charities and Correction, to appeal to the public and encourage their humanitarian support of institutions by demonstrating the positive results of institutional treatment. Godding wrote, "the burden once resolutely taken up, continuously borne, and bearing fruits in the improved condition of these afflicted ones, it will no longer seem a burden, a twice blessed, ennobling charity rather, that 'Blesseth him that gives, and him that takes.'" Orpheus Everts wrote that the relationship between doctors and society was an educational issue. According to Everts, physicians had an "official" responsibility to inform and educate the public on the causes of, treatments of, hospitals for, and prevention of insanity "by which society may be, or believe itself to be, benefited medicinally, and hygienically: and faithfully and skillfully apply their knowledge in the performance of official functions." If the public recognized the positive outcome of asylum treatment and the benefits they received from insanity education, they would financially and expressively support the institutions.[46]

Another attempt to satisfy the public was through the creation of lunacy commis-

45. "Proceedings of the Association," *American Journal of Insanity* 48 (July 1891): 104; Godding, "Aspects and Outlook," 8; "Sixteenth Annual Report of the Board of Trustees and Officers of the Athens Asylum for the Insane" (1889), 10, Canaday Center; "Thirtieth Annual Report of the Board of Trustees and Officers of the Cleveland Asylum for the Insane" (1884), 17, OHS; "Notes and Comments," *American Journal of Insanity* 54 (July 1897): 143–44; and "Annual Report, Cleveland" (1879), 12–16, OHS.

46. W. W. Godding, "The State in the Care of Its Insane," *Journal of Insanity* 46 (Jan. 1890): 325; Orpheus Everts, "Obligations of the Medical Profession to Society and the Insane," *American Journal of Insanity* 47 (Oct. 1890): 123; and "Address of Governor Andrew L. Harris," "The Ohio Bulletin of Charities and Correction Containing the Proceedings of the Seventh Annual State Conference of Charities and Correction" (1907), 9, OHS.

sions. These groups of men served as inspectors, counselors, advisers, publishers, and informers to promote "higher standards of excellence" by doctors, hospitals, and the government. Henry P. Stearns wrote in his paper titled "Lunacy Commissions" that these groups would be permanent and influential sources of publication that would "inspire confidence in reference to the utility and importance of hospital care and treatment." Lunacy commissions attended to the interests of the hospital, the government, and the public.[47] Through the aid of the professional committees, doctor's prevention and education programs, and the establishment of lunacy commissions, the public was provided with valuable information to encourage their physical and financial participation in caring for the less fortunate members of society.

During the late nineteenth century, institutionalization of the insane was molded by the interactions of physicians, state government, and the public. Concerns for cost-effective buildings based on the cottage plan, lunacy legislation that provided treatment centers and sheltered society from the insane, commitment laws that protected the insane individuals, the severance of politics and hospital management, and the communication between doctors and society provided the insane population in Ohio with the appropriate avenues of recovery through institutionalization, moral treatment, and humanitarianism.

47. Henry P. Stearns, "Lunacy Commissions," *American Journal of Insanity* 51 (July 1894): 2.

The Trial and Deposal of Bishop William Montgomery Brown, 1921–1925

RON CARDEN

William Montgomery Brown, Ohio native and Episcopal bishop of Arkansas from 1899 to 1912, was deposed for heresy in October 1925. He had become a materialist and Marxist, proclaiming, "Darwin is my Moses and Marx my Christ!" He put that theme into a 184-page book in 1920, *Communism and Christianism: Banish Gods from Skies and Capitalists from Earth*,[1] a volume he self-published. During his widely publicized trial in Cleveland for heresy in 1924, was he "railroaded" out of the church because of his communism as he subsequently claimed? Did the church set out deliberately to remove him? He had irritated many in 1907 when he argued for a separate black Episcopal Church and in 1910 when he argued for acceptance of all other Protestants under the umbrella of the Episcopal Church, denying apostolic succession and priestly sacerdotalism. Subsequently, he became a Darwinist and Marxist.

Born on a farm west of Orrville, Ohio, in 1855, Brown was the son of a maid and a day laborer.[2] His father died in the Civil War, and his mother farmed him out at the age of six to a harsh taskmaster, a German-speaking Dunkard.[3] Neighbors noticed how badly he was treated and prevailed on authorities to help, and subsequently a kindly farmer and his wife, Jacob and Rachel Gardner, took the boy in. He was well treated and given work

---

1. William Montgomery Brown, *Communism and Christianism: Banish Gods from Skies and Capitalists from Earth* (Galion, Ohio: Bradford-Brown Educational Co., 1920–32). The book had fourteen printings and, with the addition of appendices that argued with critics, grew from 184 to 243 pages by the final 1932 edition.

2. William Montgomery Brown, *My Heresy: The Autobiography of an Idea* (New York: John Day Co., 1926), 9.

3. In an early account of his life from about 1907, Brown said he was bound out to "Dutch Omish Tunkerds." "Autobiographical Sketch," box 1, folder 30, Omar and Dorothy Ranney Papers, Episcopal Church Archives (hereafter ECA), Austin, Texas.

Ohio History, Vol. 114 © 2007 by The Kent State University Press

he could easily do.[4] He attended the Methodist Church in Orrville and sought to prove he was saved and hoped to become a minister but could not work up enough emotion to prove to the congregation he was among the elect.[5] It was a bad start for a career as a Methodist preacher.

He left his foster family in 1873 for Omaha, Nebraska, where he worked for a local judge driving a carriage and entered school at the fourth grade and progressed to the eighth.[6] Returning to Ohio in 1876, he sought to enter Mount Vernon College in Alliance, Ohio, a Methodist institution, but failed due to lack of money. His foster "brother," John Gardner, suggested he apply to Cleveland matron and wealthy heir Mary Scranton Bradford for a job driving her carriage and for aid in ministerial study. An enthusiastic convert to the Episcopal Church, she had a reputation of supporting young men for the Episcopal ministry. Gardner thought Brown would like a less emotional church.[7] He got the job and became acquainted with Mrs. Bradford, the wealthy heir to property in Scranton Flats. She financed his studies at Bexley Hall at Kenyon College in Gambier, Ohio, from 1880 to 1883.[8] Adept at his studies, usually rote memorization, he finished in record time and took charge of Grace Church at Galion.

Meanwhile, he married Mrs. Bradford's adopted daughter, Ella, and they settled down for the start of his ministerial career. His mother-in-law built a mansion for them in Galion and provided a generous allowance. He was successful in his clerical duties, and Ohio's bishop, William Andrew Leonard, appointed him archdeacon for missionary work for the diocese. Impressed by Brown's energy and his sermons, Leonard wanted him to deliver lectures at Bexley Hall on the beliefs of the Episcopal Church.[9] Assisted by Professor David Davies of Bexley Hall, he wrote the lectures that became the basis for his first book, *The Church for Americans,* which extolled the Episcopal Church as best for the nation. Emphasizing the superiority of the Anglo-Saxon race and the Episcopal Church, it went through eighteen printings and was popular among Episcopalians. It also brought him to the attention of Bishop Henry Niles Pierce of Arkansas.[10]

Pierce, an elderly cleric, wanted a coadjutor to help him in Arkansas and ultimately take over the diocese, which was the whole state. Pierce engineered the election of Brown against the objections of Christ Church, a significant congregation in Little Rock. After

4. Fay Hempstead *Historical Review of Arkansas: Its Commerce Industry and Modern Affair,* 3 vols. (Chicago: Lewis Publishing Co., 1911), 1:985.

5. Brown, *My Heresy,* 12.

6. Ibid., 12–13; and *Omaha City Directory,* box 3, folder Omaha, Ranney Papers.

7. Brown, *My Heresy,* 14.

8. Omar Ranney's interview with William Airhart, n.d. (ca. 1957), box 3, folder Church Angle, Ranney Papers. Airhart, the son of Brown's half-sister, suggested that Brown go to Akron to ask his mother if he should accept Mrs. Bradford's offer and that she supposedly replied, pragmatically, that one church was as good as another. It is unclear if he actually did this.

9. Brown, *My Heresy,* 26.

10. Henry Niles Pierce, *Diary, January 1, 1894–March 23, 1898,* Feb. 26, 1897, 286, Arkansas Diocesan Archives, Trinity Cathedral, Little Rock. I used only this last of Pierce's four volumes of a handwritten diary.

a stormy process to get confirmation of his election, Brown finally got the necessary approval. He was consecrated coadjutor in Cleveland in June 1898; in September 1899 Bishop Pierce died, and Brown became the bishop of the diocese.[11] He set out to appease Christ Church which had opposed his election and which detested racial equality in the diocese. Pierce was very progressive and had created St. Phillip's parish, the only black one in the state. Brown reduced it to a mission with no say in the annual diocesan council.[12] He went so far as to argue for a completely separate black church for Episcopalians in the nation in his *The Crucial Race Question* of 1907.[13] He got support in Arkansas and in the south for his idea, but northerners declared him unchristian for his views. In 1908–09, he argued that a separate church for black people led him to believe that all white Protestants should have their own bishops and unite under the umbrella of the Episcopal Church.[14] This book was almost the opposite of his first one. He said anyone could say the communion service and rejected Apostolic Succession, a major belief of the Episcopal Church.[15] His new direction may have been due to ill health. Hard work in directing the diocese drained him of strength, and he showed the symptoms of type II diabetes and heart disease. He expressed his newfound ideas in his *The Level Plan of Church Union* in January 1910. That volume caused outrage in the national church and in Arkansas. After a major dispute with the cathedral in Little Rock, Trinity, he angered almost all churchmen in Arkansas and was pressured to leave. He returned to Galion in June 1911.

On the advice of his personal physician, he began studying comparative religion and the works of Darwin. His reading convinced him that literal understanding of scriptures and of the doctrines of the church made no sense. He demanded other bishops prove the literal truth of Christian tenets, but they ignored him. He thus evolved his eccentric view of a "symbolical" Christianity in which, he said, the Trinity reflected the physical laws of the universe. He saw it as "force, motion, and matter." Jesus was only an idea of the good, a symbol, not a literal person who lived. The miracles were philosophical truths and not literal events. He prayed, but only to his best self. The veil of superstition had been lifted from his eyes. Darwin was a secular Moses leading to the explanation of the origin of human life. The account in Genesis had no literal basis.[16]

11. *Arkansas Democrat,* Sept. 6, 1899, 1.

12. William M. Brown to Joshua Kimber, Philadelphia, Mar. 2, 1900, Domestic and Foreign Missionary Society, New York, Brown, William, 1899–1901, ECA.

13. William Montgomery Brown, *The Crucial Race Question* (Little Rock: Arkansas Churchman's Publishing Co., 1907), 161–65. Brown's segregationist attitudes are described in David E. Finch, "Little Rock's Red Bishop Brown and His Separate Black Church," *Pulaski County Historical Review* 20 (Sept. 1972): 27–31.

14. Brown, *The Crucial Race Question,* 161–65.

15. William Montgomery Brown, *The Level Plan for Church Union* (New York: Thomas Whittaker, 1910), 133. His work was not original; almost all he said came from the work of Adolf Harnack, a theologian at the University of Berlin. See Wilhelm Pauck, *Harnack and Troeltsch: Two Historical Theologians* (New York: Oxford Univ. Press, 1968), 5, 22–33. Pauck summarized Harnack's great work *History of Dogma* (London: Williams and Norgate, 1896).

16. Most of his ideas came from Ernst Haeckel, *The Riddle of the Universe* (New York: Harper and Brothers, 1900), 328–29. Haeckel was the German exponent of Darwinism.

His attraction to Marxism was more complicated. He never paid much attention to national political events but was especially concerned over the loss of life in the First World War. He never said anything about the Church Socialist League or about Progressive reform in his letters but adamantly opposed American intervention in the war in 1917. He read a letter to the editor that said the socialist perspective explained the origins of the conflict.[17] He sent for socialist literature and decided to join the party. He set up a Socialist Club in Galion and handed out its literature on Saturday evenings. In October 1917 he became entranced by the Bolshevik Revolution in Russia. One of his correspondents was the founder of the American Communist Party, Charles Ruthenberg of Cleveland. He abandoned the Socialist Party and switched his allegiance and fervor to the Communists.[18] Thereafter he found the answers to his questions on salvation in Marxian "laws" of economic development and Darwinian biological evolution.

The purpose of human life was to create the best life possible in the here and now. Once dead there was no afterlife. There was no heaven or hell, only the present. Darwin showed how humans came to exist by natural laws of evolution, not godly fiat. Marx showed the evolution of human society that followed economic laws and the rule of the proletariat. The result was *Communism and Christianism: Banish Gods from Skies and Capitalists from Earth!* The story of his two trials and ultimate removal as a bishop in the Protestant Episcopal Church suggests church conservatives decided to remove him mainly because of his heresy but partly because of his communism.

From 1920 to late 1922, Brown happily distributed his book and was quite sanguine about his prospects. A note of concern crept into his letters to friends in early 1921 when asked what effect his book would have on his standing in the church. He replied he had left the field of work in the diocese of Arkansas but remained in the House of Bishops and was a member and communicant of the church.[19] In the meantime, he attracted supporters who streamed into his home. Among them were Theodore Schroeder, a lawyer and psychologist who "psychoanalyzed" Brown Joseph McCabe, an Englishman and writer for the London Rationalist Society and Joseph W. Sharts, attorney for the Local Dayton, Ohio, Socialist Party and defender, among others, of Eugene Debs in 1918 for sedition.

In Fort Smith, Arkansas, in 1921, Bishop James Rideout Winchester, Brown's successor, met with the diocese's Annual Council in January and immediately remarked upon the "spiritual death of the Rt. Rev. William Montgomery Brown, D.D.," and suggested to the presiding bishop and the Executive Council, to Bishop Leonard of Ohio (Brown's

17. Brown, *My Heresy,* 65–66. He did not name the newspaper. In 1924 he said it was the socialist paper, *Rip Saw.* See Protestant Episcopal Church, *In the Trial of a Bishop, In the Matter of the Presentment of Bishop William Montgomery Brown, Record of the Proceedings on the Trial of Bishop Brown at Cleveland, Ohio, May 27–31, 1924,* pp. 359–63, Record Group 115, Typescript Record of the Trial of Bishop William Montgomery Brown, ECA (hereafter Typescript Record).

18. Alfred Wagenknecht to Brown, Apr. 13, 1918, MSS 780, box 5, folder 7, William Montgomery Brown Papers, Ohio Historical Society (OHS), Columbus (hereafter MSS 780). Wagenknecht and others in Cleveland wrote to Brown and introduced him to Ruthenberg.

19. Bishop Brown to Mr. Baukel of Winnipeg, Manitoba, Canada, Apr. 28, 1921, MSS 780, box 5, folder 10.

mentor), and "to others," to remove the "cloud on his deluded mind" and to bring him back "to patriotic citizenship which the virus of Marxian Socialism has poisoned."[20] A year later the Arkansas Council voted to appeal to the House of Bishops for Brown's removal, thus starting the path that led to a deposition.[21]

Brown was keenly aware of the Arkansas Council's demand for presentment (indictment for heresy) and, as early as February 1922, wrote to Thomas Gailor, the executive of the House of Bishops, explaining his position in great detail and ended up remarking that if his ideas were not acceptable, then at least "I might be tolerated."[22] Gailor rejected his request and expressed his disapproval of Brown's communism.[23] Always prolix, Brown sent a twenty-page letter to Bishop Winchester asking to meet with him, Gailor, and Bishop Leonard. But Winchester said Brown was in a "perturbed condition in body, mind and spirit"[24] and refused to deal with him. Gailor ignored him.

The House of Bishops met in advance of the formal opening of the General Convention in Portland, Oregon, in 1922, and Arkansas' petition for an indictment of Brown arrived immediately, in August 1922.[25] Almost frantically, Brown wrote to his mentor, Ohio bishop William A. Leonard, practically pleading with him to derail the attempt to present him,[26] but Leonard disliked Brown's new course, and *The Churchman*, a national church journal, reported that on September 13 the diocese of Arkansas asked the House of Bishops meeting in Portland to take action against Bishop Brown for his book. A committee of five bishops reported on September 19 and, having no inclination for heresy trials, said, "it is the general feeling that Bishop Brown can hardly be held accountable."[27] That initial effort to avoid the whole issue shifted, however, under the pressure of the conservatives, including Bishop Leonard, and the House appointed three bishops to persuade Brown to resign due to his mental incompetence, in hopes thereby of sidestepping any messy trial.[28]

Brown defiantly rejected any idea that fellow bishops could examine him concerning his sanity.[29] He said in no uncertain terms that he would not resign unless other hereti-

---

20. Appendix A, "The Bishop's Annual Address to the Forty-Ninth Council of the Diocese of Arkansas," *Journal of the Forty-Ninth Annual Council of the Church in the Diocese of Arkansas Held in St. John's Church, Fort Smith, on the Twenty-sixth and Twenty-seventh of January* (1921): 33, ECA (hereafter *Journal of the Diocese of Arkansas*).

21. Ibid., 31–32.

22. Bishop Brown to Rt. Rev. Thomas F. Gailor, Apr. 14, 1922, MSS 780, box 6, folder 10.

23. Presiding Bishop and Council, Thomas Gailor to Bishop Brown, Apr. 18, 1922, MSS 780, box 6, folder 10.

24. Bishop Brown to Bishop Winchester, Apr. 20, 1922, and Bishop Winchester to Bishop Brown, May 22, 1922, MSS 780, box 6, folder 11.

25. Protestant Episcopal Church, *Journal of the General Convention of the Protestant Episcopal Church of the U.S.A., Portland, Oregon, 1922* (New York: Abbott Press, 1923), 24.

26. Bishop Leonard was a good friend of Mary Scranton Bradford and took an interest in her son-in-law and his career.

27. *The Churchman* 126 (Oct. 7, 1922): 22.

28. William Montgomery Brown, *Heresy: Before the Trial* (Galion, Ohio: The Bradford-Brown Educational Co., 1924), 20. This would be the quieter, more Anglican way to deal with a person who had been a thorn in the flesh of the American Episcopate since 1910, if not 1898.

29. Bishop Brown to *Galion Inquirer*, Sept. 26, 1922, MSS 780, box 6, folder 12. See also *Galion Inquirer*, Sept. 26, 1922, Theodore Schroeder Papers 17/13/3, Special Collections, Morris Library, Southern Illinois University, Carbondale.

cal bishops were removed too.[30] He was convinced that no other bishop of the church believed in the Bible literally. Angry, he said he would only submit to a psychological examination by psychologists from Yale, Columbia, and Johns Hopkins.[31] No one who knew him at the time ever remarked on any lack of sanity; instead, they noticed his modesty and extreme kindness to workers who came to his home asking for help.[32]

Meanwhile, in the summer through the fall of 1923, a major quarrel had broken out among Episcopal priests and bishops in various sections of the country between the "modernists" and the "traditionalists." It was a quarrel that had reverberations across the country and was part of the larger modernist versus fundamentalist battle of the 1920s, although for the Episcopal Church the issues were different and more sedate than the carnival surrounding the Scopes trial. Bishop William Lawrence of Massachusetts in his book *Fifty Years* caused a sensation with his comments in October 1923. His literal beliefs eroded during his university days; he had read Darwin's *Origin of Species* and ended up firmly on the side of science, no longer believing in the inerrancy of the scriptures or in their absolute inspiration. The Old Testament taught not science and history but spiritual truths. In the New Testament he saw in the life of Jesus the character of God. He stunned many when he said he thought there was no need to require a postulant for orders to say he believed in a literal virgin birth.[33] Brown believed Lawrence thought exactly as he did.

A major row had erupted in Fort Worth, Texas, over a Palm Sunday sermon by the Reverend Lee W. Heaton, who suggested that each generation had to interpret theology for itself. He argued that there was room for those who believed in a literal virgin birth and for those who saw Jesus as both the Incarnation and the son of Joseph. His comments sparked a sharp retort from the powerful Reverend J. Frank Norris of Fort Worth's First Baptist Church, known as" two-gun Norris" because he shot and killed a parishioner in his study during a dispute.[34] Episcopal Church laymen in Fort Worth heeded Norris and angrily demanded Bishop Harry T. Moore initiate a heresy trial of Heaton. This case and others like it set Bishop Winchester fulminating again about Brown and the modernists.[35]

The House of Bishops prepared to meet in a special session in Dallas in November 1923 to deal with relatively mundane matters. The meeting coincided with Bishop Lawrence's book and the Heaton case. Prominent laymen, including U.S. senator George W. Pepper (R-Pa), sent a petition to the presiding bishop, complaining about the "Unitarian"

30. Bishop Brown to the House of Bishops, Oct. 5, 1922, MSS 780, box 6, folder 10.

31. Brown, *Heresy: Before the Trial,* 19–20. This is a printed copy of a letter dated Sept. 25, 1922, and sent to the House of Bishops.

32. Ibid.; and Bishop Brown to Editor of *Syracuse Telegram,* Feb. 15, 1924, 26. Brown mentioned in a 1924 unpublished booklet, "Winter, 1921–2," that he and Ella spent nearly $1,000 on the unemployed in the "Panic of 1919–1920." See also Mary Marcy, "A Biographical Sketch of Bishop Brown," p. 6, MSS 780, box 10, folder 5.

33. William Lawrence, *Fifty Years* (Boston: Houghton Mifflin, 1923), 13, 19, 23, 74–75.

34. Barry Hankins, *God's Rascal: J. Frank Norris and the Beginnings of Southern Fundamentalism* (Lexington: Univ. Press of Kentucky, 1996.), 118–20. Another account by a friend of Norris is E. Ray Tatum, *Conquest or Failure? A Biography of J. Frank Norris* (Dallas: Baptist Historical Foundation, 1966), 221. It was a complicated story, and Norris said he acted in self-defense. He was acquitted. He was wildly anti-Catholic and anti-Semitic.

35. *Journal of the Diocese of Arkansas,* Jan. 23, 1923, 43–44.

comments of Lawrence.[36] The bishops gave the petition to a special committee of conservatives, Arthur Hall of Vermont, Joseph Cheshire of North Carolina, Thomas F. Gailor of Tennessee, Reginald Weller of Wisconsin, and William Manning of New York. Their report became the pastoral letter that demanded a literal acceptance of the Nicene Creed, ostensibly adopted unanimously. Although sixty-five bishops out of 143 were at Dallas, and at least one said that he had not voted at all and that others may have done the same.[37]

After dealing with the Nicene Creed, the bishops indicted Bishop Brown for heresy. Their comments about a literal creed were aimed at Bishop Lawrence, but he was too significant to be charged with heresy, so Brown was a convenient scapegoat for the conservatives. He had to go because of his challenges to both traditional beliefs and capitalism. Too, he had demanded they examine his ideas so that they could see he was quite rational. In Dallas's St. Matthew's Cathedral Parish House at 9:30 Thursday, November 15, 1923, the Executive Council met to discuss the presentment of Brown for heresy.[38] Thereafter, in January 1924 the canonically required number of bishops—three, all from the Dallas meeting—set in motion a trial for heresy of a fellow bishop. They formally filed a request for a presentment of Brown. Church liberals criticized the pastoral letter as "ill-advised"[39] and noted that such a pronouncement had never been made in a special session of the House of Bishops but in the church's triennial general conventions. Almost no liberal in the church wanted to try Brown for heresy. They felt that doing so would only advertise his eccentric views. Bishop Winchester in Arkansas, however, enthusiastically endorsed Brown's indictment.[40]

Brown, meanwhile, encouraged by his widespread support, pored over invitations to speak at leftist gatherings and read enthusiastic letters praising *Communism and Christianism.* The Workers' Party in Chicago asked him to deliver a speech on his views in November 1923,[41] and letters from the northwest and Canada asked for more copies of his book[42] A supporter in Toledo, Ohio, sold the book on street corners, and large crowds heard it discussed in the Temple of Reason.[43] Brown described his volume as "our little preacher of the Marxian and Darwinian gospel."[44] In these jubilant days he became a charter subscriber to the *Daily Worker.*[45]

The Court for the Trial of a Bishop, the formal name of the entity bent on removing

36. A petition signed by "hundreds of clergymen and lay members of the church, including Senator George W. Pepper of Pennsylvania, was read at the secret session of the House last night, setting forth alleged 'Unitarian' utterances of Bishop Lawrence and asking the House to answer them" (*New York Times,* Nov. 16, 1923, 10).

37. Hugh Jansen Jr. "Heresy Trials in the Protestant Episcopal Church, 1890–1930" (Ph.D. diss., Columbia University, 1965), 234–36. See Protestant Episcopal Church, "Appendix: Special Meetings of the House of Bishops: Dallas, Texas, November 14 and 15, 1923," *Journal of the General Convention* (1925): 471, ECA.

38. Norman F. Furniss, *The Fundamentalist Controversy, 1918–1931* (New Haven: Yale Univ. Press, 1954), 168.

39. Jansen, "Heresy Trials," 241; and Furniss, *The Fundamentalist Controversy,* 166.

40. *Journal of the Diocese of Arkansas,* May 14, 1924, 54.

41. Bishop Brown to Eugene Berchthold, Nov. 19, 1923, MSS 780, box 6, folder 2.

42. Jack Junker to Bishop Brown, Nov. 22, 1923, MSS 780, box 6, folder 3.

43. Comrade Karl Pauli to Bishop Brown, Oct. 29, 1923, MSS 780, box 6, folder 5.

44. Bishop Brown to W. E. Stache, Nov. 20, 1923, MSS 780, box 6, folder 6.

45. Bishop Brown to Comrade J. Louis Engdahl, editor, *Daily Worker,* Dec. 10, 1923, MSS 780, box 6, folder 3. Brown sent a check for $25 as a contribution to the cause and $12 for a one-year subscription.

him, chose Bishop John Gardner Murray of Maryland as president or presiding official for the trial,[46] and, after a last minute effort to get Brown to resign,[47] Murray proclaimed that the trial would proceed.[48] The "Red Bishop," as he was called, asked the brilliant Joseph W. Sharts of Dayton, Ohio, to defend him. Murray rejected all of Sharts' pleas for more time[49] and allowed only two months to prepare for this unique case. No bishop had been tried for heresy before, and no precedents existed. The only concession was that it would take place in Cleveland at Trinity Cathedral, close to Brown's home in Galion, where he had begun his clerical career.

The bishop's supporters included his faithful sidekick, the Reverend Arthur Whatham from Kentucky, his "theological advisor" who focused on symbolic Christianity and another aide, Col. Emery West, a retired army officer who provided "expert" testimony on the effects of the sun myths on the development of Christianity.[50] Symbolic Christianity meant the use of the laws of nature that fitted Christian theological concepts. Brown and the others discussed their Trinity as "force, motion, and law." Theodore Schroeder, a friend and "alienist" or psychologist, also sat at the defense table as Brown's "psychological advisor." The most capable person in Brown's camp (what he termed his "official family") was, however, Joseph W. Sharts.

Members of the 1924 Trial Court were Thomas D. Bratton of Mississippi, Benjamin Brewster of Maine, (ironically a charter member of the Church Socialist League founded in 1911), William F. Faber of Montana, John D. McCormick of western Michigan, and John Gardner Murray of Maryland, court president,[51] and Edwin M. Lines of Newark (a friend of Brown and opponent of heresy trials, who chose not to appear),[52] finally Herman Page of Michigan, Edward M. Parker of New Hampshire, and Frederick F. Reese of Georgia. Church law stated that six bishops would be a quorum, so the eight who appeared were enough. Bishop Reese had been particularly active in the special meeting of the House of Bishops in November 1923 and clearly wanted Brown out. None of the bishops left any record of the trial in their respective dioceses,[53] and all seemed to take the trial and the results, deposal, as foreordained.

---

46. Protestant Episcopal Church, "In the Trial of a Bishop," Typescript Record, pp. 5–7.

47. *New York Times,* Feb. 24, 1924, 7. Theodore Schroeder acted as the press agent for Brown and released the statement to the newspapers.

48. Bishop Murray to Bishop Brown, Mar. 7, 1924, MSS 780, box 7, folder 1.

49. Bishop Murray to Bishop Brown, Mar. 24, 1924, Protestant Episcopal Church in the United States of America, Brown Documents 6, General Convention, Registrar, ECA. Canon 31.I. said that the president of the trial court "shall call the Court to meet . . . not to be less than two nor more than six calendar months from the day of mailing such notice." See Protestant Episcopal Church in the United States (PECUSA), *Constitution and Canons for the Government of the Protestant Episcopal Church in the United States of America Adopted in General Conventions 1789–1922* (New York: Abbott Press, 1922), 95.

50. Bishop Brown to Theodore Schroeder, Apr. 16, 1924, Schroeder Papers. This is the first mention of Colonel West in papers relating to Brown.

51. PECUSA, *Constitution and Canons,* 89.

52. Bishop Brown to Bishop Edward Cross of Spokane, Dec. 23, 1926, MSS 780, box 7, folder 4. Bishop Lines was from Newark, N.J., the diocese of former Bishop John Spong, a maverick in the church in the 1990s.

53. The author wrote to all of the dioceses of the eight bishops, and while all responded most courteously, none could provide any in-depth record of his predecessor concerning the trial.

Sharts seemed to know that a presentment and then trial meant the accused was already considered guilty. The bishops had suffered Brown's ideas since his days as a bishop in Arkansas[54] and after 1920 had tried to ignore him or ease him out voluntarily. Sharts used the predestined nature of the trial to criticize the Protestant Episcopal Church.

Meanwhile Bishop Brown and his "theological advisor," Whatham, prepared a questionnaire for all bishops in lieu of witnesses. They wanted eighty-one questions focusing on proving their point that no bishop believed the creeds literally; included were 327 quotes of miracles from both the Old and New Testaments, requiring the bishops to state if they believed literally in all of them and to explain why or why not.[55] Murray and the church advocate rejected the questionnaire and its addendum, so Brown was deprived of a major part of the preparation for his defense.[56]

Brown and his entourage arrived in Cleveland on May 24 and stayed in the New Amsterdam Hotel, a luxury establishment close to Trinity Cathedral. The trial was held in the Trinity Cathedral House, and 400 people were present, mostly reporters and some clergymen.[57] The number tapered off as the trial ground on with technicalities, but it was reported daily on the front page of the *New York Times.* The proceedings began on Tuesday May 27, 1924, and went through Saturday May 31, 1924.[58]

Beginning at 2:00, everyone stood as Bishop John Gardner Murray opened the proceedings with the Apostles' Creed and a prayer.[59] The clerk called the roll, and all bishops, except Lines, were present. Court members avoided eye contact with Brown when the trial began.[60] Sharts immediately claimed that the court had no jurisdiction because the 1919 General Convention had failed to appoint the requisite bishops for the three year staggered terms as set forth in canon law. The House of Bishops had appointed the others in 1922, and Sharts argued that they were chosen because they detested Brown and were expected to depose him. Sharts argued that Brown did not have a diocese and so could not be tried, as he must have a canonical residence. He also suggested that only two months preparation time was an effort to deny him time to mount his defense.[61] Brown had no recourse to any ultimate court of appeals as mentioned in the church's constitution.

54. In 1916 Brown asked 122 bishops to prove to him their ideas of literal Christianity; most ignored him.

55. In the Bishops Court, PECUSA, *Presentment of Bishop Brown, Stipulation for Deposition,* 1–28, ECA.

56. Charles Dibble to Joseph Sharts, telegram, May 12, 1924, Typescript Record, p. 51.

57. In a special story, the *New York Times* described the scene in which three unpainted kitchen tables were arranged in a horseshoe shape with the presiding judge and the other bishops seated together and the president on a dais in front of a red curtain. At one table sat the church advocate, and to his left were the reporters. At the other table were Brown and his "official family." "The hall was dimly lighted by sunlight that filtered in through small leaded panes, and clergymen, communists and the curious, occupied 400 seats," reported Louis Stark, (June 8, 1924, 8:13).

58. *The Searchlight* of Redding, Calif., reported there were 400 people in the hall when the court entered and the proceedings began. Also, the *Cleveland Plain Dealer* on May 27 said the crowds "swept into Trinity Cathedral to get a glimpse of the first heresy trial in centuries against a bishop but that one fourth of the seats were vacant after the trial got underway because the technicalities 'chilled' them." MSS 780, box 11, folder 7.

59. *Cleveland Plain Dealer,* May 27, 1924, MSS 780, box 11, folder 7.

60. *New York Times,* June 8, 1924: "The principals in the case regarded each other frigidly across the counsel table. The accusing bishops studiously avoided recognizing Bishop Brown" (8:13).

61. Typescript Record, 5–6, 17, 9.

Charles Dibble, the church advocate, said other bishops for the trial of a bishop had the authority to fill the vacancies. Any idea these three were chosen by the others just to ensure a conviction was mere speculation. Dibble pointed out the court would have been willing to go to Little Rock, where Brown actually had his canonical resident, but were never asked. He ignored the issue of an ultimate court of appeals.[62]

At 5:00, Bishop Murray stopped the proceedings and announced that the evidence would be taken under "careful and prayerful consideration" and adjourned court until Wednesday morning at ten. Brown, looking gaunt and worn, said nothing. The next morning Bishop Murray announced that the court overruled the objections Sharts had made about the composition of the court and its jurisdiction. Sharts then proposed a voir dire or questioning of whether any of the bishops, sitting as a jury and judges, had any prejudice toward Brown.[63] But Bishop Murray insisted the clerk read the present-ment (indictment) before he would consider the challenge, and the twenty-three charges were read, quoting from *Communism and Christianity*, the edition of April 15, 1923.

Sharts then set out the heart of Brown's defense. What exactly were the doctrines of the Protestant Episcopal Church? Precisely what statements were heretical according to the *Book of Common Prayer?* What was heretical according to the Apostles' and Nicene Creeds? He said there were no specifics as to just what Brown had done and exactly when and where. He then read the table of contents of the *Book of Common Prayer* (1892 ed.) and proceeded to analyze the Apostles' Creed, asking if the charges applied specifically to each part.[64]

He knew the Episcopal Church was not a "confessional" church, and there was really no specific doctrinal statement anyone could point to as the dividing point between an Epis-copalian and a non-Episcopalian. He built his case on the argument that scripture could be accepted only in a symbolical way, as a Christianity devoid of anything supernatural. It could not be taken literally. He did, however, admit that Brown went further than others in the symbolical vein. He alluded to the real issue when he remarked, "the real foundation of this accusation against Bishop Brown is not error of doctrine that is to say of religious teaching. It is the purpose of a certain faction within the Church that are undertaking to expel from the Church those that they disagree with politically and economically." [65]

Church advocate Dibble, focusing on the Brown's religious heterodoxy, quoted from *Communism and Christianity*, "Within the social realm, humanity is my new divinity, my old one, a symbol of it, or less, as I think, it is at best a fiction and at worst a superstition." John Smart, Dibble's associate, argued that Brown convicted himself by denying the divin-ity of Jesus. Sharts shot back that one could not use a defendant's own words as a form of indictment and quoted another section "If you ask whether I am still a professing Chris-tian, I shall answer yes." Sharts said one example could be juxtaposed with another.[66]

62. Typescript Record, 56.
63. Typescript Record, 78.
64. Typescript Record, 26–29.
65. Typescript Record, 104.
66. Typescript Record, 106–14

Sharts wanted to query the court bishops about their prejudice, the voir dire process, and about whether or not they had read the book *Communism and Christianity*.[67] Murray immediately said Sharts had no right to question the integrity of the bishops. Only an affidavit showing a reason for disqualification would be entertained. Sharts immediately asked for acceptance of his earlier motion for depositions from all bishops of the church for their views. Murray denied it too. Sharts then asked for specifics of church doctrine that Brown had violated. Murray quickly denied the request. Sharts announced that he had sent by mail a questionnaire to each juror-bishop asking if the bishop had read the book, had formed an opinion on it, and whether or not he was competent to sit as a fair and impartial judge. Only one bishop had answered, Bratton of Mississippi. Murray ignored everything Sharts had said and then told him to plead. Sharts said "not guilty." The church advocate then presented his case.[68]

Dibble gave a brief overview of the points considered heretical. He did not repeat the specific points taken from the twenty-three charges but, focusing on Brown's heterodoxy, read out the denial of God as a personal objective reality, the denial of the Trinity, the denial of the very life of Jesus and any connection with a Godhead. He carefully avoided any mention of communism. Murray recessed the court at noon to reassemble at 2:00.[69]

Meanwhile, Bishop Brown had a "mild" heart attack. When the court convened, Sharts asked for a brief stay for a half-hour for Brown to appear, noting that the bishop had been in precarious health. Sharts used the time, however, to discuss how commissioners would take depositions from bishops on the points asked in the previous questionnaire. Sharts reminded Bishop Murray that the court could authorize depositions when it was in session. Dibble recommended the motion be overruled and Murray asked the assessors, advisers on the law, what they should do, and they told him it was within the sole discretion of the court, so Murray overruled Sharts on the call for depositions and adjourned until 10:00 Thursday, May 29, 1924.[70] Thus ended the first three days of Shart's brilliant efforts to get the case dismissed. Clearly he faced a hostile court.

On Thursday morning, the trial bishops and Bishop Brown all took part in Communion on Ascension Day,[71] and the trial continued. Sharts, unable to get depositions, read the questions and gave what he anticipated would be the answers. He answered hypothetically, as he and Brown thought the bishops would do, showing that the bishops did not have a literal understanding of matters of scripture or of the creeds and that the locations of the doctrines of the church were neither in the prayer book nor in the creeds.[72] He probably was right, but the court wanted Brown removed as a clergyman and did not care to hear what other bishops thought.

67. Typescript Record, 132.
68. Typescript Record, 104, 132.
69. Typescript Record, 138.
70. Typescript Record, 168.
71. *New York Times*, May 30, 1924, 6.
72. Typescript Record, 161–64.

Dibble and his aides took each of the questions and gave a specific answer as to why it should not be considered. Their basic point was that the court took notice of the church's doctrine just as any court would take notice of the law, but the answers of the bishops would be their opinions only and therefore immaterial to the matter at hand. Sharts insisted that the doctrines were contained in every official utterance of the bishops. Dibble answered that experts' opinions do not make the doctrine of the church. Murray, like Dibble, knew the views of most bishops were probably liberal and would possibly reflect the flexibility that Sharts and Brown wanted. Murray then recessed the Court until 2:00 and announced that they would meet through the next day, Friday, May 30, Memorial Day.[73]

When the Court reconvened that Thursday afternoon, Murray announced that the opinion of witnesses as to the doctrine of the church was not acceptable. He said, as did the church advocate, that the court for the trial of a bishop had the duty to determine the doctrine of the church, not take depositions from witnesses. He said the doctrine was found in the *Book of Common Prayer,* and the "most important formularies of doctrine are the Apostles' and Nicene Creeds."[74] He insisted it was common knowledge that doctrine is not formulated in the Holy Scriptures but is supported by them as interpreted by the church in its corporate capacity. Sharts immediately asked where the doctrine of the church had been interpreted in the corporate capacity of the church. He noted he had wanted additional time for taking depositions as well as producing evidence and had been blocked in that effort. Murray overruled the defense entirely and told Dibble to present his case.[75]

Dibble put *Communism and Christianism* into evidence, using the 1923 edition to illustrate Brown's recalcitrance and opposition to the House of Bishops. He read from that edition a letter of September 25, 1922, showing Brown rejected any consultation with the three bishops appointed to persuade him to resign. He showed a cartoon of Brown being pursued by a porcupine labeled the "House of Bishops." He also noted the Latin inscription underneath a photograph of Brown, *Episcopus in partibus Bolshevikium et Infidelium* (A bishop in part a bolshevik and an infidel). The court and the audience erupted into laughter even the trial bishops chuckled. Dibble read the back of the book where it stated that anyone who bought the book under the impression Brown was orthodox in religion or in economics was wrong.[76]

Dibble wanted to read those parts of the prayer book that constituted doctrine. Sharts immediately took exception and insisted that the prayer book was intended for worship and not doctrine, and he then started to read the entire *Book of Common Prayer,* asking just where the doctrine of the church was. Sharts read and stopped to ask Bishop Murray if he had discovered the doctrine of the church. Sharts went on at great length, and Murray, exasperated, asked him just what he was doing, and Sharts explained that he was

73. Typescript Record, 173–94, 200.
74. Typescript Record, 201.
75. Typescript Record, 205.
76. Typescript Record, 225–31.

trying to find the doctrine. The courtroom erupted into laughter and applause. Sharts shouted out that he was serious. Murray banged down his gavel and demanded silence.[77] After this lengthy presentation, Murray adjourned the court until 10:00 the next day, Friday, May 30, 1924, the climactic day when Brown offered his own testimony.

That morning, Sharts, on bad terms with Murray, who questioned the defense attorney's loyalty to the church, demanded pointblank just what the doctrine of the church was. Murray declined to answer. Sharts pursued the matter, but Murray warned that he would prevent any more argument over how the prayer book reflected doctrine. Sharts objected but was overruled and Murray told him to present his case. Sharts then had Theodore Schroeder, the psychologist, set out his considerable qualifications as an expert witness, but Dibble objected, saying that Schroeder's views as to the intent of those who wrote the creeds was immaterial to the issue at hand. Murray sustained Dibble and Sharts proceeded to read into the record all of the points he expected Schroeder to make. He went over the ideas that fourth-century concepts of a heaven and earth, for example, were quite different from the modern understanding of cosmology. He emphasized that the meaning of words by one individual is quite different from that of another person. Dibble objected to all that had been read and Murray sustained him.[78]

Dibble did not cross-examine Schroeder who stepped down, and Sharts called on Reverend Arthur Whatham, a friend of Brown and a prolific letter writer, as an expert on theology. Putting Whatham on the stand as an expert in theology was difficult because he was not a recognized authority but a good friend of Brown and quite verbose.[79] Sharts tried to establish Whatham's qualifications by asking him to recite the books he had read on the subject. Dibble recognized Sharts's problem and objected that having read several books on theology did not make Whatham an expert. Dibble also objected to what appeared to be Sharts leading Whatham's testimony. Murray sustained the church advocate's objection. Sharts read into the record what he anticipated Whatham would say,[80] especially the many authorities for symbolical, or nonsupernatural interpretations of various aspects of Christianity.

Next Col. Emery W. West, self-styled as an expert on archeology of the Near East, testified, and Sharts had the same problem he had with Whatham: West was not a recognized authority in anything and was merely an amateur. Dibble objected to the testi-

---

77. Typescript Record, 250; and *New York Times,* May 30, 1924, 6. The official transcript and Brown's account record the laughter but not Sharts's comment that he was serious.

78. Typescript Record, 254–58, 264–72. Schroeder was an autodidact in psychology but was well-trained as a lawyer and had written many authoritative works on free speech, including his classic *"Obscene" Literature and Constitutional Law: a Forensic Defense of Freedom of the Press* (New York: Privately printed, 1911). His law work showed concern for those with different religious views, especially Protestants among the Mormons.

79. Educated in England and serving parishes in England and Canada and the U.S., ending up in Louisville, Ky. Whatham had no standing among scholars, as Schroeder certainly did. Whatham had published one short pamphlet of eight pages, *Neo-Malthusianism, Defence: Being a Reply to a Paper Read before the London Junior Clergy Society* (London, 1887), which is available only in the University of London Library.

80. Typescript Record, 286–307.

mony because Sharts cast his questions in such a way that the witness had to judge his own qualifications. Dibble also pointed out that the testimony about the nature of Near Eastern society in the ancient world was not relevant to the case. President Murray sustained the objections, and Sharts read into the record all he expected West to show. In the meantime, Brown asked to be excused, apparently exhausted and perhaps frustrated because the case was not going well. Both Sharts and Murray agreed that Bishop Brown could go and that they would continue in his absence. Sharts read into the record West's lengthy remarks about Christianity and sun worship,[81] wearying Bishop Murray who insisted that Sharts simply mark passages that would thereafter be printed in the record.

Refreshed, Brown returned, and Sharts announced he wanted to put the bishop on the stand. Murray offered the courtesy of waiving the oath, but Brown chose not to waive it. What followed was the strangest part of a very strange trial. Brown appeared wan and tense, and his mind wandered often from the questions put to him. Observers thought he was not in his right mind or was senile; contemporary accounts described him as nervously running his hand through his white hair and fingering a red rose in his buttonhole as he walked slowly to the witness stand smiling at the eight bishops trying him.[82]

Sharts gently asked Bishop Brown questions, establishing his background and getting around to why he wrote the books he did. Brown recited his life's history and pointed out the connections between *The Crucial Race Question* (1907) and then *The Level Plan for Church Union* (1910). He said he thought his heresy began with the first book because it proposed an idea that many objected to two bishops in the same geographical territory one for blacks and one for whites. Similarly, he said the idea of bishops for all denominations under the leadership of the Episcopal Church was his second heresy because many people really disliked it. He described his return to Galion in 1911 and his dejection and how he began to read Darwin. He said he drifted from his Christianity and tried to get the church's leaders to set him back on the right path. He said he got many responses from the bishops but none convinced him. He turned to Marxism after reading a socialist paper, *The Rip Saw,* and sent for socialist literature and saw that in socialism there are natural laws as there are in the physical world.[83]

It was then 6:00, but Brown said he wanted to continue. Sharts asked if he had examined the higher criticism, and Brown said he had done so but dismissed it with a wave of his hand, saying it just said what we had thought about the scriptures was not always

---

81. West had written one booklet of eighty pages in 1923, entitled *Impeachment of the Bible; A Brief offering the Bible in Evidence in the Cause; Twentieth Century Intelligence vs. Ignorance and Superstition* (Chicago: n.p., 1923.) The other book West said he was going to publish never saw the light of day. West could never be taken as an expert on archeology; he certainly had no standing in that scientific community. See also Typescript Record, 286–307, 310, 311.

82. Typescript Record, 358. This was thought of as the climax of the trial and merited front-page treatment in the *New York Times* on May 31, 1924. For the red rose see ibid., June 8, 1924, 8:13.

83. Typescript Record, 359–63. In his *The Crucial Race Question* of 1907, Brown was a rabid racist and segregationist. Later, in 1930, he wrote *America's Race Problem* and repudiated all he had said earlier. As a Communist he was totally colorblind.

the case. It revealed the inconsistencies of the accounts of Jesus's ministry and inaccurate translations of Greek words. Brown said he dealt with an account of a miracle by making a parable out of it; a miracle was never real, but only a symbol for a higher meaning. He felt he could make a parable out of all of what passed for typical Christian doctrine, including heaven and hell. He said he wrote *Communism and Christianism* to tell the truth as he understood it, and he hoped the bishops would allow him the liberty of teaching as he saw fit.[84] Sharts never referred to the communism in Brown's book.

Sharts gently drew Bishop Brown's attention to the Apostles' Creed and led him through it to the end. Brown recited all of it and said he believed all of it but only in a symbolical way. He had hoped to bring religion from an impossible basis to a possible one; that is, he wanted to take religion from a supernatural position to a natural one. Brown was clearly exhausted and asked that he be let off. Bishop Murray then adjourned the proceedings until 10:00 the next day, Saturday, May 31, 1924.[85]

When the court reconvened, Sharts continued his direct examination of Bishop Brown who said he thought he had given the impression he had admitted he was a heretic in the previous day's testimony but was not one. In cross-examination, Dibble asked Brown if his recitation of the creed meant he had retracted his book. Brown answered immediately, "Oh no, not a word of it," shaking his head vigorously and ending Dibble's examination. Subsequently, Dibble's associate, John Smart, refuted the points Sharts' witnesses had given, saying that Brown could think as he pleased but that he could not associate his ideas with the Protestant Episcopal Church.[86]

Sharts gave his summary, focusing on the failure of the church advocate to demonstrate just what the doctrine of the Episcopal Church really was, and emphasized the modern character of Darwinism and the effects of the World War on Brown. Sharts summarized the major tenets of Marxism, especially the need for common ownership of the major means of production, and connected that idea with a quote from Isaiah, "They shall not build, and another inhabit; they shall not plant and another eat." In an eloquent ending, Sharts depicted Brown as a church worker in Arkansas who fell in the harness and had to renew his beliefs, and his studies and books provided that renewal.[87]

Bishop Murray turned to Brown and asked him if he had anything to say. Brown said, curiously, "I believe I will let things stand just as they are, except perhaps to thank the Court for their lovely attitude toward me, and the press, and the presenters, and my prosecutors. I am thankful to you all for the lovely treatment I have received."[88] The whole case was anything but lovely, but Brown, from this point on tended to be extremely magnanimous toward his antagonists.

Dibble summarized the church's case. He said he felt he was like Alice in Wonderland because the case revolved around a man who said he was a Christian atheist. Dibble

---

84. Typescript Record, 384.
85. Typescript Record, 387–92.
86. Typescript Record, 394, 396.
87. Typescript Record, 436–58.
88. Typescript Record, 458.

quoted a part of Brown's book in which the bishop seemed to say he stood for atheistic rationalism. The book had been on the market for four years, and Brown had insulted the House of Bishops in its attempt to get him to resign. He mentioned, correctly, that Brown had really demanded this trial to determine if his doctrine was compatible with that of the Protestant Episcopal Church, and clearly it was not.[89]

Dibble took pains to deny that the trial had anything to do with fundamentalism versus modernism. He defined fundamentalism as the view that argued for the inerrancy of scripture and repeated the complex view of the Episcopal Church that the Nicene Creed contained the church's doctrine, as did the Bible and the Articles of Religion. Few Episcopalians would, however, deny the truth of the theory of evolution. He reiterated that the church did adhere to the concept of a personal God and that Brown denied it.[90]

Dibble only obliquely alluded to Brown's communism, saying Brown rejected orthodox "Christianism," quoting the British Socialist Party's view that any religion was anathema to the "socialist faith." Dibble suggested Brown would do just as well outside the church even though he said he wanted to remain inside it. Brown's socialist views would lead him to destroy Christianity by reinterpreting it as Christian atheism. Bishop Murray then overruled Sharts's motion to dismiss the case and said that the court would adjourn until 3:00 when the verdict would be rendered.[91]

When the court reconvened that Saturday afternoon, Murray specified the main charges against Brown and pronounced the defendant guilty on all counts. The trial court bishops unanimously agreed and signed the document declaring Brown guilty of heresy. Murray said the actual sentence, presumably deposal, would be announced later, and if he wished, Brown could give his rejoinder then. Sharts promptly gave notice he would appeal the verdict and sentence.[92]

Sharts appealed, and the subsequent review court, meeting for four days in January 1925, was quite different from the trial. President of the review court, Bishop Leonard of Ohio and Brown's mentor and chief protagonist, ran a tight ship and set down absolute time limits for both lawyers, creating an atmosphere of tension and hostility. Even Brown's expurgated version reveals sharp tension. The *New York Times* did not take the review court very seriously; most articles about the review were on the inside of the first section and no reports were front-page news, as they had been in May 1924. The review court, however, was just as determined as the trial court to eject Brown, and the results were almost foreordained; the decision of guilty was reiterated, and it recommended Brown be removed from the ministry of the church.[93]

---

89. Typescript Record, 459–62.

90. Typescript Record, 474–76.

91. Typescript Record, 475–77.

92. Typescript Record, 479.

93. The Protestant Episcopal Church, "Record of the Proceedings on Appeal from the Court for the Trial of a Bishop, The Protestant Episcopal Church in the United States of America, In the Court of Review: In the Matter of the Presentment of William Montgomery Brown" (Jan. 13–15, 1925), 240, Record Group 115, PECUSA, C.C. Registrar, Brown Documents, ECA.

Brown gained much sympathy in the review court because his lawyer, Mr. Sharts, and Brown himself carefully presented the most reasonable aspects of the latter's ideas. At the end Brown gave a concise, eloquent explanation of how he accepted the creeds in a spiritual sense, his "Confession of Faith," which sounded orthodox. His "literary advisors," Joseph McCabe, a member of the British Rationalist Society of Johnson's Court, and Theodore Schroeder may have written it, but Brown reprinted and repeated it often, making the church look quite ridiculous. It was a bit of legerdemain, because few people really read *Communism and Christianism* and thereby never understood his disjointed religious ideas and clear commitment to communism.

Public opinion just after the review court was partly positive for Brown, thus encouraging him. The first to comment on the review court and its decision was the communist *Daily Worker* which observed, "A man with his [Brown's] views should feel just about as much at home with his [former] associates in the vineyard of superstition, as an ear of sweet corn in a barrel of dung." It also said, "William Montgomery Brown has our respect, but not our sympathy. We believe the punishment has added to his manhood. It is further testimony to his sterling character."[94] The Communist Party thus viewed the trial with amusement and was never too sure about how to take him. The *Literary Digest* of February 14, 1925, gave a summary of the major issues of the trial and quoted approvingly his "Confession of Faith."[95]

Brown sought unsuccessfully to gain adherents among liberal churchmen in New York City in April, and in June 1925 he accepted consecration into the Old Catholic Church of "Archbishop" William Henry Francis, a "wandering bishop." He announced his new position when he arrived in New Orleans in October for the final settlement of his case, most likely removal as a bishop in the Episcopal Church. But now he could still claim the title of "bishop" through his new connection.[96] The title was always of utmost importance to him.

Brown's finances improved just before the convention at New Orleans. He and his wife sold land in Cleveland's Scranton Flats for a railroad station for $80,000, enabling him and his entire "official family"—including Archbishop Francis, Arthur Whatham, and Theodore Schroeder—to go to New Orleans on October 3, 1925, and lodge in the venerable St. Charles Hotel. Brown, meanwhile, wrote presiding bishop Ethelbert Talbot and revealed his consecration into the Old Catholic Church, implying that his orders would be valid whether he was deposed or not.[97] The announcement impressed no one.

94. *Daily Worker,* Jan. 17, 1925, 4, as quoted in Ralph Lord Roy, *Communism and the Churches* (New York: Harcourt, Brace, 1960), 25.

95. *Literary Digest* 84 (Feb. 14, 1925): 30–31.

96. Julie Ann Stevens, "Heresy in the Twentieth Century: The Protestant Episcopal Church vs. William Montgomery Brown" (honors thesis, Denison College, 1968), 65. Stevens quoted Sharts: "the defendant admitted his Episcopal bishopric was more important to him than the heresy issue. He sacrificed the dignity of the case."

97. Bishop Brown to Bishop Ethelbert Talbot, n.d. The complete text of this remarkable and lengthy epistle is in the Schroeder Papers.

The Old Catholics, whose headquarter was in Holland, had broken from Rome in the early nineteenth century, but their orders were recognized by the Church of England and the American Episcopal Church. Unfortunately for Brown, Archbishop William Henry Francis's line of consecration for the Old Catholics had been revoked. Brown was blissfully unaware of that fact.

The case was taken up by the church's General Convention in New Orleans on October 8, 1925, just as the proceedings got under way, and Tennessee's Bishop Gailor asked the bishops to affirm the findings of the trial and review courts. Bishop Brown spoke for thirty minutes; he could not get through his characteristically lengthy remarks in the time allotted and asked for the bishops' indulgence for more time and for an ultimate court of appeals. Massachusetts's bishop William Lawrence moved to deny both and was upheld. A vote on Bishop Gailor's motion was taken, and the findings of the two courts were upheld. The bishops went into executive session that afternoon, excluding reporters and spectators, and voted to depose Brown by a vote of 95 to 11. One who voted to support Brown was Bishop Lines of Newark,[98] who argued that suspension would be sufficient. The presiding bishop, Ethelbert Talbot, was to depose him.

Talbot summoned Brown to a formal ceremony of deposition on Monday, October 12, 1925, at 9:30 in St. Paul's Episcopal Church, New Orleans. Theodore Schroeder was present as an observer and, in a sense, as Brown's proxy. Some two hundred people witnessed the scene. After calling Brown's name three times and getting no reply, the presiding bishop declared him deposed. The House of Bishop's secretary solemnly drew a line through the name of William Montgomery Brown, Fifth Bishop of Arkansas.[99] Thus the "Red Bishop" was formally removed as a prelate in the Protestant Episcopal Church.

Brown, now in the national limelight, continued his efforts to "propagandize" his views. From 1925 to 1935 he went on a series of lecture tours for Communist groups and made a reputation as America's "Red Bishop." Wealthy because of his wife's inheritance, he paid his English friend, Joseph McCabe, to ghostwrite most of the approximately thirty books and pamphlets that Brown published to show the House of Bishops the errors of its ways and to advance communism. He and his wife, Ella, had no children. She preceded him in death in July 1935. He died of a cerebral hemorrhage on October 31, 1937, at age eighty-two, and left a Last Will and Testament that provided money for "indigent communists" and for propagating communism. His home, Brownella Cottage, is today a museum and tourist attraction in Galion, Ohio, and his estate still exists and is administered out of Cleveland.

The church was slow to indict Brown for heresy, and the driving force behind the effort to remove him was his successor in the diocese of Arkansas, Bishop Winchester. Brown refused to resign as demanded on account of mental instability and angrily insisted on

---

98. The diocese of Newark has a tradition of liberality; Bishop John Spong, author of many controversial books, was the bishop of Newark until his retirement in 2000.

99. John L. Keyser, "The Deposition of Bishop William Montgomery Brown in New Orleans, 1925," *Louisiana History* 8 (Winter 1967) 50.

competent psychologists to evaluate him. Liberal church leaders had pronounced viewpoints that conservatives in the church disliked, and in 1924 they indicted him as an example to others and to express their discomfiture with the "Red Bishop." After two trials, the courts clearly denied him an extensive defense and found him guilty and recommended deposal.

The results of heresy trials are usually preordained and accomplish nothing. The church would have been far better off had it ignored William Montgomery Brown. He was retired, had no see, and no one had paid any attention to his eccentric ideas. Bishop James R. Winchester of Arkansas was the leader of those who wanted Brown removed as a bishop, probably because the parishioners of Arkansas had a keen dislike of their former prelate. Conservative bishops agreed with Winchester. Brown's attorney, Joseph Sharts, made a brilliant defense and shifted public opinion away from communism and over to the church's refusal to let an old man express his views. Sharts played to the gallery of public opinion. The Episcopal Church was not immune to the contest between religion and science in the 1920s. In his trials Brown, however, was revealed as more radical than those who wanted to teach evolution in the public schools.

Book Reviews

The Boundaries between Us: Natives and Newcomers along the Frontiers of the Old Northwest, 1750–1850. Edited by Daniel P. Barr. (Kent, Ohio: Kent State University Press, 2006. xx, 261 pp. Cloth $52.00, ISBN 0-87338-844-5.)

The Old Northwest was first subjected to extensive historical analysis early in the twentieth century when a generation of post-Turnerian scholarship focused on its traditions of democracy and institution building. In the past fifteen years interest in the region has been revived, now with a focus on cross-cultural relations and the complexities of lived experience in a frontier setting. The eleven essays in the volume under review fall squarely into this recent tradition. They vary widely in quality, originality, and persuasiveness, but the best of them are engaging and imaginative and suggest promising avenues for additional research. All the essays deal with relations between Indians and Euroamericans. One striking feature of the volume is its expansive time frame. Ranging from the era of the Seven Years' War to that of internal improvements and Indian removal, it brings together topics that are rarely considered within a single pair of covers.

The first four essays deal with the Seven Years' War and its aftermath. Recent scholarship sees the Ohio Indians as an inchoate group from multiple backgrounds that was beginning to act together for some purposes; often it does not do enough to disaggregate the motives of those constituent groups. Ian K. Steele and Daniel P. Barr give close attention to the motives of Shawnees and Delawares, respectively, in entering the Seven Years' War and in so doing offer important clarifications to the war's origins. David Dixon's essay pushes too far in the other direction by arguing that the uprisings known as Pontiac's Rebellion, which came at war's end, offer proof of a new ethnicity shared by the Ohio and Detroit Indians. While certain concerns united these groups, they remained permanently divided in important ways as well. Matthew C. Ward persuasively counters Gregory Dowd's claim that British officers were the principal cause of Indian grievances after the Seven Years' War by highlighting officers' role as mediators and protectors of Indian interests—though he does so, curiously, without noting his disagreement with Dowd.

Lisa Brooks presents a nuanced, persuasive account of the disagreement between the Mohawk Joseph Brant and Mahican Hendrick Aupaumut in their efforts to lead the Ohio and Detroit Indians to a workable settlement with the United States following the Revolution. Rooting each man's vision in a geographic analogy that drew on his own people's traditions and historical experiences, Brooks powerfully illustrates the complexities of their attempts to mediate peace on the post-Revolutionary frontier. Frazer Dorian McGlinchey highlights the disparity between the ideal vision of Marietta, Ohio, articulated by the leaders of the Ohio Company and the messy actuality of their efforts. Donald H. Gaff emphasizes the fluid boundaries of identity and experience in the lives of Little Turtle, Jean Baptiste Richardville, and William Wells. Bruce P. Smith offers a highly suggestive analysis of the ways criminal law was used to adjudicate cases of cross-cultural homicide on the Illinois frontier. Far from being the equitable, well-ordered system that some scholars have argued for, Smith's analysis of two such cases suggests that frontier dwellers, both Indian and Euroamerican, resorted all too easily to extralegal violence to resolve their disputes.

Phyllis Gernhardt, Ginette Aley, and Thomas J. Lappas consider the era of removal. Gernhardt's essay examines the experiences of Potawatomi and Miami Indians in the vicinity of Fort Wayne, where the United States trading factory accumulated debts that the federal government could leverage to secure parcels of land. In the 1830s and 1840s, after the factory system was abandoned, private traders were briefly able to do essentially the same thing, serving as middlemen who accumulated Indian debt and then negotiated land transfers with the government. Aley uses the example of the Wabash and Erie Canal to highlight the importance of internal improvements in converting the landscape of the Old Northwest into commercially viable property. In the book's final essay, Lappas praises the Sac leader Keokuk for his ability to defend the interests of his people through mediation, in contrast with the better-known Black Hawk who led his followers in a futile effort to resist United States expansion by force.

One wishes that the contributors to this volume had been pressed to consider and respond to one another's arguments more explicitly and also that they were more consistently attentive to the historiographical contexts in which they were writing. Taken together, though, these essays highlight the extraordinary dynamism of the Old Northwest during a century of unprecedented change. *The Boundaries between Us* amply illustrates the continuing vitality of the Old Northwest as a focus of historical inquiry.

ERIC HINDERAKER
University of Utah

Mapp v. Ohio: Guarding Against Unreasonable Searches and Seizures. By Carolyn N. Long. (Lawrence: University Press of Kansas, 2006. xii, 228 pp. Cloth $35.00, ISBN 0-7006-1441-9.)

A Place of Recourse: A History of the U.S. District Court for the Southern District of Ohio, 1803–2003. By Roberta Sue Alexander. (Athens: Ohio University Press, 2005. xx, 417 pp. Cloth $60.00, ISBN 0-8214-1602-2.)

Carolyn Long skillfully traces the judicial path of Cleveland's Dollree Mapp's case from police intrusion into her home without a warrant to the United States Supreme Court's declaration of her freedom and an exclusionary rule for illegally obtained evidence. Roberta Sue Alexander masterfully details the impact of the United States District Court for the Southern District of Ohio, provides biographies of its judges, and analyzes its impact on Ohio and the nation. Both books significantly advance our knowledge of American constitutional and legal history, provide historiographically nuanced interpretations of law's impact, and furnish readers with easy access to the complex nature of judicial process.

The federal District Court for the Southern District of Ohio opened for legal business in 1803 to afford litigants a place to enforce federal law and assert rights under the United States Constitution. The federal district judges brought federal law home to the people of southern Ohio. These judges handled nationally significant cases such as *Osborn v. Bank of the United States* (1824), part of the Jacksonian war against the national bank using state taxing authority to destroy the institution. Admiralty was another important part of the court's litigation calendar. Deciding disputes on the inland waterways of Ohio was important for the commerce of Ohio and the nation. *Ex parte Vallandigham,* a Civil War–era case of treason, also had its origins in the district. Later in the century, Judge George R. Sage was the first in 1891 to issue a labor injunction against a union boycott starting a national trend that lasted until the New Deal. In 1913 the court made national headlines sentencing the president of National Cash Register to jail time for illegal business practices under the Sherman Act. Prohibition flooded the court with enforcement cases and the New Deal litigants forced the judges to deal with statutory interpretation and administrative law problems. The judges consistently upheld New Deal statutes and administrative agency intervention in the economy. By the 1960s the court was very much a part of the lives of average residents of the district. The judges made rulings on school desegregation, civil rights, and federal regulation of the economy including equal employment opportunity. The court was an arbiter, interpreter, and innovator in statutory interpretation, mass tort litigation, products liability, and settlement procedures. In 1985 the District Court for the Southern District of Ohio was the busiest federal court in the nation.

Alexander goes beyond narrative by providing strong historical context for each period of time considered, rich biographies of each judge, pointed explanations of the varying jurisprudential approaches of the judges, and numerous tables setting out the criminal and civil dockets. She also marks nationally significant decisions. Judge John E. Stater in *United States v. Borkowski* (1920) established the constitutionally required elements of a search warrant. Judge John Weld Peck in *United States v. Slusser* (1921) set out the nature and extent of a consent search. Both established precedent.

The problem for Dollree Mapp was that the Cleveland police did not have a warrant, and she never consented to a search. The police forcibly broke into her home over her protests, ransacked the premises, and found allegedly obscene materials. They arrested her and refused to show her or her lawyer on the premises a warrant required by the Ohio constitution. Yet the Cleveland police were little different from police in half of the states. Regardless of state law or constitutions, police searched without warrants, and, as in Ohio, illegally seized evidence could be admitted into evidence in a criminal proceeding. In 1958

Ohio v. Mapp was heard in the Cuyahoga County Court of Common Pleas. Convicted of violating the Ohio anti-obscenity law, the judge sentenced her to seven years in the Ohio Reformatory for Women. Her lawyers, joined by the Ohio Civil Liberties Union, appealed through the Ohio court system to the United States Supreme Court. In 1961 the Warren Court announced the exclusionary rule throwing out Mapp's conviction.

Political scientist Carolyn Long then traces the police, district attorney, state, and federal reactions to the decision. She reviews various studies of the impact of the decision on police as well as state and federal judicial acceptance of the ruling. Interestingly, the United States Supreme Court erodes the initial impact of *Mapp*. Presidents Nixon and Reagan appointed conservative jurists to the United States Supreme Court. The Berger and Rehnquist Courts create a long list of exceptions to *Mapp*. Ironically, state courts using independent state constitutional grounds jurisprudence have been far more faithful to the promise of *Mapp* of giving Americans full protection against unreasonable searches and seizures.

Both books provide important insight into how the federal legal system impacts life in America. It is unfortunate that Professor Long does not confront the implications of the Patriot Act on freedom from unreasonable searches. Perhaps that is the subject of her next book.

GORDON MORRIS BAKKEN
California State University, Fullerton

No Taint of Compromise: Crusaders in Antislavery Politics. By Frederick J. Blue. (Baton Rouge: Louisiana State University Press, 2005. xii, 301 pp. Cloth $54.95, ISBN 0-8071-2976-3.)

Fredrick Blue's collective biography of ten antislavery activists adds a fresh and important dimension to our understanding of the antislavery movement in the 1840s and 1850s. Focusing on less-prominent figures, Blue greatly enhances our understanding of the antislavery movement generally and the politics of sectionalism in particular. Examining the private and public lives of individuals as diverse as Alvan Stewart and Jessie Benton Frémont and Charles Langston and David Wilmot, Blue analyzes their motivation to become politically active in politics, their antislavery ideology, and their varying commitments to equal rights for African Americans. He places them on a spectrum that ranges from an early commitment to the Liberty Party (Stewart and John Greenleaf Whittier, for example) to those who came to the antislavery movement later with the advent of the Republican Party (Frémont and Benjamin Wade). Each, however, was intensely committed to stopping the expansion of slavery and saw politics as the means to that end.

Common threads bind together the lives of these activists. Central to their commitment to antislavery was a religious background that issued in the conviction that slavery was immoral. This sets them apart from other more conservative—or less enlightened—opponents of slavery who were largely concerned about the institution only as it affected white society and republican politics. These activists found their commitment to antislavery politics a difficult one, occasioned as it was by hostility and threats from those less sympathetic to the plight of the enslaved. Save for David Wilmot, they also distanced themselves but were not entirely free from nineteenth-century racial stereotypes. Although they varied in their commitment to the enfranchisement of blacks, all (again, save for Wilmot) were determined to grant African Americans basic human and political rights.

What most united these ten and set them apart from abolitionists such as William Lloyd Garrison was their conviction that political activism best served the antislavery movement. And here the Mexican-American War seemed to be a turning point, and an ironic one at that. On the one hand, it raised and made salient the question of slavery extension and thus heightened sectional tensions that focused on the institution. On the other, Wilmot's proviso had the effect (though not the intent) of blunting more radical antislavery activity by shifting its focus to restriction (not abolition) and making politics (not moral suasion) the broad-based grounds on which that contest would be fought. What Blue suggests is that "radical" antislavery activism is less a category than a continuum: if Whittier, Jane Swisshelm, and Owen Lovejoy were less extreme in their attacks on slavery than Garrison or Wendell Phillips, they were certainly no less committed to its elimination and to the advancement of equal rights.

Blue's analysis of this antislavery cohort also illuminates and gives substance to the positions of those radicals and conservatives who opposed them. Thus, he expands and enriches the political landscape of the Middle Period. Separately and together, these biographies begin to map a path by which the moral element of abolitionism intersects with the antislavery politics of Free Soil Democrats and Republicans. Finally, Blue reminds us that abolitionism and the politics of antislavery were deeply personal, intensely felt, and mutually reinforcing. This is the rare collective biography in which the whole is greater than the sum of its parts.

MICHAEL A. MORRISON
Purdue University

On Jordan's Banks: Emancipation and Its Aftermath in the Ohio River Valley. By Darrel E. Bigham. (Lexington: University Press of Kentucky, 2005. x, 428 pp. Cloth $45.00, ISBN 0-8131-2366-6.)

Darrell's Bigham's fine study of African American life on the nineteenth century's great "Borderland" (as the notable Underground Railroad conductor John P. Parker referred to it) takes its place alongside the surprisingly large number of histories of African Americans in Ohio River states and cities that have been published in the past half-century. Emma Lou Thornbrough's *The Negro in Indiana Before 1900: A Study of a Minority* (1957), David A. Gerber's *Black Ohio and the Color Line, 1860–1915* (1976), and Marion B. Lucas's *A History of Blacks in Kentucky, Volume I: From Slavery to Segregation, 1760–1891* (1992) argue generally for the multifaceted nature of the African American experience in these border states. Of course, these being studies of states that border the river but whose culture, politics, and history are hardly monolithic, the experiences of African Americans in those states was equally diverse.

More recently, several studies of Ohio River Valley cities have appeared, including George C. Wright's *Life behind a Veil: Blacks in Louisville, Kentucky, 1865–1930* (1985); Bigham's previous book, *We Ask Only a Fair Trial: A History of the Black Community of Evansville, Indiana* (1987); Henry Louis Taylor Jr.'s edited collection on Cincinnati's black community, *Race and the City: Work, Community, and Protest in Cincinnati, 1820–1970* (1993); and, most recently, Nikki Taylor's *Frontiers of Freedom: Cincinnati's Black Community, 1802–1868* (2005).

Unlike any of these works, Bigham's book is a regional study, placing it most closely with Joe William Trotter Jr.'s *River Jordan: African American Urban Life in the Ohio Valley* (1998), which compares Cincinnati, Evansville, Louisville, and Pittsburgh. Where Jordan's book relies primarily on secondary works, Bigham's balances exhaustive primary research with a full canvass of secondary literature, both published and unpublished. Moreover, Bigham expands his study, using the ribbon of fifty counties of Illinois, Indiana, Kentucky, and Ohio, urban and rural, that lie immediately north and south of the lower Ohio River to compare and contrast patterns of settlement, community development, and race relations from 1861 to 1890. As such, this is regionalism of the most valuable kind, defining a region that since the Civil War has been largely subsumed by the Midwest north of the river and the South below it. Bigham's study challenges those regional distinctions, at least in the matters of race and culture.

Of course, where Bigham's book focuses largely on the years during and after the war, it fully explains the region's earlier history, nicely confronting the periods during and after slavery, which, ironically, existed in some form in all of them during the early nineteenth century, despite the Northwest Ordinance's famous prohibition in the territories and states north of the Ohio River. The point is critical; as Bigham notes, the famous boundary between freedom and slavery was far more porous than history has offered. The Underground Railroad, after all, existed as the nation's first civil rights movement, especially after 1850, because the "free states" were anything but free. For every white resident of the western free states who opposed slavery, there were many more who supported its existence below the Ohio and opposed black freedom above it. Bigham describes in detail how these communities were shaped by the presence or absence of slavery, how the abolition of slavery and the rise of free labor became the rule of law on both banks and yet racial exclusion prevailed on both sides of the river. Proscriptive "Black Laws" before and during the war were replaced with de facto segregation above the river and de jure segregation in Kentucky afterward, both which resembled or replicated the exclusionary Jim Crow laws associated so commonly with the South. Yet Bigham demonstrates that African Americans on both sides of the river made remarkable advances in spite of being offered little with which to make their new start. Emancipation allowed for the expansion and formation of black communities, separated from other communities even while lying within the larger cities, whose families, schools, and churches sheltered their members and kept alive the "dream deferred" and thus fueled the century-long African American struggle for equality.

On Jordan's Banks offers a welcome addition to the growing historical literature on the Ohio Valley and African American life and culture and carves deeply into the perception of the existence of a static border that defined the nation's western region before and after the Civil War.

CHRISTOPHER PHILLIPS
University of Cincinnati

Ohio & the World: Essays Toward a New History of Ohio. Edited by Gregory Parker, Richard Sisson, and William Russell Coil. (Columbus: Ohio State University Press, 2005. xiv, 199 pp. Cloth $49.95, ISBN 0-8142-0939-4; Paper $22.95, 0-8142-5115-3; CD $9.95, 0-8142-9068-X.)

To honor the bicentennial of Ohio statehood in 2003, The Ohio State University sponsored a series of eight public lectures that have been collected in this text. The first chapter, by Andrew Cayton, defines themes of Ohio history, including, "to rethink the popular image of Ohio as a bastion of American normalcy, the comfortable heartland"; "the progressive story of nineteenth century Ohio turns into decline and stagnation"; and the geographical diversity of the state, particularly between north and south.

David Edmunds, in the next chapter, reconstructs Ohio in the late eighteenth century. He portrays the Native American groups as they allied with either the French or British then, later, with the Americans or British. The Indians did quite well until the collapse in the 1790s and when they were removed from the state in order to gain their land.

James Horton continues the theme of cultural intolerance in the next chapter as he emphasizes the second-class citizenship that African Americans suffered in the antebellum era. Horton contrasts liberal northeast Ohio, which was settled by New Englanders and Pennsylvanians, with southern Ohio, which was settled by Southerners, a contrast illustrated by the difference between Cleveland and Cincinnati.

Eric Foner displays the importance of Ohio during the Civil War era. Many of the major political and military leaders were sons of Ohio, and the state contributed more soldiers to the Union cause per capita than any other Northern state. As a result, the presidency was dominated by Buckeyes from 1869 to the early 1900s.

Kathryn Sklar illustrates the progressivism of Ohio in the era between the Civil War and World War I as it urbanized and industrialized as the focus of the national core. A civil society of popular culture based on democracy and justice prevented major violence in the state in the Great Railroad Strike of 1877 in Newark, unlike some other states. The national social gospel movement was led by Washington Gladden of Columbus. Tom Johnson emerged as a populist progressive mayor of Cleveland. National female leaders of the temperance movement (Eliza Stewart) and the suffrage movement (Harriet Taylor Upton and African American Hallie Quinn Brown) came from Ohio.

James Patterson discusses the strength of Ohio as late as the 1950s, with its booming industry based on steel, oil, and automobile manufacturing. Ohio was still a place of choice in the American Union, with its stalwart small-town conservative values represented by Republican Robert Taft in contrast with the more cosmopolitan and liberal Atlantic coast. Nonetheless, racial tensions were an issue, particularly in the larger Ohio cities in the 1950s and 1960s.

Herbert Asher depicts Ohio in 2003 as in a state of decline economically and politically. Globalization has led to deindustrialization, and the average educational attainment in Ohio is among the worst in the nation. Ohio is no longer a place of choice, giving way to more vibrant regions like the Sunbelt and he two coasts. In the last chapter, William Kirwin echoes Asher in his formula for reviving Ohio economically by 2053, emphasizing higher education focused on the sciences and computer technology. However, as Asher pointed out, Ohio is no longer geographically central to the national economy as it once was in the nineteenth and early twentieth century.

This book will work well in Ohio history courses as a supplement to a more detailed central text. The writing is enhanced by many illustrations, particularly the New Deal post office murals that are examples of popular imagery of the state. All in all, other states would do well to produce a similar text as they celebrate their history.

BRUCE BIGELOW
Butler University

American Vanguard: The United Auto Workers during the Reuther Years, 1935–1970. By John Barnard. (Detroit: Wayne State University Press, 2004. xiv, 607 pp. Cloth $49.95, ISBN 0-8143-2947-0.)

In accepting the presidency of the United Auto Workers (UAW) in 1947, Walter Reuther hailed the union as "the vanguard in America in that great crusade to build a better world." John Barnard describes the origins, development, and achievements of the UAW from its inception in 1935 to 1970, the year that Reuther died. Drawing on extensive research in the voluminous UAW collections at the Archives of Labor and Urban Affairs in Detroit and the large secondary literature on the union, Barnard offers a judicious, even-handed, and not uncritical assessment of this quintessential industrial union and its commitment to industrial democracy and social justice.

If not quite the leader of the postwar liberal quest for social improvement and equity, the UAW certainly was the pacesetter for union gains that boosted blue-collar workers and their families into the middle class. Barnard devotes nearly half the book to the UAW's history before Walter Reuther became president. Noting that the union "grew from the bottom up and it grew through contact of one worker with another" (103), Barnard evokes the excitement, energy, and democratic impulse of the union's early history. He captures the challenges and triumphs of the sit-down era and the legacy of struggle and success that characterized and shaped the union in the years that followed. In this half of the book, Barnard not only brings to life the rank and file as well as the leadership of the fledgling union, but he also provides an excellent guide to the different ideological and political groups that flourished within the UAW in the 1930s and 1940s. The second half of the book examines Reuther's rise to power and his leadership of the nation's largest industrial union. Promoting "teamwork in the leadership and solidarity in the ranks," Reuther steered the more than one-million-member union toward collective bargaining agreements that significantly improved the quality of life for autoworkers in the United States and Canada. From cost-of-living adjustments and the annual improvement factor that gave workers a share of gains in productivity and profits to vacations and paid holidays to health insurance to early retirement and pension benefits to supplemental unemployment benefits that offset the impact of layoffs and achieved a measure of secure and predictable employment and income, the contracts negotiated by the UAW created in effect a private welfare state. In the 1950s and 1960s, the UAW, says Barnard, "functioned superbly as a bread-and-butter union" (292).

Although sympathetic to the union, Barnard is no apologist. He appraises the union's strengths but also is straightforward about its limitations. Despite the union's commitment to racial equality, Reuther did not make an active campaign for black advance within the union a major priority in the postwar era. Barnard also charges Reuther with stifling dissent and violating the union's civil liberties principles in purging the left from the union. The UAW's deference to the Democratic Party and its failure openly to oppose the war in Vietnam not only denied the union independence but also undermined the reform coalition that Reuther and other auto unionists were dedicated to creating and preserving in the 1960s. On other matters debated by labor scholars, Barnard offers fair-minded analysis. In response to those who criticize the UAW for ceding control over the workplace in exchange for high wage and benefit packages, for example, Barnard notes both the refusal of auto executives to surrender managerial prerogatives as well as the evident desire among the rank and file for the meaningful improvements in the quality of life outside the plants. Barnard also reminds us of the conservative, antiunion climate in postwar America, suggesting that there was no other realistic route for the union to follow insofar as labor relations were concerned.

Written in clear and lively prose, *American Vanguard* is the only one-volume history of this important union. Barnard does more than simply chronicle the UAW's history to 1970. Despite the title, Barnard offers astute and valuable assessments of the leadership provided by Leonard Woodcock and Doug Fraser in the decade that followed Reuther's death and of the UAW's difficulty in maneuvering through the auto industry's hard times. And although the rank and file tends to disappear from the narrative once Reuther becomes president, and the union's presence and history in regions other than southeast Michigan receive scant attention, the book is an effective blend of social and political history and an important and welcome addition to the literature on twentieth-century labor and politics.

NANCY GABIN
Purdue University

The Shawnees and Their Neighbors, 1795–1870. By Stephen Warren. (Champaign: University of Illinois Press, 2005. x, 217 pp. Cloth $35.00, ISBN 0-252-02995-X.)

In this book Stephen Warren first offers an analysis of the Shawnees living interspersed with members of other tribes before their removal to west of the Mississippi and then focuses on how the Shawnees came to see themselves as members of a nation. "The object of this book," states Warren, "is to understand how and why this shift in the political consciousness of the Shawnees took place" (9). Consequently drawing on solid primary and secondary sources as well as his own knowledge of the Shawnees, Warren has constructed an in-depth, complex account of the changes brought to Shawnee life from 1795 to 1870.

Warren examines the various relationships working among the Shawnees. He points out that the Shawnees were broken into rather autonomous, multiethnic villages. A single tribal organization did not exist. Thus, when Tenskwatawa the Prophet called for moral reform and his brother Tecumseh pursued an intertribal confederacy, neither relied on kinship as a motivator for Shawnee unity.

With the end of the War of 1812, Shawnees in Ohio attempted to coexist with the United States. American government officials demanded that they end any multitribal political association. They were pressured to select only a few prominent chiefs so that diplomacy could be easier. Whites also wanted the Shawnees to adopt "American civilization" particularly as brought to them by missionaries. Eventually, though, the goal of white politicians was to induce the natives to remove to the West.

By the 1830s, Shawnees and other Indians, facing poverty and discrimination, acceded to removal and resided in present-day Kansas. There, the internal factors of Shawnee politics and culture became more agitated. The influence of missionaries, particularly conflicting Methodists and Baptists, led to quarrelling, not just religiously but also politically. Aspiring tribal leaders, especially prosperous mixed-lineage individuals, fostered reciprocal support from the contesting missionaries and caused disputes between the various village groups. The issue of either having a national tribal organization or independent villages arose. Also, the issue of slavery that split the missionary denominations played on the Shawnees as a few held slaves while most opposed it. Fueling the feuding between the religious bodies allowed traditionally minded Shawnees to retain their independence from a central tribal authority.

During the American Civil War, most Shawnees eventually sided with the Union. Following the war, some Shawnees accepted citizenship in Kansas, but more reluctantly moved into the Indian Territory (Oklahoma). Many were placed in the Cherokee Nation as full Cherokee citizens. They became a recognized tribe in late 2000. The Black Bob Shawnees and the Absentee Shawnees purchased land from the Seminoles and received federal recognition in 1872.

After years of disputes with whites as well as among themselves, the Shawnees finally

melded into a unified people. They had been buffeted toward that end, rather than politically evolving there on their own, and Stephen Warren credibly presents this story.

THOMAS BURNELL COLBERT
Marshalltown Community College

The Papers of Robert A. Taft. Vol. 1, 1889–1938; Vol. 2, 1939–1934; Vol. 3, 1945–1948; Vol. 4,
1949–1953. Edited by Clarence E. Wunderlin Jr. et al. (Kent, Ohio: Kent State University
Press, 1997–2006. Cloth, $65.00 each: Vol. 1, ISBN 0-87338-572-1; Vol. 2, ISBN 0-87338-679-
5; Vol. 3, ISBN 0-87338-764-3; Vol. 4, ISBN 0-87338-851-8.)

If any politician was ever subject to stereotype, it was Senator Robert Alfonso Taft, whose
rimless spectacles, moonlike face, and metallic voice permitted pundits to call him "a
grapefruit with eyeglasses." To his critics, he was an arch-reactionary, a man totally out
of touch with his own nation. Many of his followers, however, literally worshipped him,
pointing continually to his intelligence, courage, and integrity.

Whatever one's opinion, there was no question that Taft was one of the major figures
of post–World War II America, part of a circle that dominated the Senate during the Truman and early Eisenhower years. Thanks to Clarence E. Wunderlin Jr. and his staff of editors, we now have the chance to allow the senator, in a sense, to speak for himself. The Taft
papers, given to the Library of Congress at his death in 1953, comprise some 520,000 items
deposited in 1,449 containers. Of necessity, the published volumes are selective, with the
first volume, for example, reproducing about 25 percent of what the editors perceived to
be the most historically significant material. The volumes not only contain significant
correspondence but also major speeches and position papers.

Volume 1 concentrates on his labors with the Herbert Hoover's Food Administration
during World War I and with the postwar American Relief Administration and then
turns to his postwar law practice in Cincinnati as well as to his stint in the Ohio House
(where he served as speaker in 1926) and Senate. One sees Taft in 1916 showing his con-
tempt for President Wilson ("a hypocrite and opportunist" [1:104]) and in 1919 revealing
his anxiety that an economically crippled Europe would turn Communist. As a state leg-
islator Taft manifested mildly progressive sympathies, backing, for example, limitations
on child labor, while always remaining a party regular.

Defeated for reelection in the Democratic landslide of 1932, Taft returned to his firm of
Taft, Stettinius and Hollister, his base for attacking much New Deal legislation. The Tennessee Valley Authority, for example, was no less than as "a step in the direction of Revolution" (1:483). Yet Taft was no dogmatist, for he supported collective bargaining, stock
exchange regulation, minimum wages, old-age pensions, and unemployment insurance.

The second volume begins with Taft's election to the U.S. Senate in 1938 and ends
with the 1944 presidential election. The senator bitterly fought Roosevelt's intervention-
ist policies and strongly endorsed the America First Committee, claiming in January 1941

that "Hitler's defeat is not vital to us" (2:218). In 1940 he made his first bid for the presidency, in the course of which he found GOP nominee Wendell Willkie "a demagogue" (2:158) who was undercutting everything he, Taft, believed in. Even during America's full-time participation in World War II, Taft maintained that FDR had gotten the nation into war, though his attention was far more focused on fighting government spending and price controls. The war itself, Taft always argued, was being fought to "make clear that national aggression cannot succeed in this world" (2:443), not to advance the Four Freedoms, the Atlantic Charter, or publisher Henry Luce's "American Century." Always fearful of a resurgent left-wing movement, he went so far in 1944 as to find Communist leader Earl Browder one of the two major figures "providing the real energy behind the Democratic campaign" (2:589).

In his third volume, Wunderlin reveals Taft's activities from 1945, the year World War II ended, through 1948, when Taft lost his second major bid for the presidency. Particularly crucial are Taft's activities from March 1947 through March 1949, when he held the post of Senate majority leader. In some ways his views became increasingly extreme, for he claimed in 1945 that Democratic party thinking was "dominated today by the policies and thinking of the CIO-PAC, derived directly from Marx via Moscow" (3:84). He opposed a federally sponsored Fair Employment Practices Commission, argued with Roman Catholic leaders over federal aid to parochial schools, and was best known for the Taft-Hartley labor law that still prevails over half a century later. Yet Taft broke with much of his party in backing federal housing and aid to education, though he always insisted any such program be administered on the state and local level. Government, he said in 1946, should "give to all a minimum standard of living," including sufficient education to give "to all children a fair opportunity to get a start in life" (3:111). In regard to foreign policy, his speeches often took a conspiratorial cast, as he blamed the Democrats for Communist domination of Eastern Europe and China. He found the new United States Charter sacrificing "law and justice" to "force and expediency," claimed that the Nuremberg trials were based on faulty ex post facto statutes, and sought to curb Marshall Plan aid on the grounds of economy.

The last volume covers Taft's career from the formation of the NATO alliance, which he found unnecessary provocation to the Soviets, until his death in 1953. Here one finds what journalist William S. White calls "the sad, worst period" of the senator's career, one during which he tolerated Joseph McCarthy, found President Truman fostering a "police state," and blamed General George C. Marshall for the "fall" of China and the subsequent Korean War. As far as politics went, it was the Ohio senator's "last hurrah," for he lost the Republican presidential nomination in a bitter struggle with Dwight Eisenhower. Particularly helpful are the letters and speeches in which he espouses his "air-sea" strategy for winning the Cold War, a posture he thought would avoid destructive land engagements. Polemical to the last, he referred to Democratic presidential candidate Adlai Stevenson as "representative of the left wingers, if not a left winger himself" (4:419).

The editing is extremely thorough, and there is hardly a person or subject that is not identified by footnote. Despite the editors' painstaking work, at times errors creep in. It was editor Felix Morley, not publisher Eugene Meyer, who wrote a controversial *Washington Post* editorial in the spring of 1939 (2:79). Herbert Hoover was more than honorary chairman of the National Committee on Food for the Small Democracies (2:259); he was its driving force. In 1942 there was no *New York Herald;* there was a *New York Herald Tribune* (2:324). Hiram Johnson was presidential candidate in 1920, not 1924 (3:70). The Knight-Ritter publishing merger took place in 1974, twenty-three years after the editors cite a supposed "Knight Ridder" editorial (4:320). In several places the editors confuse the year of senator is elected with the year that person takes office (e.g., 4:7, 77).

At times names are confused. One "Henry Luce Jackson" was never editor of *Life;* the individual's name was Charles Douglas Jackson, commonly known as "C.D." (2:50). Senator "J. Bennett" Clark is really Bennett Champ Clark (2:93, 225). "Ed Ryerson" undoubtedly refers to the prominent Republican steel manufacturer Edward Ryerson, not surgeon Edwin Ryerson (2:220). Claude R. Wickard, not "Henry Wickard," was agriculture secretary in 1942 (2:317). Lansing Hoyt, Milwaukee County Republican Chairman in 1941, should not be confused with Taft campaigner Kendall K. Hoyt (3:287). Wilfred Binkley, not "Brinley," was the professor who wrote the *Fortune* article in 1949 (4:32). Michigan senator "Arthur E. B. Moody" is really Blair Moody (4:366). Similarly, Connecticut senator "J. O. McMahon" is Brien McMahon (4:406).

All in all, however, Wunderlin and his associates have a made a great contribution to our knowledge of a figure crucial to understanding post–World War II politics. They deserve our thanks.

JUSTUS D. DOENECKE
New College of Florida

More Than One Struggle: The Evolutions of Black School Reform in Milwaukee. By Jack Dougherty. (Chapel Hill: University of North Carolina Press, 2004. xviii, 253 pp. Paper $19.95, ISBN 0-8070-5524-3.)

In *More Than One Struggle* Jack Dougherty challenges conventional civil rights narratives that depict the civil rights movement as unified and orchestrated by a few elite leaders by examining how different groups of African American activists in Milwaukee defined the struggle over racial segregation in the city's public schools between the 1930s and 1990s. Focusing primarily on the fundamental differences in the way various African Americans in Milwaukee interpreted and set out to implement the Supreme Court's 1954 *Brown* decision, Dougherty effectively exposes myriad cracks in the civil rights front on both national and local levels. For instance, he explains that school segregation in Milwaukee continued to grow even after the Court's ruling, in part because many black Milwaukeeans "did not embrace the same concept of integration as did national race leaders of the time" (40). Deep splits in Milwaukee's African American community emerged as different community leaders and groups fashioned their own understandings of the Court's decision. Some refused to equate the "racial composition" of a particular school with "inferior" education and viewed *Brown* as "all about increasing access" rather than "racial acculturation" (44). Conversely, others believed that all-black education was inherently inferior and that "integrating schools was a necessary condition" for improving African American employment opportunities and living standards (84–85). Even if all factions shared the common goal of securing "more power for blacks in Milwaukee's education system," Dougherty cautions that "their respective struggles should not be compared head-to-head but understood through a historical lens as part of a long line of cumulative, and sometimes conflicting, movements for black education" (102–3). Future civil rights studies should take note of this precaution.

On the surface this book appears to be a straightforward case study. But the masterful way in which the author teases out the tensions that existed in Milwaukee's school desegregation struggle provides an important template for reexamining many of the "conventional assumptions embedded within national civil rights history" (106). By demonstrating how generational, class, gender, and other conflicts shaped black activism in Milwaukee, Dougherty effectively broadened the cast of historical players and presents new insights on the motivations, ideologies, and strategies of civil rights activists in the urban North. This nuanced treatment of the struggle over school desegregation presents a rich picture of black activism in Milwaukee that reminds us that the civil right movement often brought together varied and disparate voices and, thus, is "best understood by weaving together the perspectives of both movement spokesmen and ordinary participants" (129). Students of civil rights history and African American urban history should pay close attention to the standard that Jack Dougherty sets in *More Than One Struggle*.

CORNELIUS L. BYNUM
Purdue University

The British Buckeyes: The English, Scots, and Welsh in Ohio, 1799–1900. By William E. Van Vugt. (Kent: Kent State University Press, 2006. xvi, 295 pp. Cloth $55.00, ISBN 87338-843-7/978-0.)

In a time when immigration policy represents a major political issue, it is good to read a book about a time and place when immigration created far less "angst." Through the eighteenth and nineteenth centuries, people from the British Isles continued to come to the United States, including Ohio, where they made a substantial impact on Ohio.

Van Vugt argues that Ohio was attractive to those from England, Scotland, Wales, and even from Man and Guernsey because of the existence of ample, cheap land. Many who came with skills, even professions such as medicine, as well as from British cities came for the opportunity to acquire farmland. England's industrialization process had created an urge in English people to continue the romantic attachment to land, and Ohio was an ideal place to continue that tradition.

The research for this book was well conceived, and the mining of county histories was done in an excellent manner. Though in places the book can get a bit tedious in review-ing immigrant after immigrant as illustrious of a larger theme, this is a nicely written and well-researched historical work. Van Vugt effectively argues the obvious that the British immigrant was more welcome than other ethnic groups in Ohio and came to be a part of the American context with an ease that was not possible for those with linguis-tic differences or significant ethnic appearances that differentiated them from the larger Anglo-American context of Ohio in the eighteenth and nineteenth centuries.

But the author also effectively documents the major contributions that came from this migration. The large and very profitable pottery industry that marked eastern Ohio came almost entirely from English origins. Many Ohio potters migrated directly from English cities to the Ohio potteries to work. Their transition was eased by their quick absorption into largely English communities of fellow potters. Similarly, the coal min-ing industry of Ohio had largely Welsh origins. Those from southern portions of Wales came to Ohio after the coal beds had been discovered and began large-scale coal mining operations in the Buckeye state in the nineteenth century.

Perhaps the most persuasive chapter, though, comes when the author writes about the complex relationships between the native population, the French, the British, and the Americans in the Ohio Territory in the eighteenth century. The Indian-friendly relation-ship with the less-intrusive English and their hostility to the Americans and their pressure to take the area is exceptionally well written and is very persuasively argued by Van Vugt.

On a more humorous side, one who reads carefully can find perhaps the earliest doc-umented case of a transgendered person in Ohio, "Sophia Gibaut: an immigrant from Guernsey."

At a time when immigration policy is in turmoil and when nativism continues to be a central point of the immigration discussion, *British Buckeyes* illustrates clearly the impact of new people on the transformation of American society.

HARRY JEBSEN JR.
Capital University

The Struggle for the Life of the Republic: A Civil War Narrative by Brevet Major Charles Dana Miller, 76th Ohio Volunteer Infantry. Edited by Stewart Bennett and Barbara Tillery. (Kent: Kent State University Press, 2004. xxiv, 301 pp. Cloth $34.00, ISBN 0-87338-785-6.)

"Many generations must pass ere so great a civil strife will furnish such wonderful mate-rial for history" (229). More than 125 years later, Charles Dana Miller's postwar memoirs finally joined the ranks of that "wonderful material" that makes up the ever-expanding corpus of Civil War history. The reasons why this veteran of the western theater decided to pen a narrative of his service remain unclear, as does the exact dating of its writing. His great-granddaughter Barbara Tillery concludes from internal evidence that Miller composed his reminiscences between 1869 and 1881. Visiting with former comrades dur-ing the Great Re-Union of the Veteran Soldiers and Sailors of Ohio, for which Miller served as secretary in the summer of 1878, might have provided the impetus for him to chronicle his experiences. Whatever the case, he presents an informative description of a soldier's three-year stint with the 76th Ohio Infantry.

Because the war dragged on past the summer of 1861, Miller felt obliged to leave his grain business in Newark, Ohio, to share in "the struggle for the life of the Republic" (4). After training at Camp Sherman, the 76th Ohio saw action in 1862 at Fort Donelson, Shiloh, and Corinth, shortly after which Miller began serving as adjutant. The grueling conditions throughout the siege of Vicksburg and the regiment's subsequent pursuit of General Joseph E. Johnston's army to Jackson, Mississippi, weakened Miller's constitution, and he contracted malaria in the fall of 1863. Even after a lengthy sick leave and thirty-day furlough for reenlisting, Miller still suffered from the effects of his illness, but he returned to the field with the rank of captain and fought commendably during the Atlanta campaign. Following a leave of absence to shore up his business affairs, Miller was unable to contact Sherman's army on its decisive march through Georgia, so he resigned his commission in November 1864.

Besides skillfully recounting military maneuvers, Miller provides an interesting perspective on topics such as the unsanitary conditions of camp, the suffering of Southern civilians, and practical jokes played on contrabands. In 1863, he had the opportunity to become an officer in a black regiment being formed, but he declined, citing his preference to earn promotion in the 76th. Like many Union officers, Miller adopted a personal servant from among the liberated slaves. He took his fifteen-year-old mulatto north with him in 1864 and recalled that "Johnny" was "impressed" by the prosperity of Cincinnati and "the superiority of the great yankee people" (225). Although he often referred to African Americans in a condescending manner, Miller nonetheless affirmed their right to freedom.

Editor Stewart Bennett superbly contextualizes the account, even inserting quotations from other members of the 76th to substantiate Miller's report. Instead of appending only three of Miller's personal letters written during the war, it would have been beneficial to include a broader sampling in order to compare his postwar views with his contemporary opinions. Despite this omission, Miller's reminiscences provide an excellent framework for rehearsing the exploits of the 76th Ohio.

SEAN A. SCOTT
Purdue University

The Black Laws: Race and the Legal Process in Early Ohio. By Stephen Middleton. (Athens: Ohio University Press, 2005. xii, 363 pp. Cloth $59.95, ISBN 0-8214-1623-5; Paper $26.95, ISBN 0-8214-1624-3.)

During a three-day period in April 2001, the City of Cincinnati was gripped by racial unrest that resulted from the shooting death of Timothy Thomas, a young African American male, by a white police officer. A subsequent investigation revelaed an ongoing pattern of racial hatred and violence in a city in which fourteen black males had been killed by police officers over the previous six years. Yet as the work under review indicates, a problematic relationship between black and white is not new in the annals of Ohio history. Barely a year after admission into the union, the State of Ohio passed legislation endorsing the so-called "Black Laws." Labeled as "an act to regulate black and mulatto persons," the Black Laws in essence institutionalized racism in the state. Stephen Middleton's *The Black Laws: Race and the Legal Process in Early Ohio* is an important study on this subject. Based on extensive primary sources, Middleton's book chronicles the origins, impact, and eventual repeal of the Black Laws. These notorious laws contained residency requirements designed to restrict the immigration of blacks into Ohio. In order to take up residence in the state, blacks were required to show proof of their freedom and also pay a bond to ensure "proper behavior." The language used to describe blacks was consistent with the new laws: blacks were "worse than drones to society, "and a few of them will multiply "like locusts" (50). Black Laws excluded African Americans from voting, owning firearms and property, participating on juries and militia, attending public schools, and testifying in court against a white person. The implications of the laws were far reaching: they justified anti-black violence and established the bedrock foundation of the state's contemporary de facto segregation. Black Laws, Middleton persuasively argues, mirrored Southern slave codes.

Despite laws regulating racial behavior, the construction of racial identity remained a thorny issue. Beyond physical attributes and other social constructs, it was unclear how to determine who qualified as black. To resolve the problem, the court, Middleton argues, added its own interpretation to what it means to be black. Progressive judges relied more on "fairness in the court room" and as a result began to undermine aspects of the black (4). For example, the court considered as white "a mixed-race individual with more than 50 percent Caucasian blood" (57). Such a person was accorded all the rights and privileges that came with whiteness. The court, Middleton concludes, was at the forefront of the emerging challenge to the Black Laws.

Perhaps the most significant contribution of this book is Middleton's discussion of how ordinary citizens, both black and white, student and nonstudent, joined the anti-racist, antislavery, and anti–Black Laws crusade. They had witnessed, observed, and read about abolitionist activities in other states. They petitioned, demonstrated, and protested against racial injustice. They joined the struggle against the fugitive slave laws. Colleges such as Oberlin and Ohio University opened their doors to blacks, who in turn provided leadership to the emerging civil rights movement. The Ohio Anti-Slavery Society was forceful in its anti–Black Laws arguments. The laws, the Society argued, were vicious and psychologically harmful to blacks. Pro–civil rights activities and petitions from the various groups soon paid off. By the end of 1849, aspects of the Black Laws had been repealed. However, portions of the Black Laws would remain in place until the passage of the Arnett Bill of 1877, which repealed the final remnants.

Middelton's book is thorough, well-researched, and makes a significant contribution to the literature on race relations. But there are some shortcomings. The author should have included data on the population of African Americans at different points in the narrative. Did the African American population increase or decrease at different times in the nineteenth century? Because ensuring and promoting black ignorance was an integral part of the Black Laws, Middleton could have devoted more attention to the nature and content of education for blacks. Even though Wilberforce University is mentioned, there is little discussion about its role (if any) in the civil rights struggle during this time. Additionally, race relations and racial strife in Ohio did not occur in a vacuum. In what ways did the racial practices in Ohio fit within the broader national context? The author also fails to address the topic's contemporary relevance, to wit, the enduring legacy of the Black Lawws in the state. In race relations, a significant portion of Ohio is still trapped in the mindset of the Black Laws.

JULIUS A. AMIN
University of Dayton